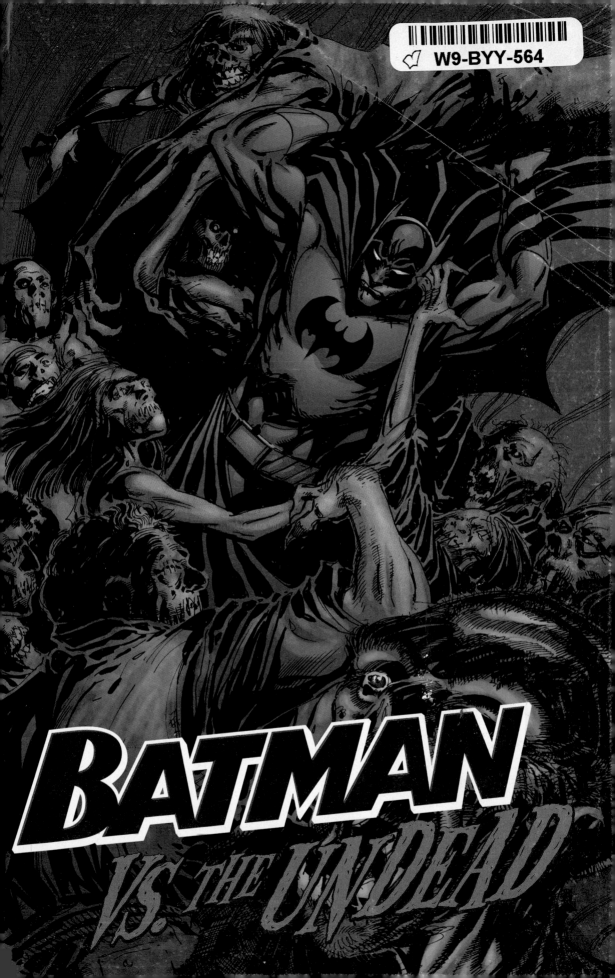

BATMAN

VS. THE UNDEAD

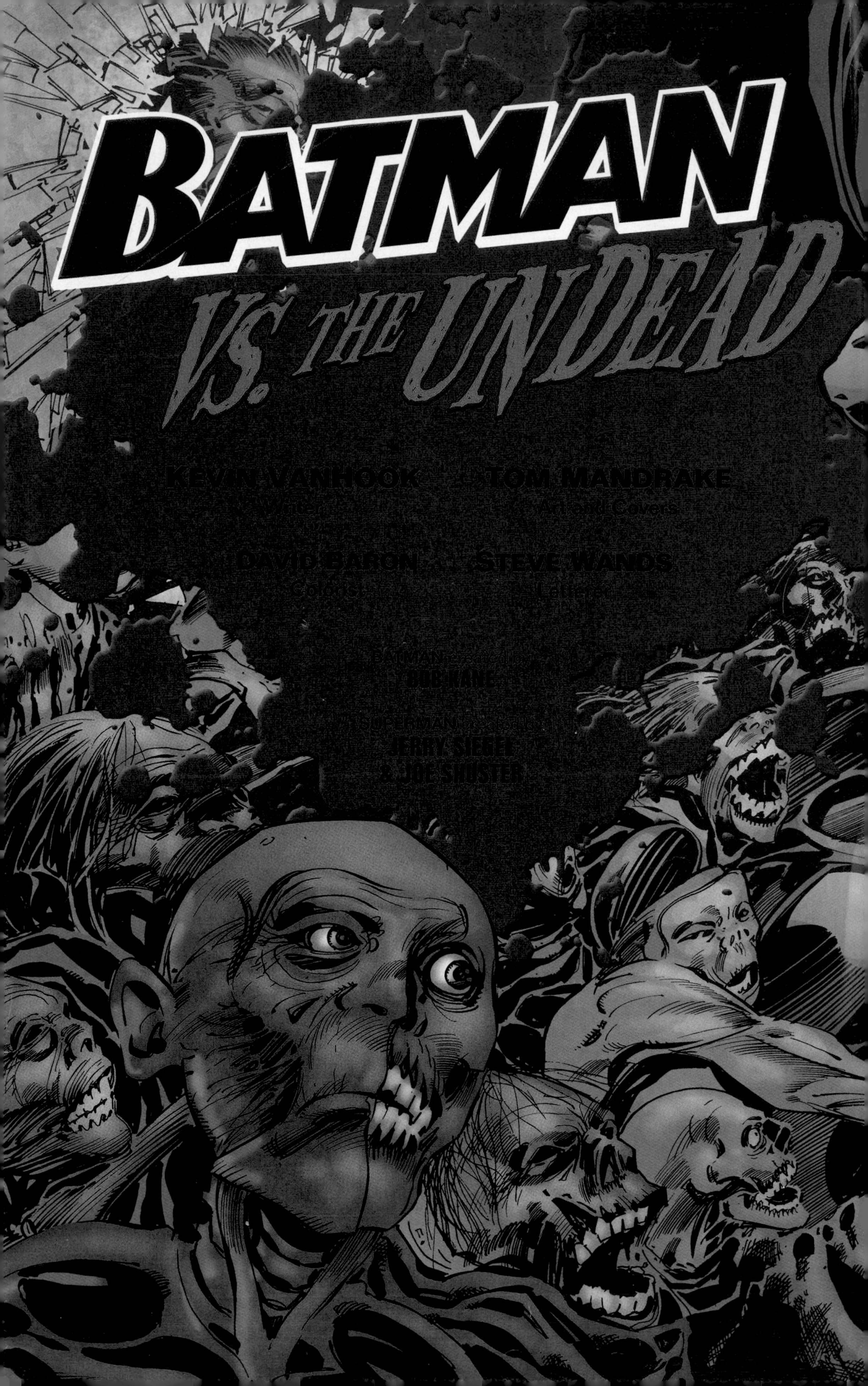
BATMAN
VS. THE UNDEAD
KEVIN VANHOOK
Writer
TOM MANDRAKE
Art and Covers
DAVID BARON
Colorist
STEVE WANDS
Letterer
BATMAN created by
BOB KANE
SUPERMAN created by
JERRY SIEGEL
& JOE SHUSTER

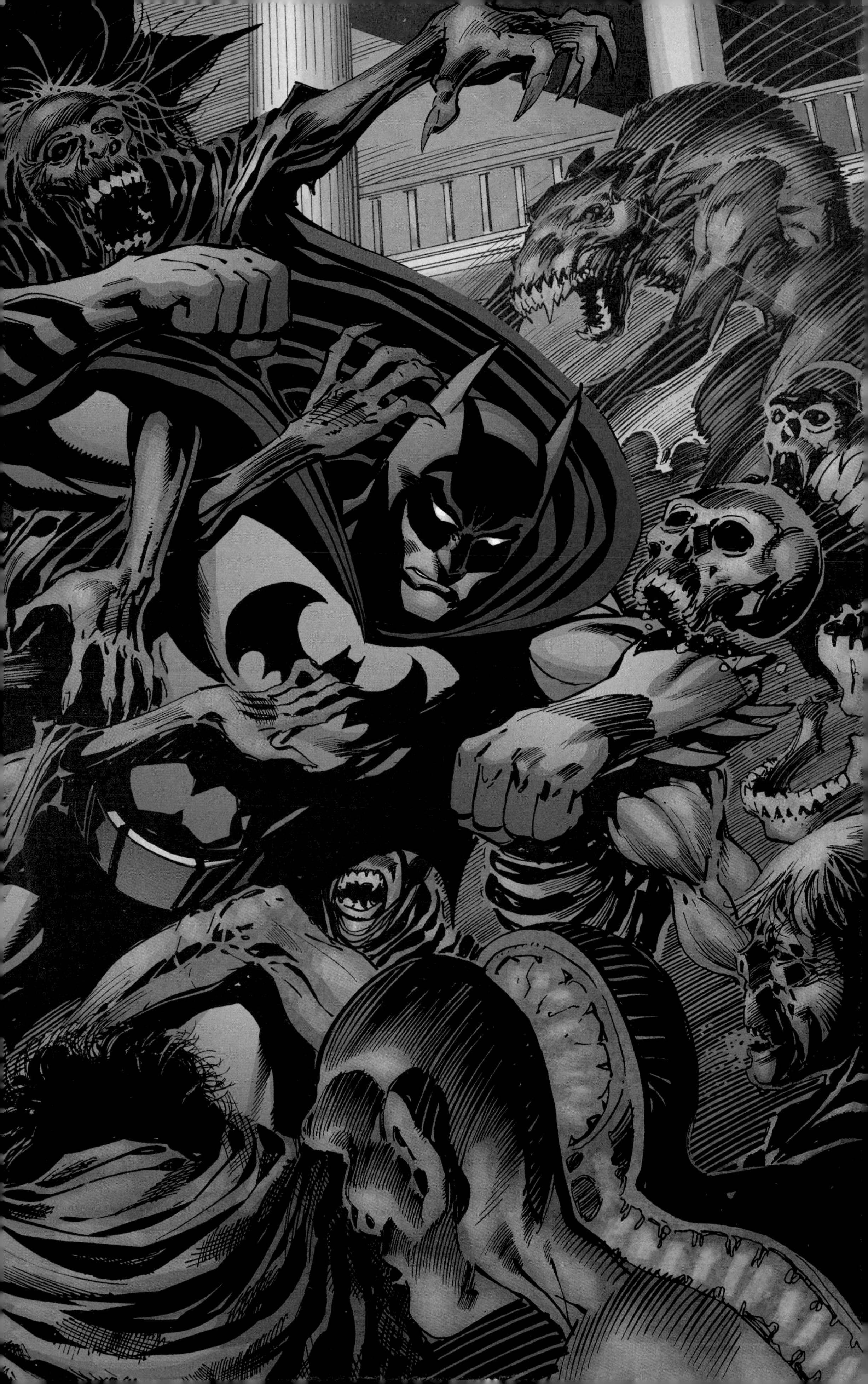

Michael Siglain *Editor-original series*
Harvey Richards *Assistant Editor-original series*
Bob Harras *Group Editor-Collected Editions*
Robbin Brosterman *Design Director-Books*
Curtis King Jr. *Senior Art Director*

DC COMICS
Diane Nelson *President*
Dan DiDio and **Jim Lee** *Co-Publishers*
Geoff Johns *Chief Creative Officer*
Patrick Caldon *EVP-Finance and Administration*
John Rood *EVP-Sales, Marketing and Business Development*
Amy Genkins *SVP-Business and Legal Affairs*
Steve Rotterdam *SVP-Sales and Marketing*
John Cunningham *VP-Marketing*
Terri Cunningham *VP-Managing Editor*
Alison Gill *VP-Manufacturing*
David Hyde *VP-Publicity*
Sue Pohja *VP-Book Trade Sales*
Alysse Soll *VP-Advertising and Custom Publishing*
Bob Wayne *VP-Sales*
Mark Chiarello *Art Director*

DC Comics, 1700 Broadway, New York, NY 10019
A Warner Bros. Entertainment Company
Printed by Quad/Graphics, Dubuque, IA, USA. 12/22/10. First printing.
ISBN: 978-1-4012-3035-7

SUSTAINABLE
FORESTRY
INITIATIVE

Certified Chain of Custody
Promoting Sustainable
Forest Management

www.sfiprogram.org

Fiber used in this product line meets the sourcing requirements
of the SFI program. www.sfiprogram.org PWC-SFICOC-260

PART ONE: **THE BIG EASY**

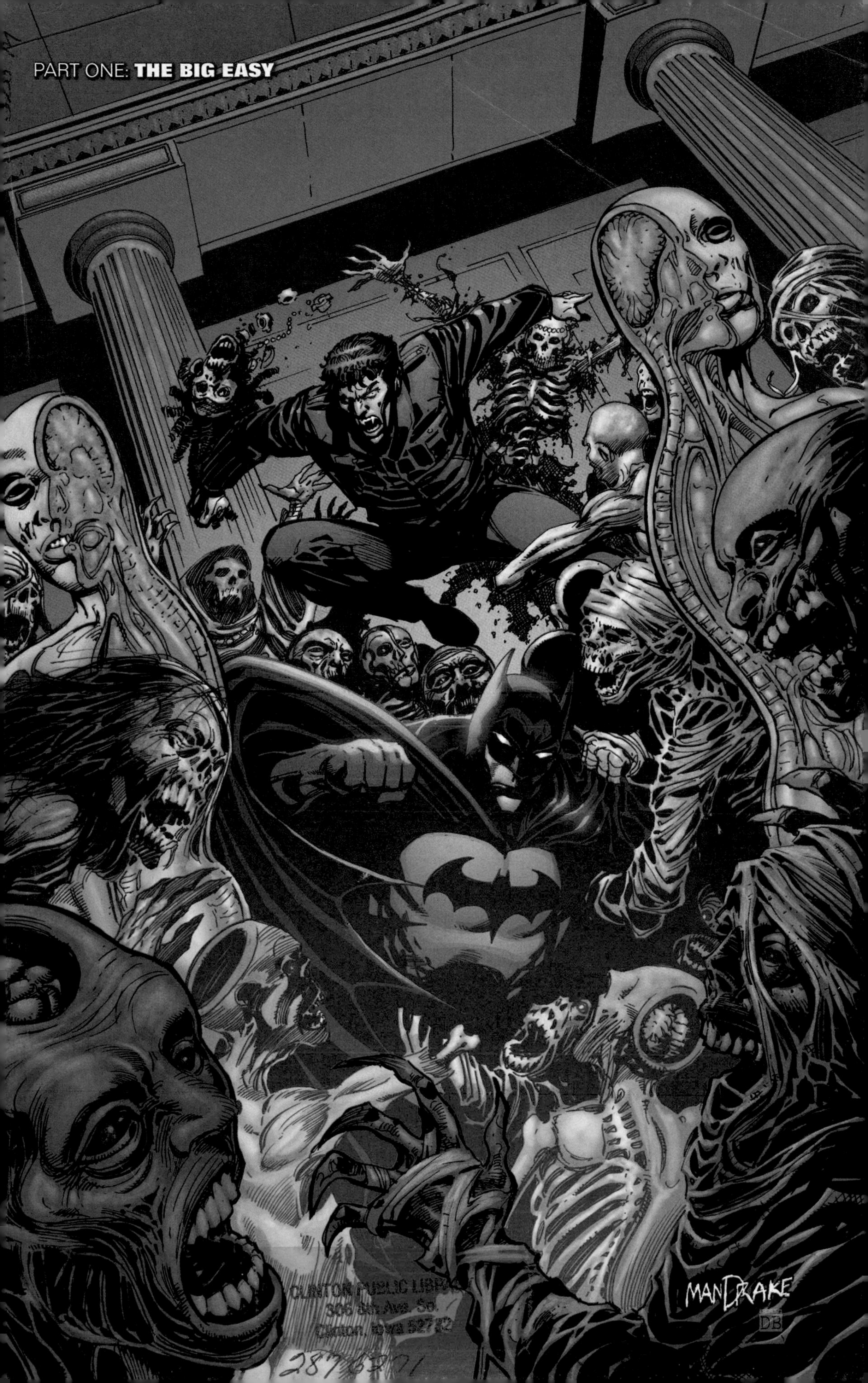
MANDRAKE
DB

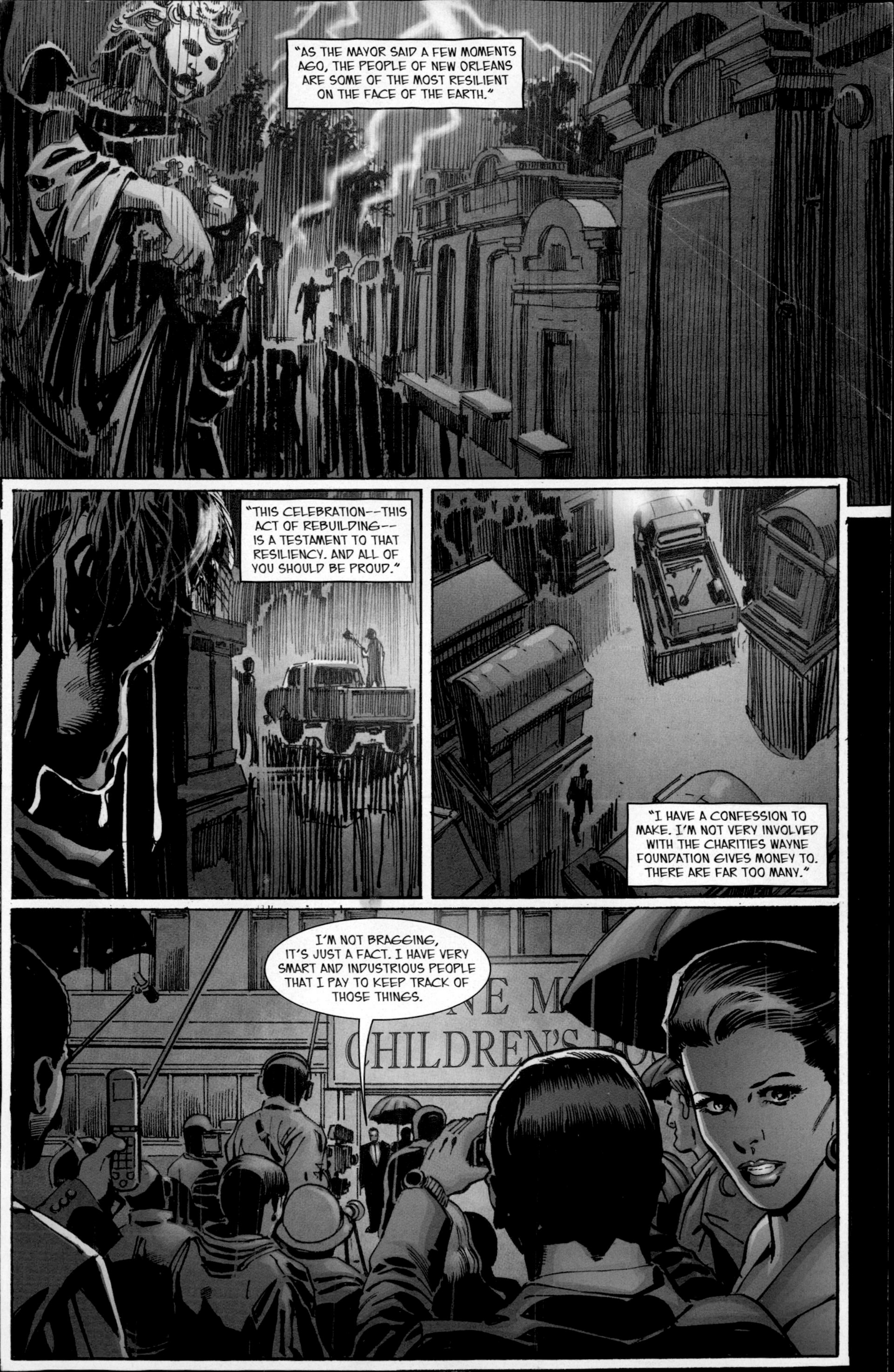
"AS THE MAYOR SAID A FEW MOMENTS AGO, THE PEOPLE OF NEW ORLEANS ARE SOME OF THE MOST RESILIENT ON THE FACE OF THE EARTH."
"THIS CELEBRATION--THIS ACT OF REBUILDING-- IS A TESTAMENT TO THAT RESILIENCY. AND ALL OF YOU SHOULD BE PROUD."
"I HAVE A CONFESSION TO MAKE. I'M NOT VERY INVOLVED WITH THE CHARITIES WAYNE FOUNDATION GIVES MONEY TO. THERE ARE FAR TOO MANY."
I'M NOT BRAGGING, IT'S JUST A FACT. I HAVE VERY SMART AND INDUSTRIOUS PEOPLE THAT I PAY TO KEEP TRACK OF THOSE THINGS.
CHILDREN'S

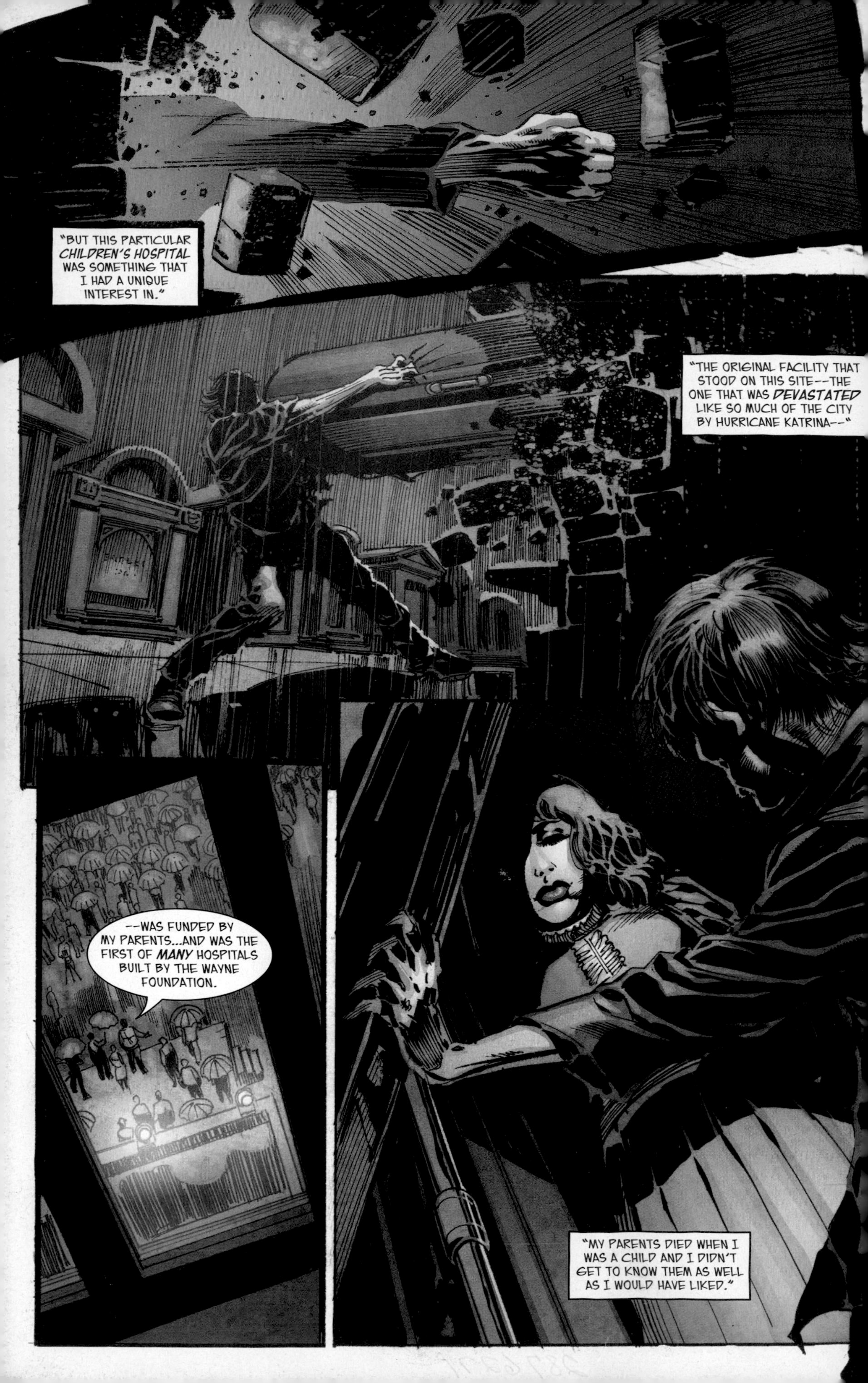
"BUT THIS PARTICULAR CHILDREN'S HOSPITAL WAS SOMETHING THAT I HAD A UNIQUE INTEREST IN."
"THE ORIGINAL FACILITY THAT STOOD ON THIS SITE--THE ONE THAT WAS DEVASTATED LIKE SO MUCH OF THE CITY BY HURRICANE KATRINA--"
--WAS FUNDED BY MY PARENTS...AND WAS THE FIRST OF MANY HOSPITALS BUILT BY THE WAYNE FOUNDATION.
"MY PARENTS DIED WHEN I WAS A CHILD AND I DIDN'T GET TO KNOW THEM AS WELL AS I WOULD HAVE LIKED."

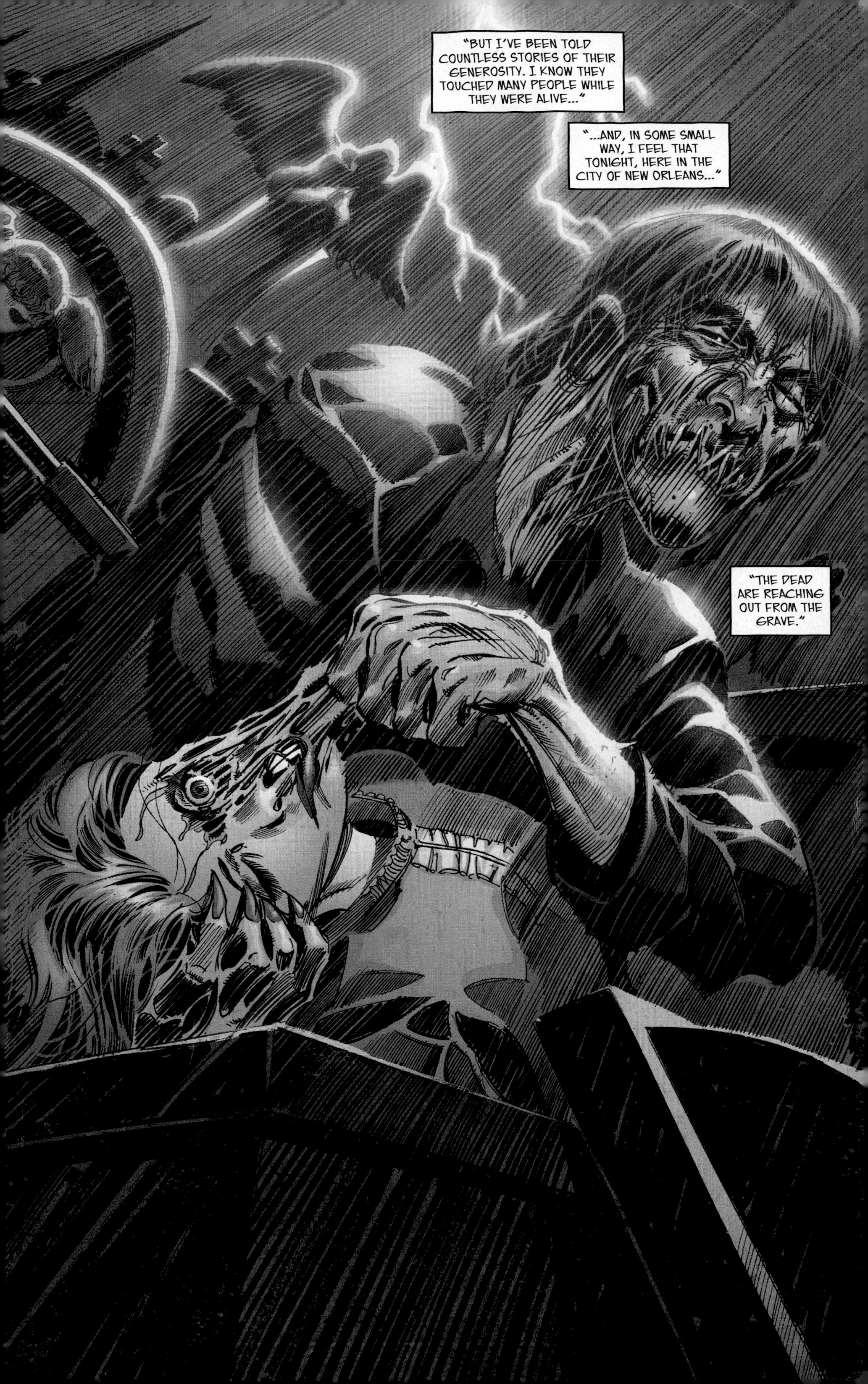
"BUT I'VE BEEN TOLD COUNTLESS STORIES OF THEIR GENEROSITY. I KNOW THEY TOUCHED MANY PEOPLE WHILE THEY WERE ALIVE..."
"...AND, IN SOME SMALL WAY, I FEEL THAT TONIGHT, HERE IN THE CITY OF NEW ORLEANS..."
"THE DEAD ARE REACHING OUT FROM THE GRAVE."

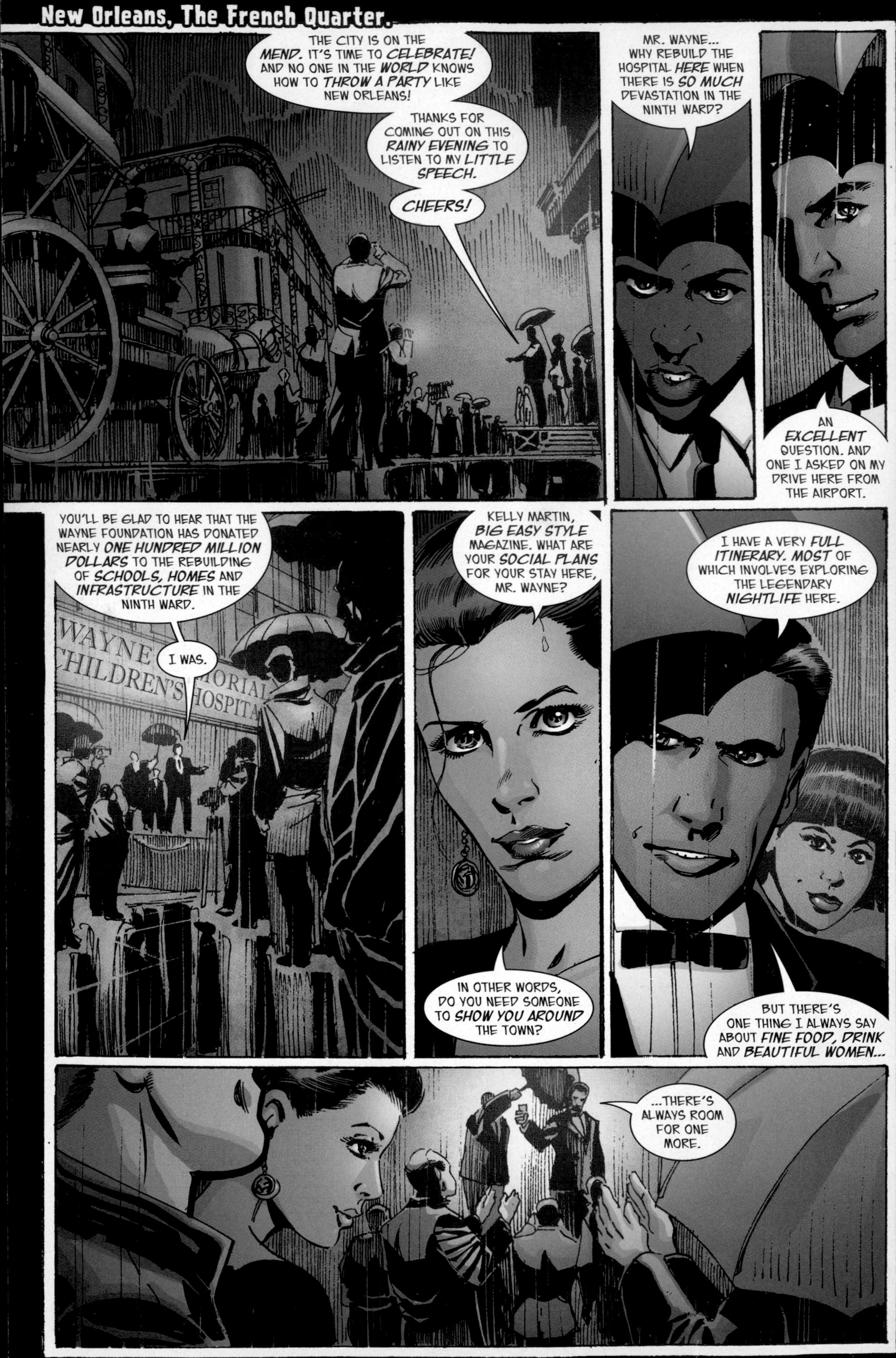
New Orleans, The French Quarter.
THE CITY IS ON THE MEND. IT'S TIME TO CELEBRATE! AND NO ONE IN THE WORLD KNOWS HOW TO THROW A PARTY LIKE NEW ORLEANS!
THANKS FOR COMING OUT ON THIS RAINY EVENING TO LISTEN TO MY LITTLE SPEECH.
CHEERS!
MR. WAYNE... WHY REBUILD THE HOSPITAL HERE WHEN THERE IS SO MUCH DEVASTATION IN THE NINTH WARD?
AN EXCELLENT QUESTION. AND ONE I ASKED ON MY DRIVE HERE FROM THE AIRPORT.
YOU'LL BE GLAD TO HEAR THAT THE WAYNE FOUNDATION HAS DONATED NEARLY ONE HUNDRED MILLION DOLLARS TO THE REBUILDING OF SCHOOLS, HOMES AND INFRASTRUCTURE IN THE NINTH WARD.
I WAS.
WAYNE MEMORIAL CHILDREN'S HOSPITAL
KELLY MARTIN, BIG EASY STYLE MAGAZINE. WHAT ARE YOUR SOCIAL PLANS FOR YOUR STAY HERE, MR. WAYNE?
IN OTHER WORDS, DO YOU NEED SOMEONE TO SHOW YOU AROUND THE TOWN?
I HAVE A VERY FULL ITINERARY. MOST OF WHICH INVOLVES EXPLORING THE LEGENDARY NIGHTLIFE HERE.
BUT THERE'S ONE THING I ALWAYS SAY ABOUT FINE FOOD, DRINK AND BEAUTIFUL WOMEN...
...THERE'S ALWAYS ROOM FOR ONE MORE.

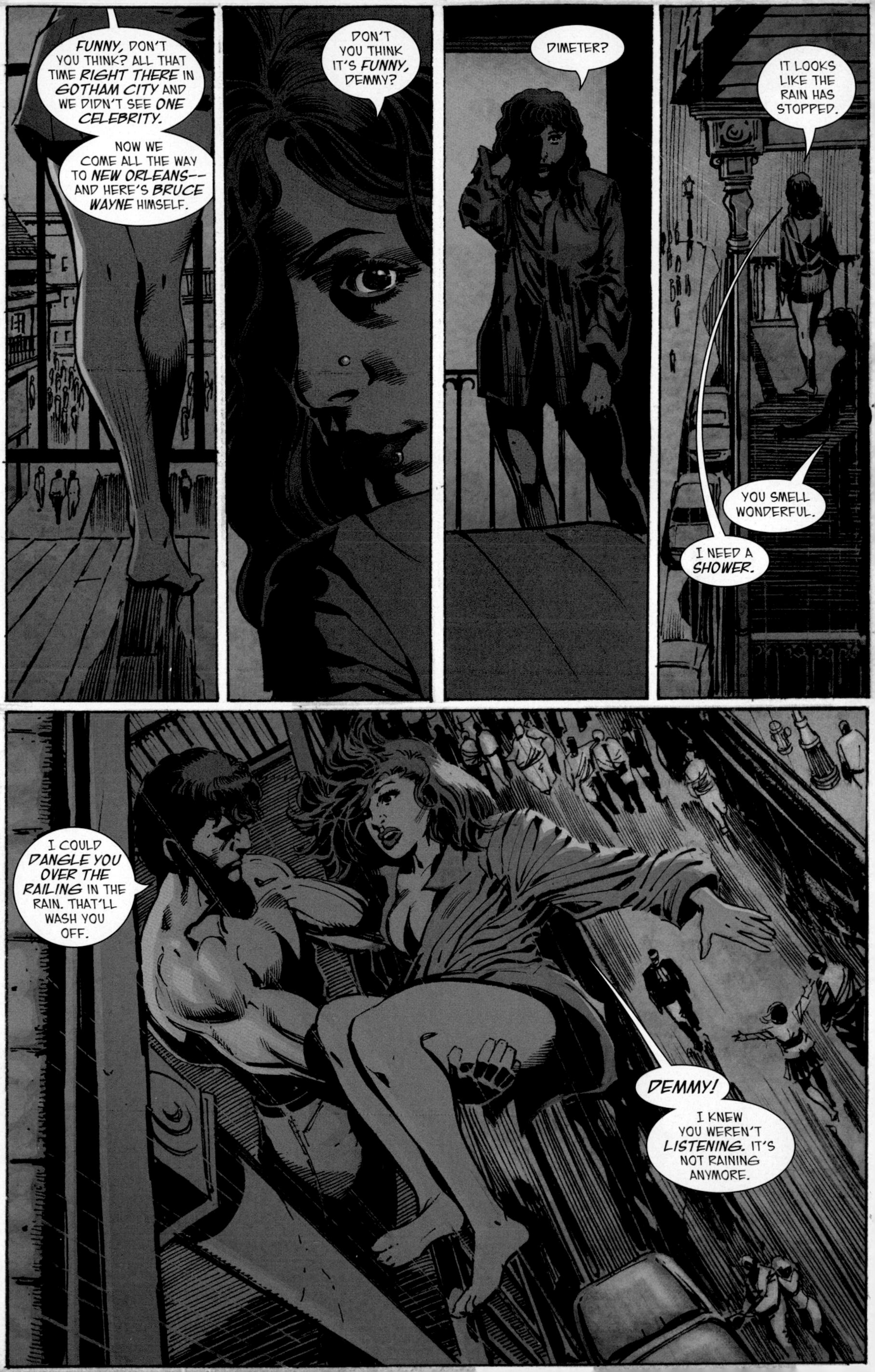
FUNNY, DON'T YOU THINK? ALL THAT TIME RIGHT THERE IN GOTHAM CITY AND WE DIDN'T SEE ONE CELEBRITY.
NOW WE COME ALL THE WAY TO NEW ORLEANS-- AND HERE'S BRUCE WAYNE HIMSELF.
DON'T YOU THINK IT'S FUNNY, DEMMY?
DIMETER?
IT LOOKS LIKE THE RAIN HAS STOPPED.
YOU SMELL WONDERFUL.
I NEED A SHOWER.
I COULD DANGLE YOU OVER THE RAILING IN THE RAIN. THAT'LL WASH YOU OFF.
DEMMY!
I KNEW YOU WEREN'T LISTENING. IT'S NOT RAINING ANYMORE.

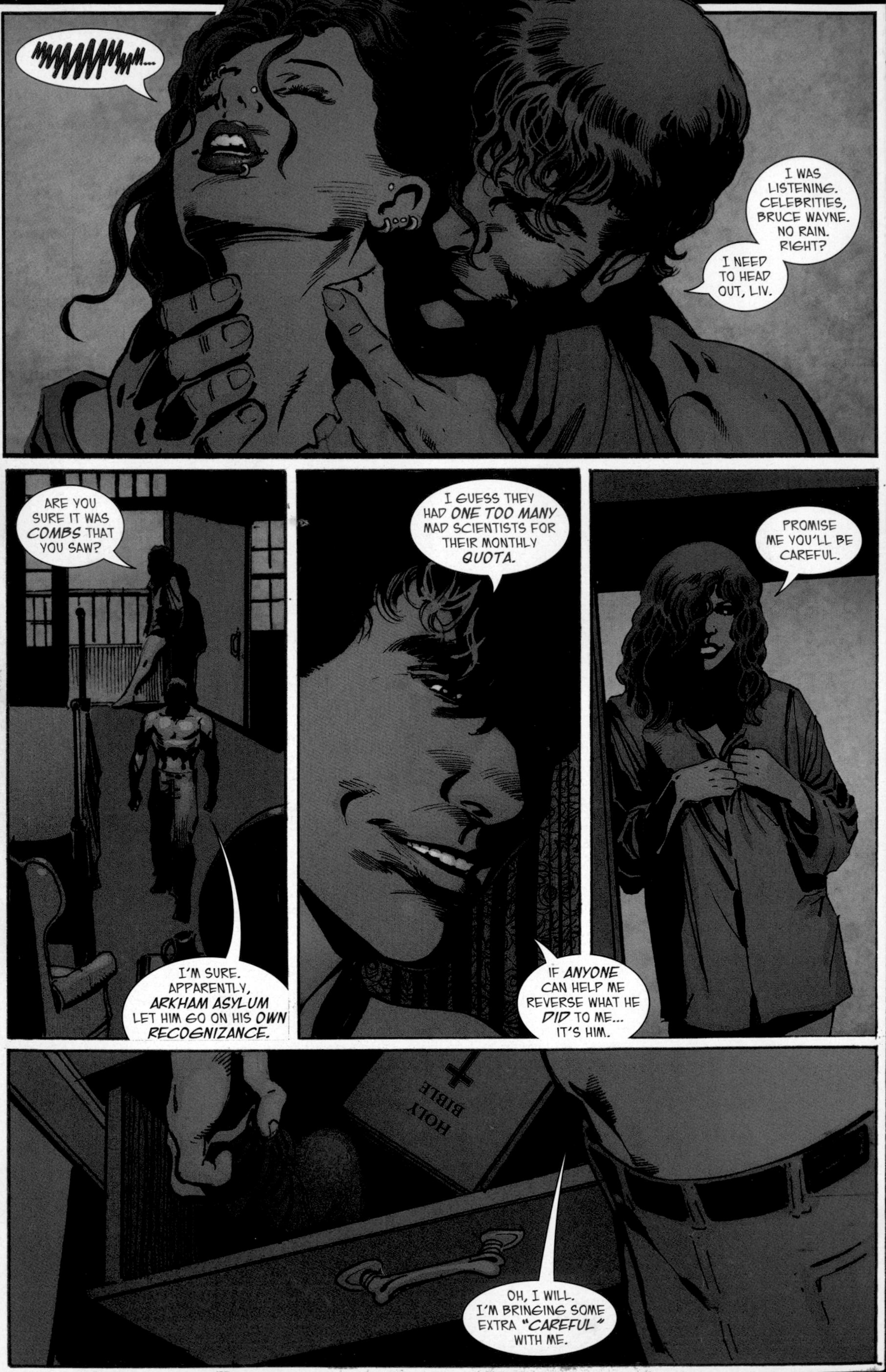
MMMMMMMMmmm...
I WAS LISTENING. CELEBRITIES, BRUCE WAYNE. NO RAIN. RIGHT?
I NEED TO HEAD OUT, LIV.
ARE YOU SURE IT WAS COMBS THAT YOU SAW?
I'M SURE. APPARENTLY, ARKHAM ASYLUM LET HIM GO ON HIS OWN RECOGNIZANCE.
I GUESS THEY HAD ONE TOO MANY MAD SCIENTISTS FOR THEIR MONTHLY QUOTA.
IF ANYONE CAN HELP ME REVERSE WHAT HE DID TO ME... IT'S HIM.
PROMISE ME YOU'LL BE CAREFUL.
HOLY BIBLE
OH, I WILL. I'M BRINGING SOME EXTRA "CAREFUL" WITH ME.

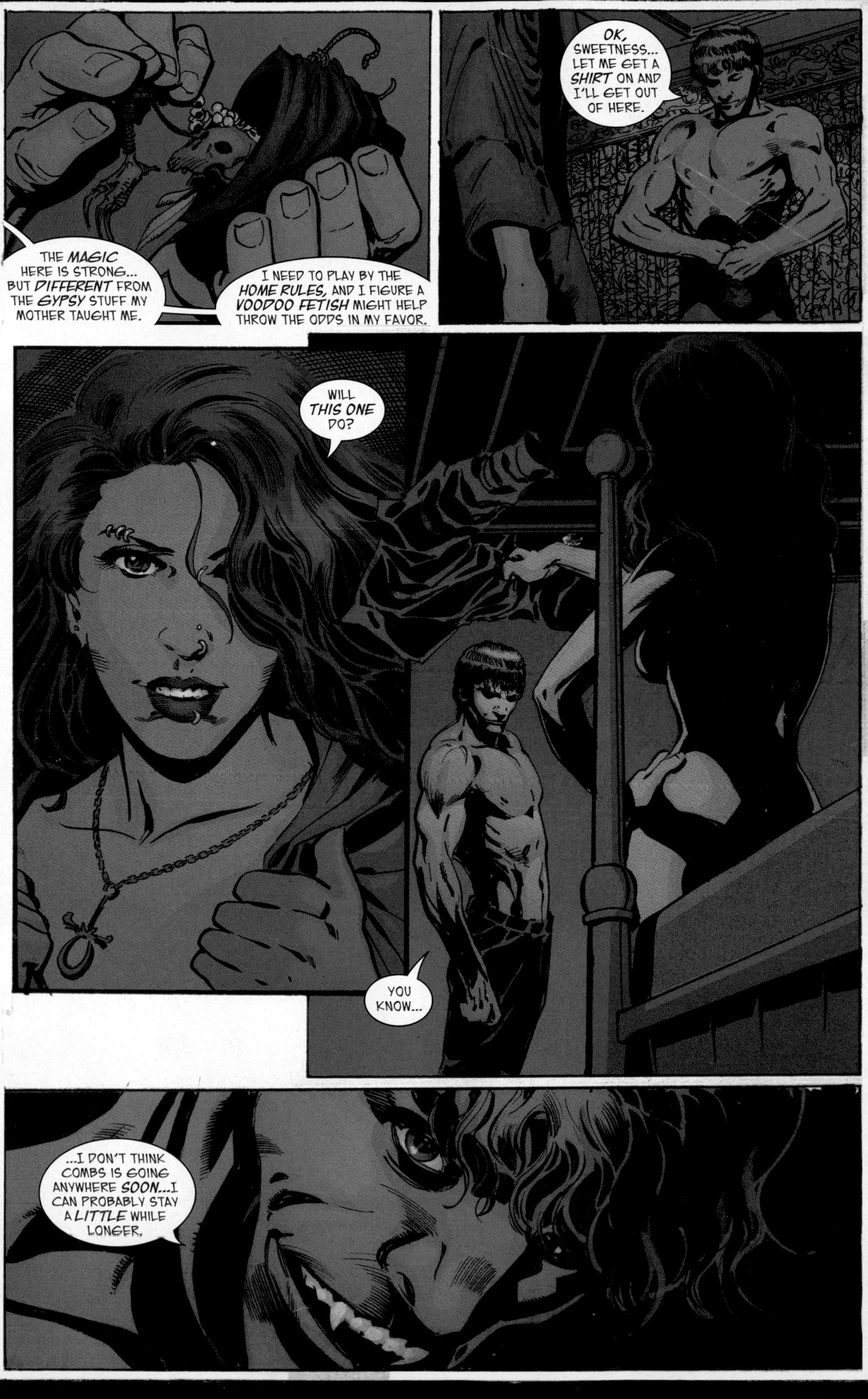
THE *MAGIC* HERE IS STRONG... BUT *DIFFERENT* FROM THE *GYPSY* STUFF MY MOTHER TAUGHT ME.
I NEED TO PLAY BY THE *HOME RULES,* AND I FIGURE A *VOODOO FETISH* MIGHT HELP THROW THE ODDS IN MY FAVOR.
OK, SWEETNESS... LET ME GET A *SHIRT* ON AND I'LL GET OUT OF HERE.
WILL *THIS ONE* DO?
YOU KNOW...
...I DON'T THINK COMBS IS GOING ANYWHERE *SOON*...I CAN PROBABLY STAY A *LITTLE* WHILE LONGER.

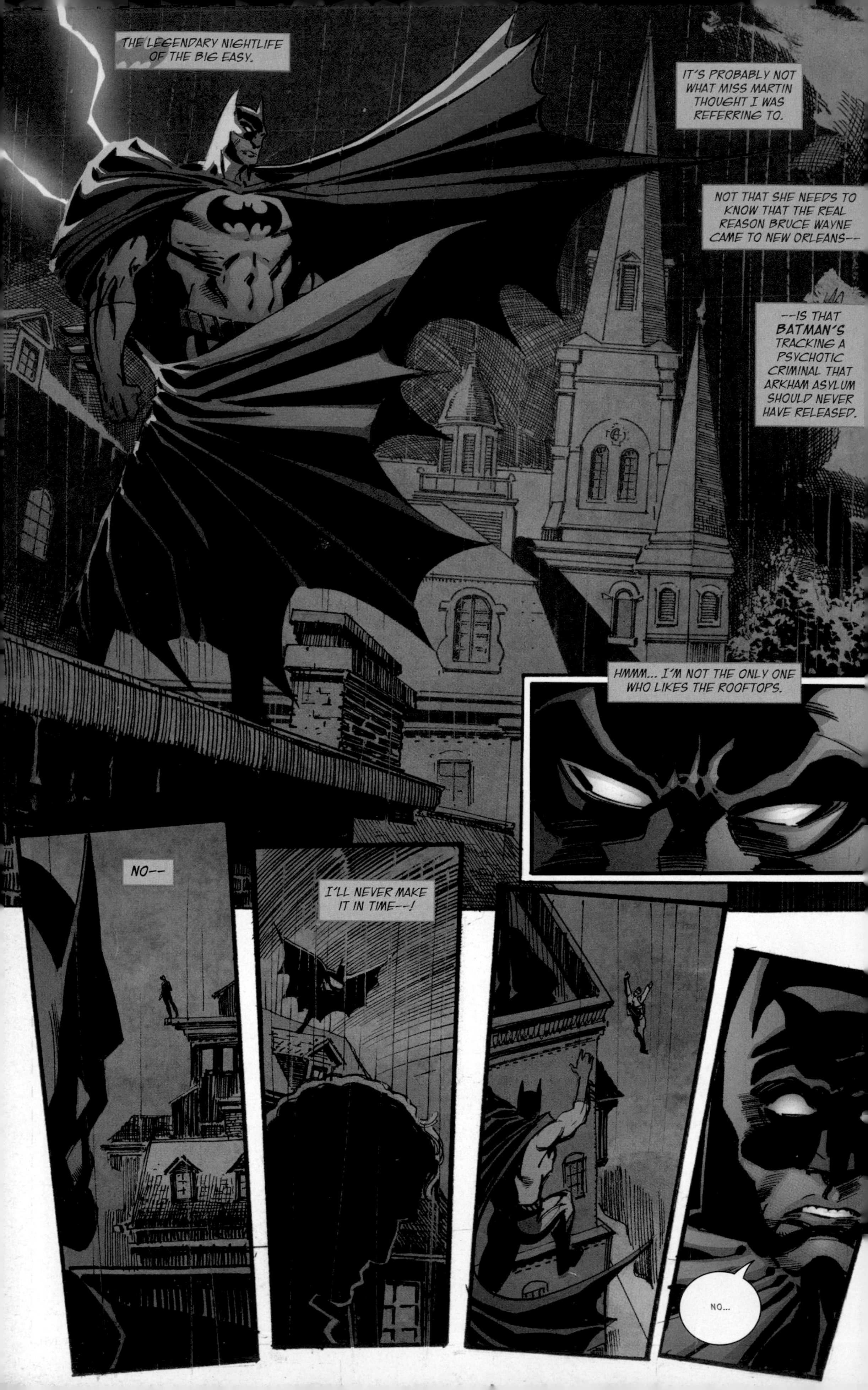
THE LEGENDARY NIGHTLIFE OF THE BIG EASY.
IT'S PROBABLY NOT WHAT MISS MARTIN THOUGHT I WAS REFERRING TO.
NOT THAT SHE NEEDS TO KNOW THAT THE REAL REASON BRUCE WAYNE CAME TO NEW ORLEANS--
--IS THAT BATMAN'S TRACKING A PSYCHOTIC CRIMINAL THAT ARKHAM ASYLUM SHOULD NEVER HAVE RELEASED.
HMMM... I'M NOT THE ONLY ONE WHO LIKES THE ROOFTOPS.
NO--
I'LL NEVER MAKE IT IN TIME--!
NO...

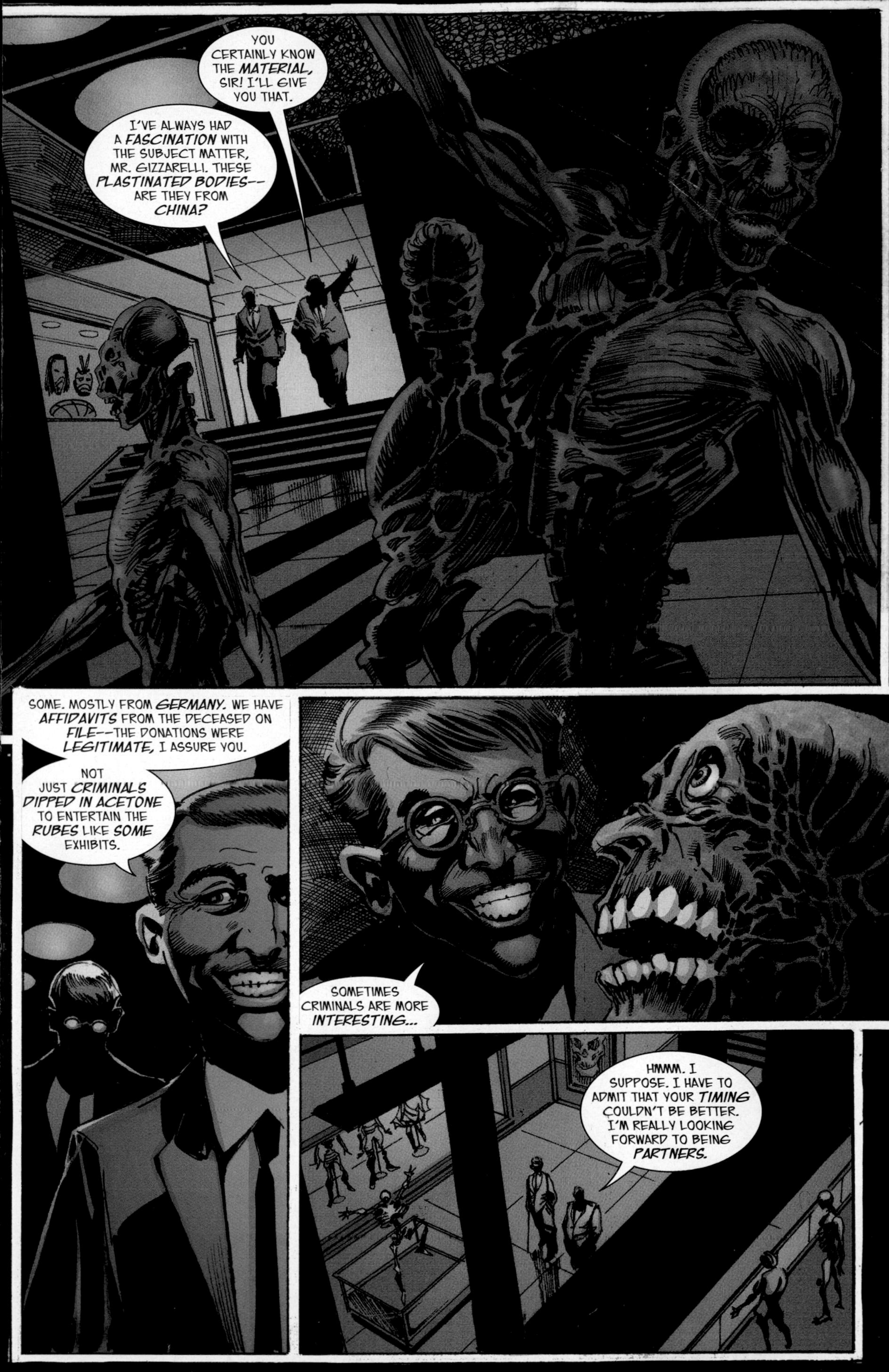
I'VE ALWAYS HAD A FASCINATION WITH THE SUBJECT MATTER, MR. GIZZARELLI. THESE PLASTINATED BODIES-- ARE THEY FROM CHINA?
YOU CERTAINLY KNOW THE MATERIAL, SIR! I'LL GIVE YOU THAT.
SOME. MOSTLY FROM GERMANY. WE HAVE AFFIDAVITS FROM THE DECEASED ON FILE--THE DONATIONS WERE LEGITIMATE, I ASSURE YOU.
NOT JUST CRIMINALS DIPPED IN ACETONE TO ENTERTAIN THE RUBES LIKE SOME EXHIBITS.
SOMETIMES CRIMINALS ARE MORE INTERESTING...
HMMM. I SUPPOSE. I HAVE TO ADMIT THAT YOUR TIMING COULDN'T BE BETTER. I'M REALLY LOOKING FORWARD TO BEING PARTNERS.

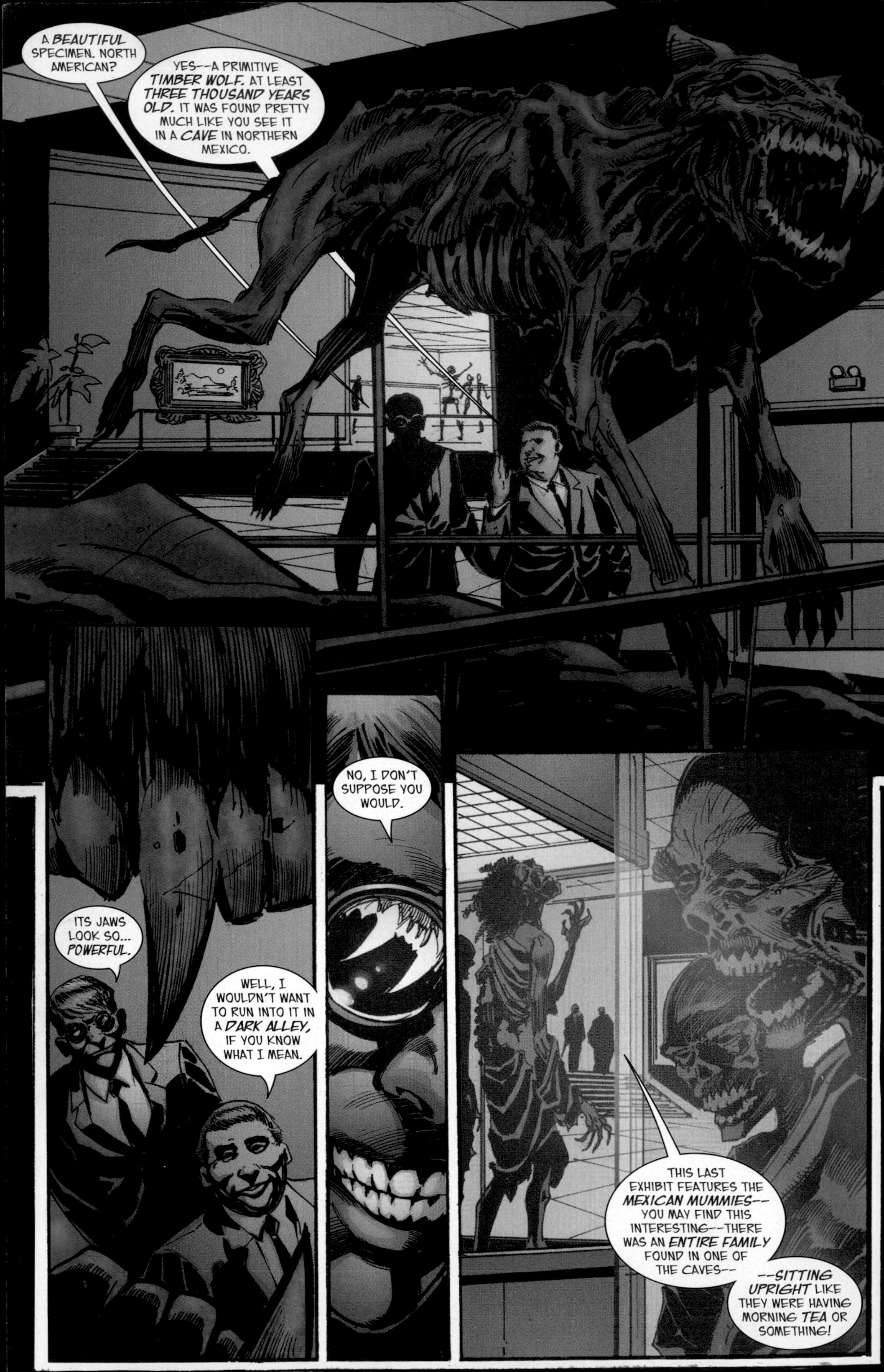
A BEAUTIFUL SPECIMEN. NORTH AMERICAN?
YES--A PRIMITIVE TIMBER WOLF. AT LEAST THREE THOUSAND YEARS OLD. IT WAS FOUND PRETTY MUCH LIKE YOU SEE IT IN A CAVE IN NORTHERN MEXICO.
ITS JAWS LOOK SO... POWERFUL.
WELL, I WOULDN'T WANT TO RUN INTO IT IN A DARK ALLEY, IF YOU KNOW WHAT I MEAN.
NO, I DON'T SUPPOSE YOU WOULD.
THIS LAST EXHIBIT FEATURES THE MEXICAN MUMMIES--YOU MAY FIND THIS INTERESTING--THERE WAS AN ENTIRE FAMILY FOUND IN ONE OF THE CAVES--
--SITTING UPRIGHT LIKE THEY WERE HAVING MORNING TEA OR SOMETHING!

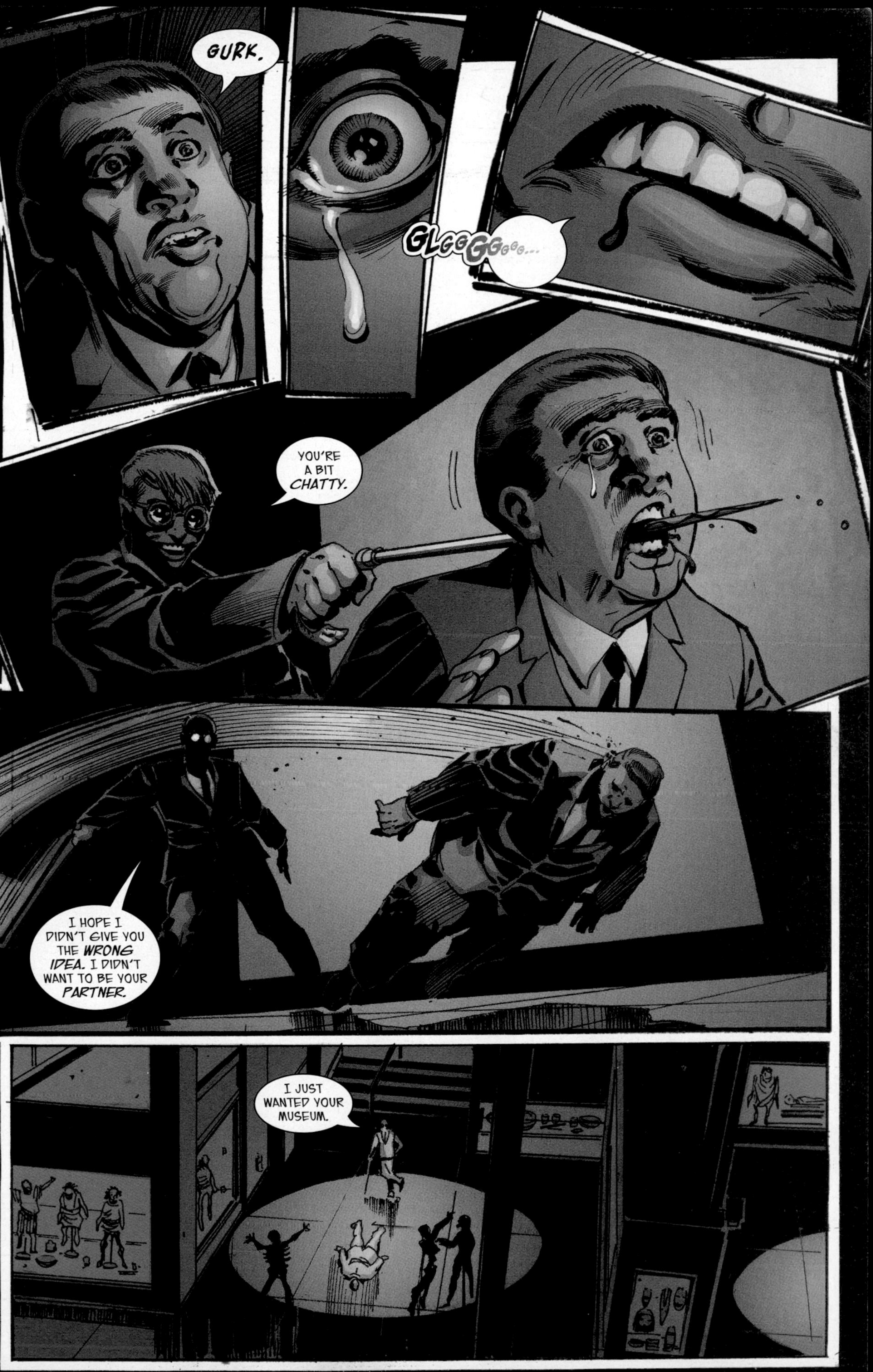
GURK.
GLGGGGGGG...
YOU'RE A BIT CHATTY.
I HOPE I DIDN'T GIVE YOU THE WRONG IDEA. I DIDN'T WANT TO BE YOUR PARTNER.
I JUST WANTED YOUR MUSEUM.

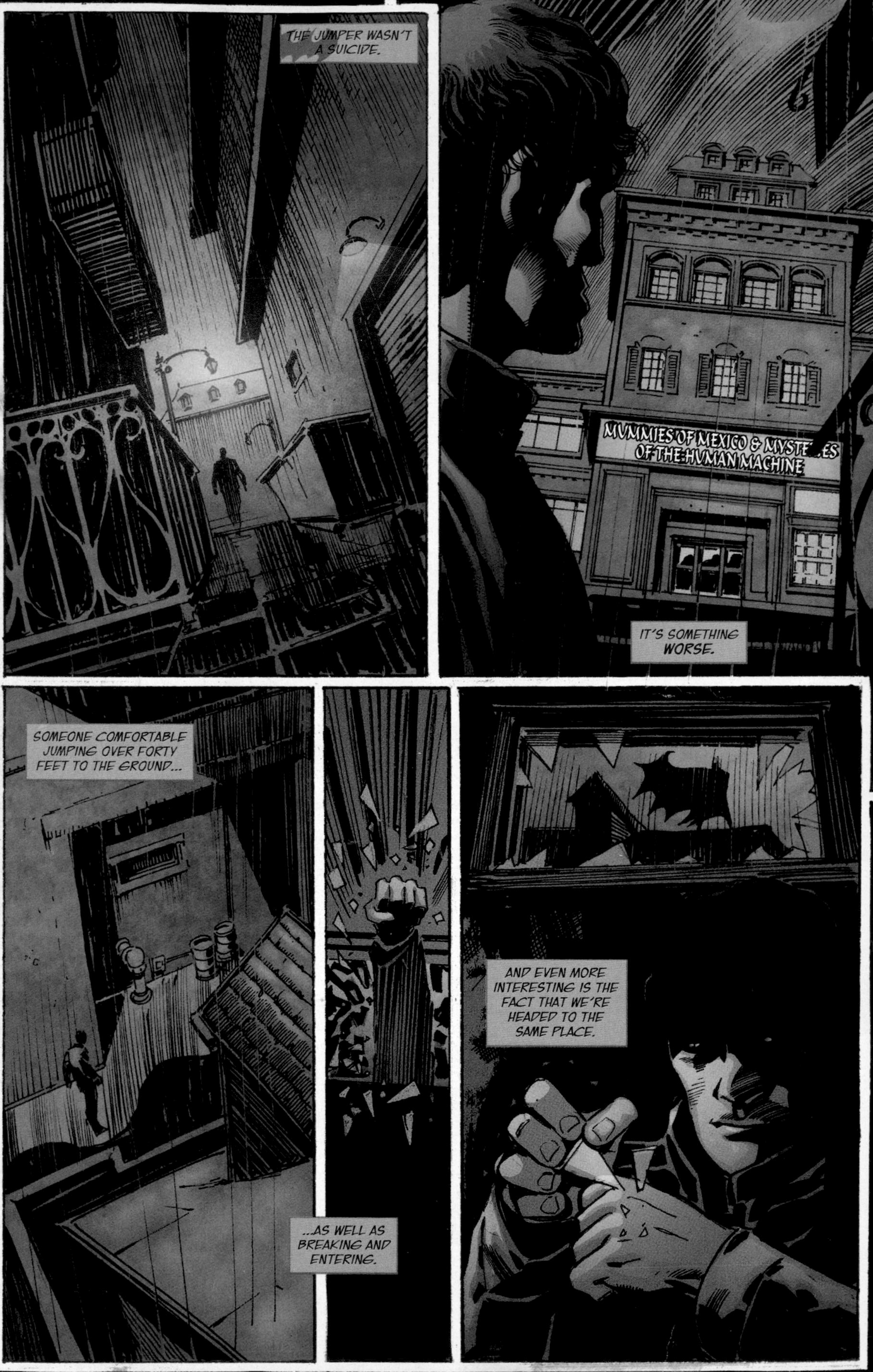
THE JUMPER WASN'T A SUICIDE.
MUMMIES OF MEXICO & MYSTERIES OF THE HUMAN MACHINE
IT'S SOMETHING WORSE.
SOMEONE COMFORTABLE JUMPING OVER FORTY FEET TO THE GROUND...
...AS WELL AS BREAKING AND ENTERING.
AND EVEN MORE INTERESTING IS THE FACT THAT WE'RE HEADED TO THE SAME PLACE.

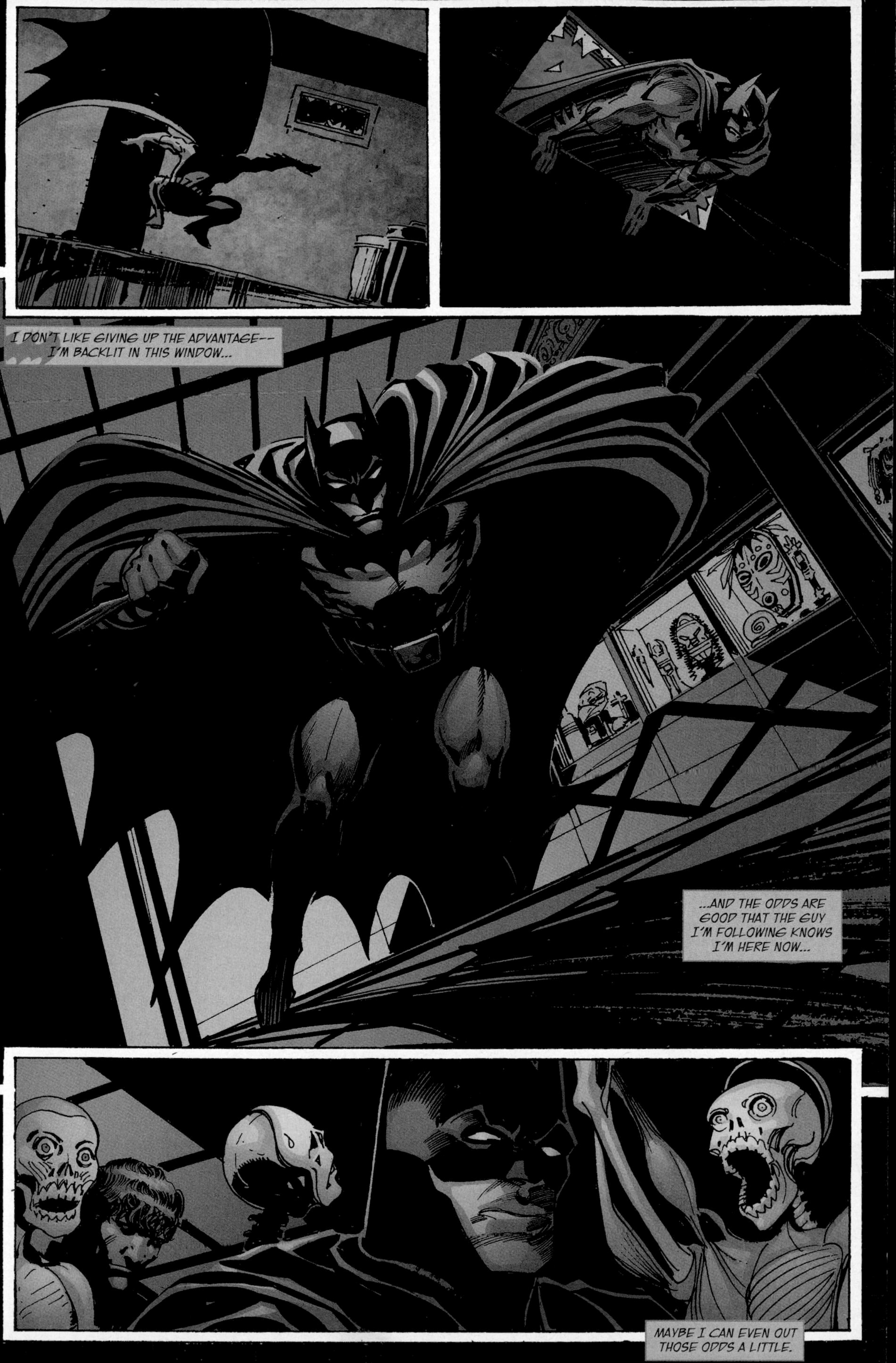
I DON'T LIKE GIVING UP THE ADVANTAGE-- I'M BACKLIT IN THIS WINDOW...
...AND THE ODDS ARE GOOD THAT THE GUY I'M FOLLOWING KNOWS I'M HERE NOW...
MAYBE I CAN EVEN OUT THOSE ODDS A LITTLE.

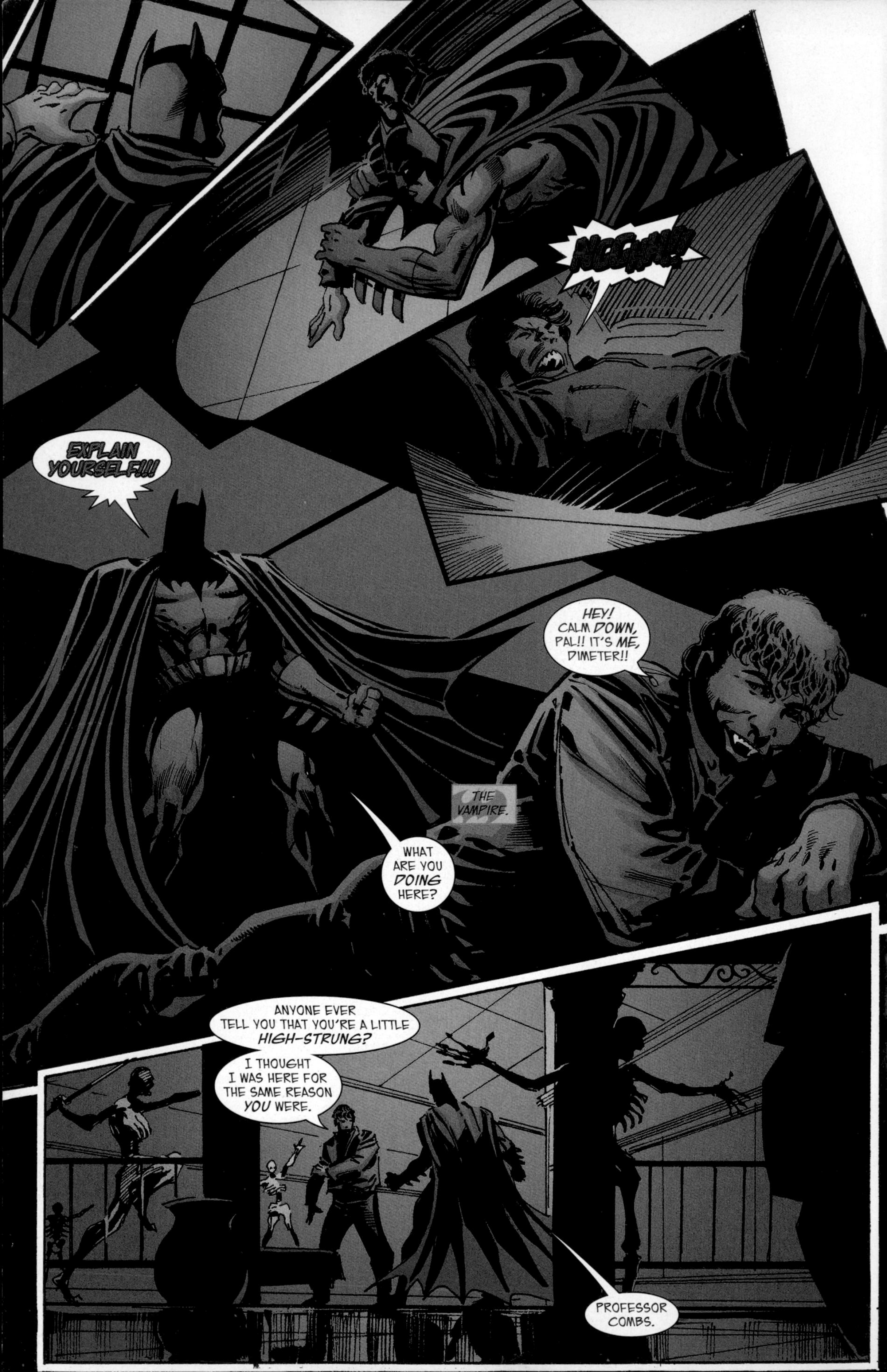
EXPLAIN YOURSELF!!!
HEY! CALM DOWN, PAL!! IT'S ME, DIMETER!!
THE VAMPIRE.
WHAT ARE YOU DOING HERE?
ANYONE EVER TELL YOU THAT YOU'RE A LITTLE HIGH-STRUNG?
I THOUGHT I WAS HERE FOR THE SAME REASON YOU WERE.
PROFESSOR COMBS.

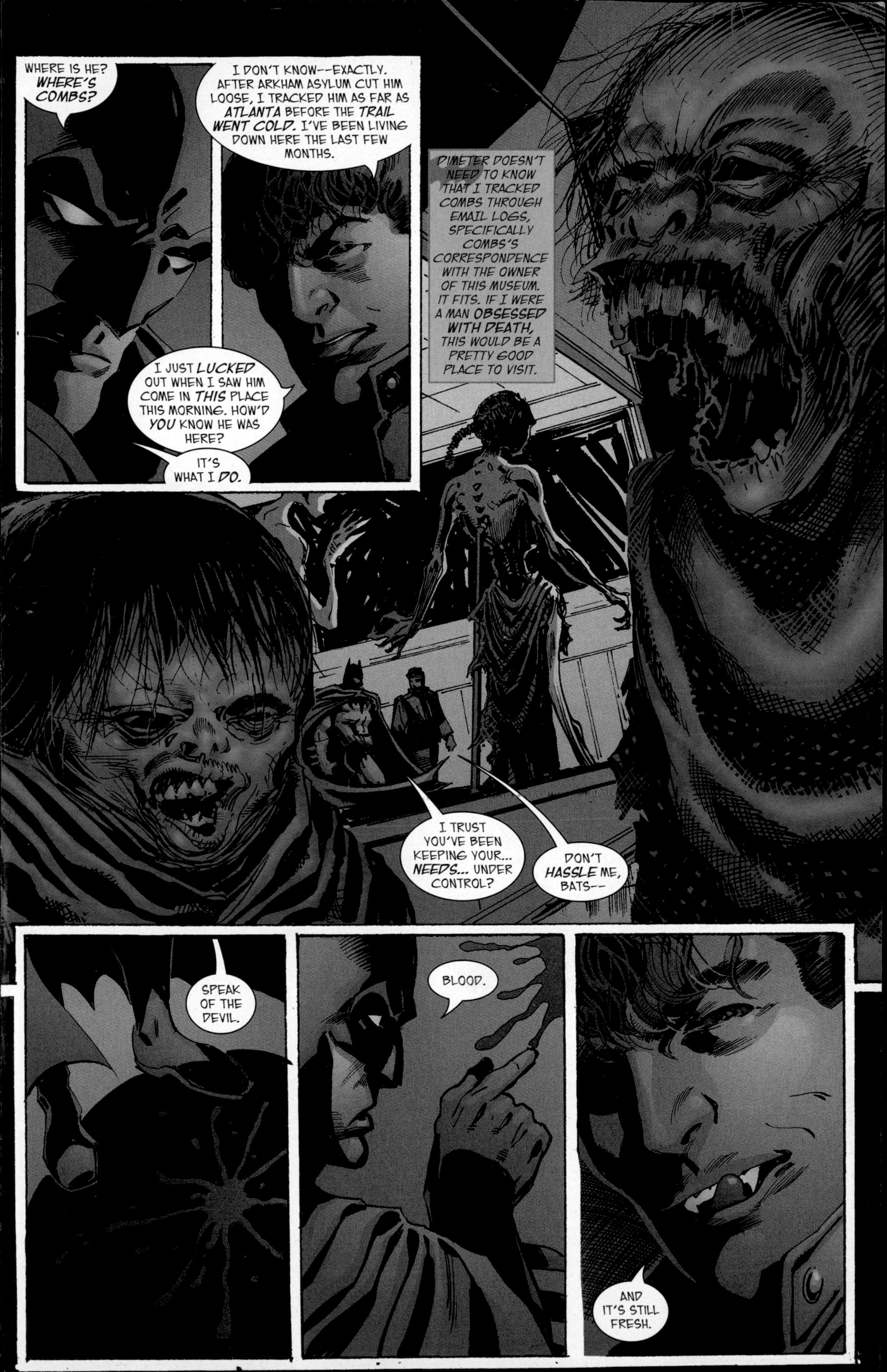
WHERE IS HE? WHERE'S COMBS?
I DON'T KNOW--EXACTLY. AFTER ARKHAM ASYLUM CUT HIM LOOSE, I TRACKED HIM AS FAR AS ATLANTA BEFORE THE TRAIL WENT COLD. I'VE BEEN LIVING DOWN HERE THE LAST FEW MONTHS.
I JUST LUCKED OUT WHEN I SAW HIM COME IN THIS PLACE THIS MORNING. HOW'D YOU KNOW HE WAS HERE?
IT'S WHAT I DO.
DIMETER DOESN'T NEED TO KNOW THAT I TRACKED COMBS THROUGH EMAIL LOGS, SPECIFICALLY COMBS'S CORRESPONDENCE WITH THE OWNER OF THIS MUSEUM. IT FITS. IF I WERE A MAN OBSESSED WITH DEATH, THIS WOULD BE A PRETTY GOOD PLACE TO VISIT.
I TRUST YOU'VE BEEN KEEPING YOUR... NEEDS... UNDER CONTROL?
DON'T HASSLE ME, BATS--
SPEAK OF THE DEVIL.
BLOOD.
AND IT'S STILL FRESH.

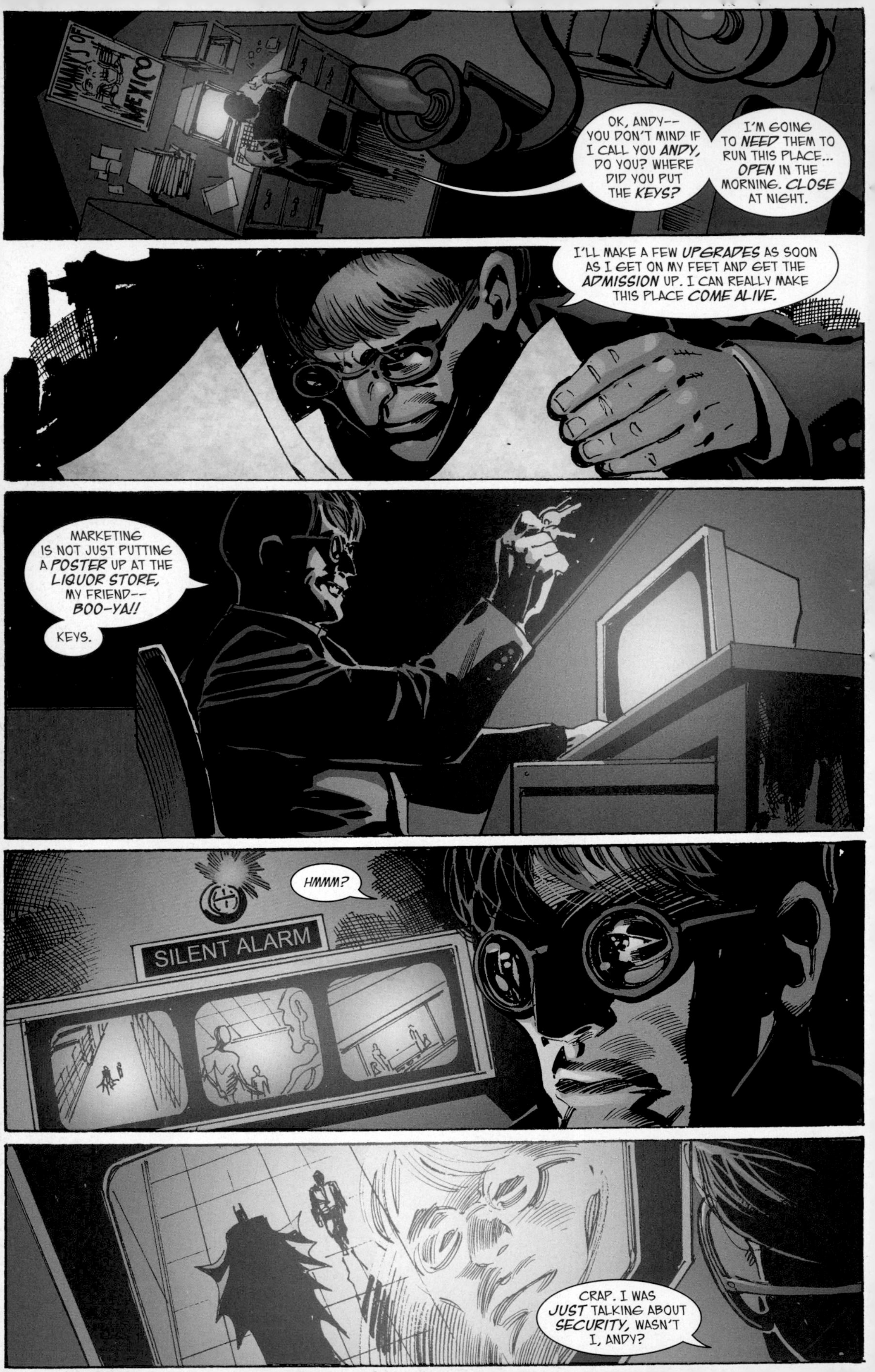
MUMMY'S OF MEXICO
OK, ANDY-- YOU DON'T MIND IF I CALL YOU ANDY, DO YOU? WHERE DID YOU PUT THE KEYS?
I'M GOING TO NEED THEM TO RUN THIS PLACE... OPEN IN THE MORNING. CLOSE AT NIGHT.
I'LL MAKE A FEW UPGRADES AS SOON AS I GET ON MY FEET AND GET THE ADMISSION UP. I CAN REALLY MAKE THIS PLACE COME ALIVE.
MARKETING IS NOT JUST PUTTING A POSTER UP AT THE LIQUOR STORE, MY FRIEND-- BOO-YA!!
KEYS.
HMMM?
SILENT ALARM
CRAP. I WAS JUST TALKING ABOUT SECURITY, WASN'T I, ANDY?

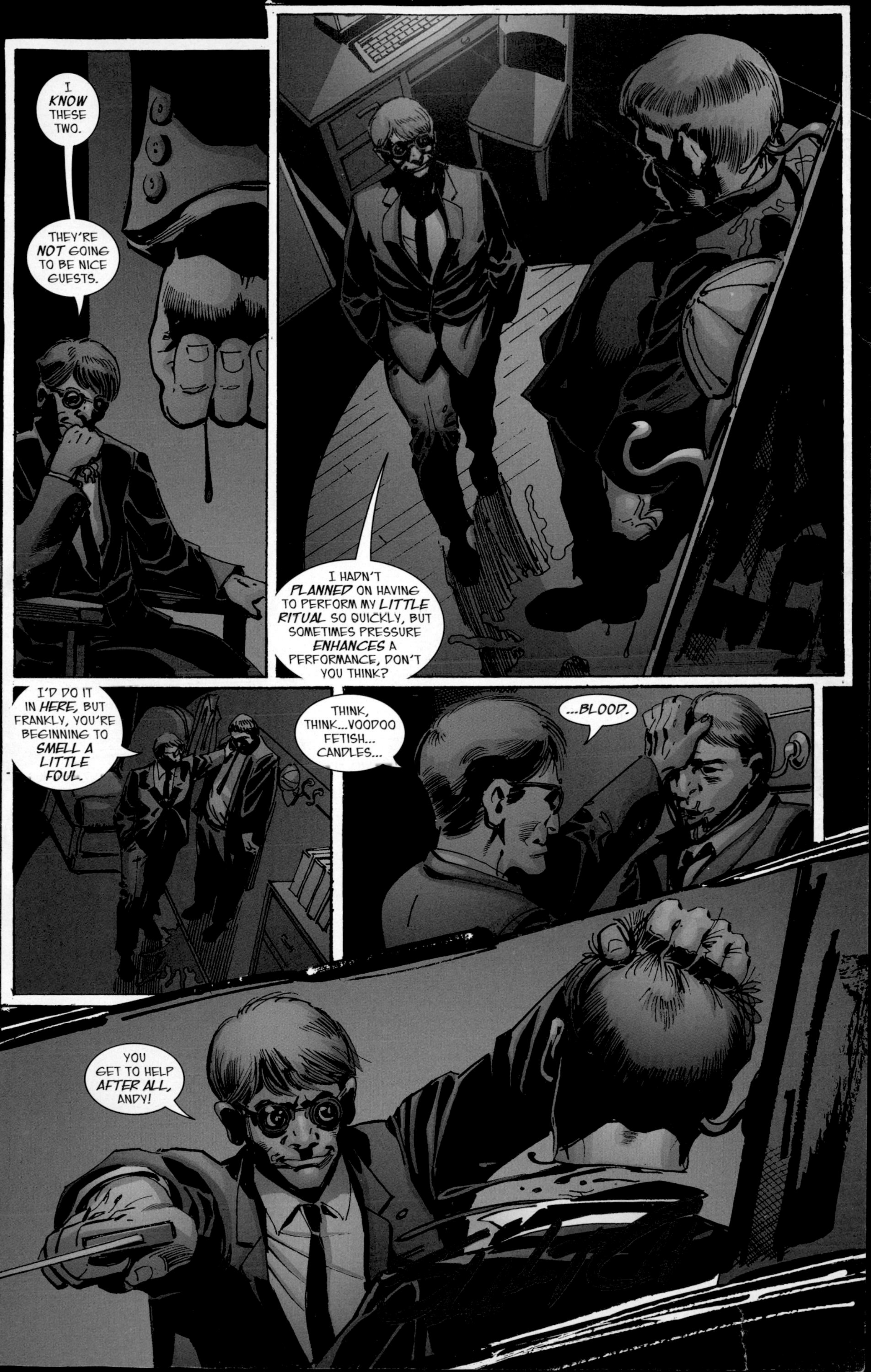
I KNOW THESE TWO.
THEY'RE NOT GOING TO BE NICE GUESTS.
I HADN'T PLANNED ON HAVING TO PERFORM MY LITTLE RITUAL SO QUICKLY, BUT SOMETIMES PRESSURE ENHANCES A PERFORMANCE, DON'T YOU THINK?
I'D DO IT IN HERE, BUT FRANKLY, YOU'RE BEGINNING TO SMELL A LITTLE FOUL.
THINK, THINK...VOODOO FETISH... CANDLES...
...BLOOD.
YOU GET TO HELP AFTER ALL, ANDY!

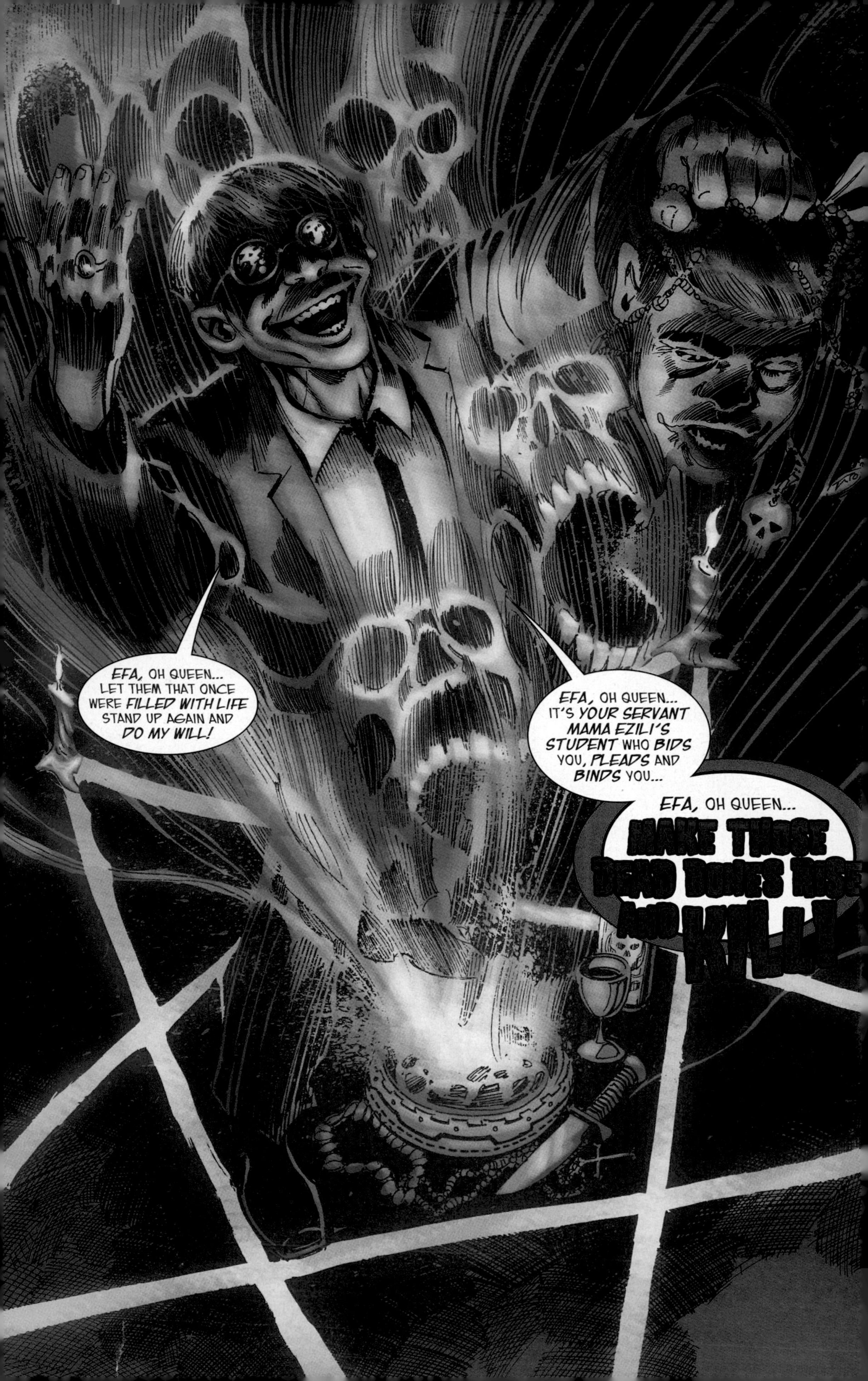
EFA, OH QUEEN... LET THEM THAT ONCE WERE FILLED WITH LIFE STAND UP AGAIN AND DO MY WILL!
EFA, OH QUEEN... IT'S YOUR SERVANT MAMA EZILI'S STUDENT WHO BIDS YOU, PLEADS AND BINDS YOU...
EFA, OH QUEEN... MAKE THOSE DEAD BONES RISE AND KILL!

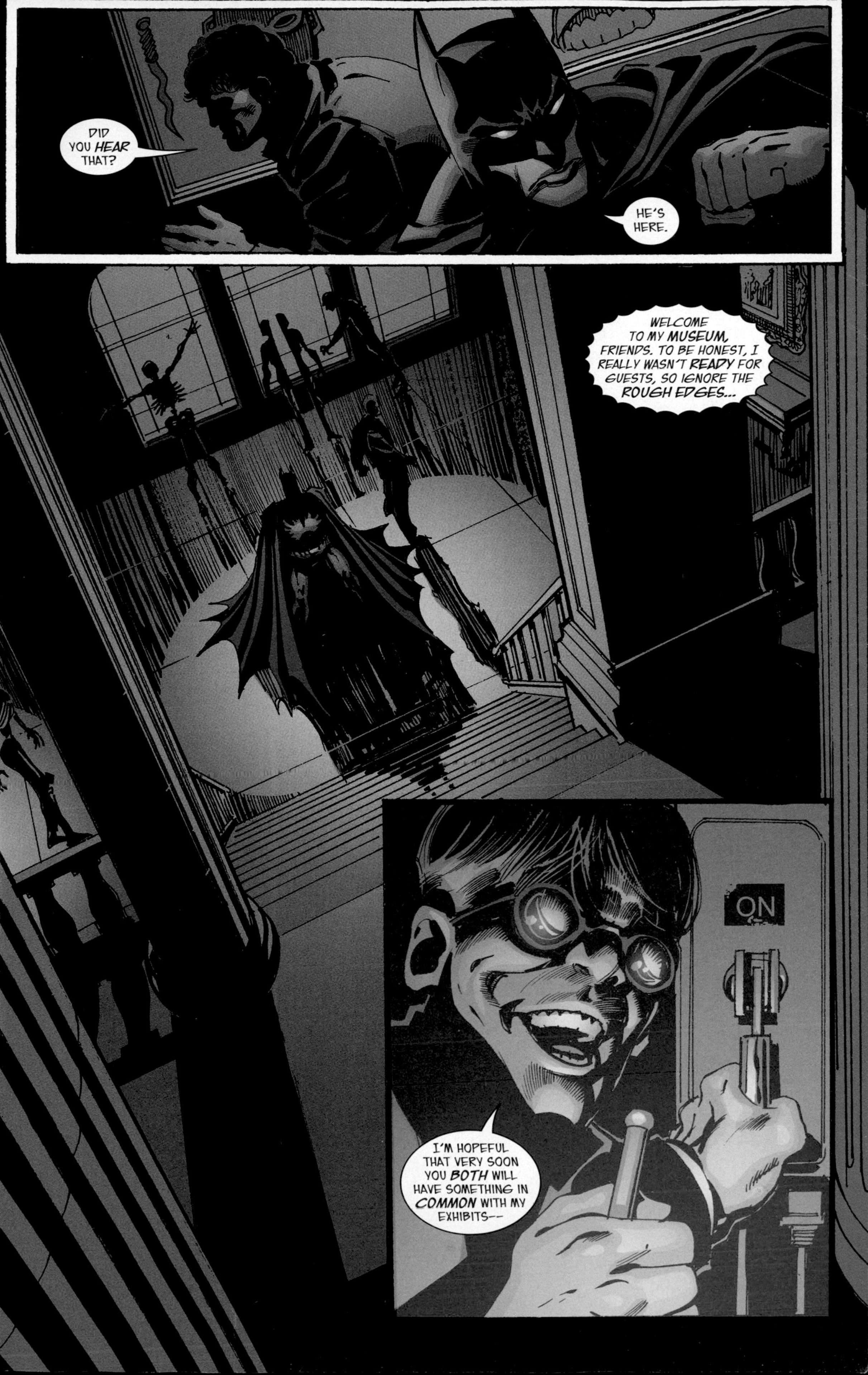
DID YOU HEAR THAT?
HE'S HERE.
WELCOME TO MY MUSEUM, FRIENDS. TO BE HONEST, I REALLY WASN'T READY FOR GUESTS, SO IGNORE THE ROUGH EDGES...
ON
I'M HOPEFUL THAT VERY SOON YOU BOTH WILL HAVE SOMETHING IN COMMON WITH MY EXHIBITS--

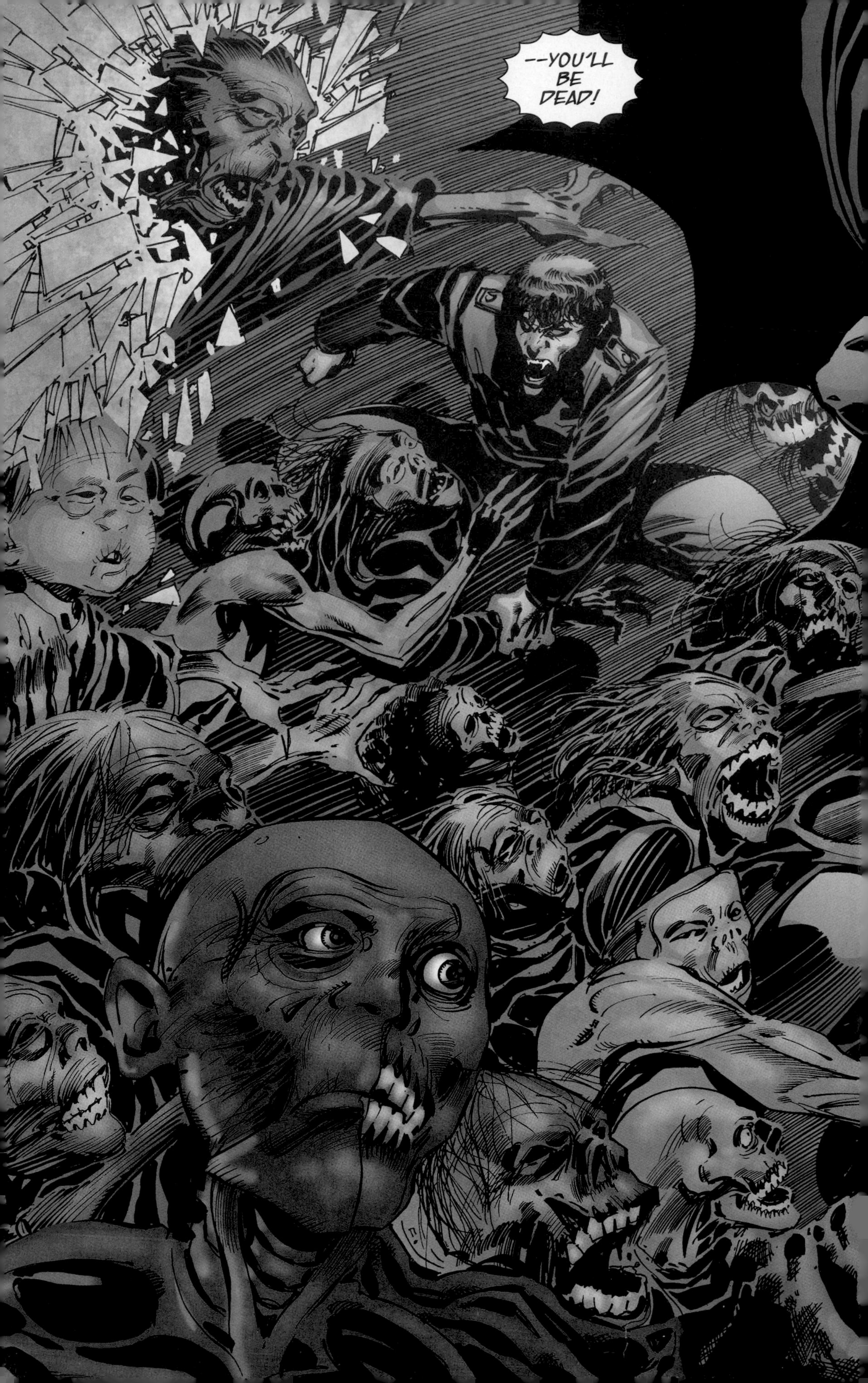
--YOU'LL BE DEAD!

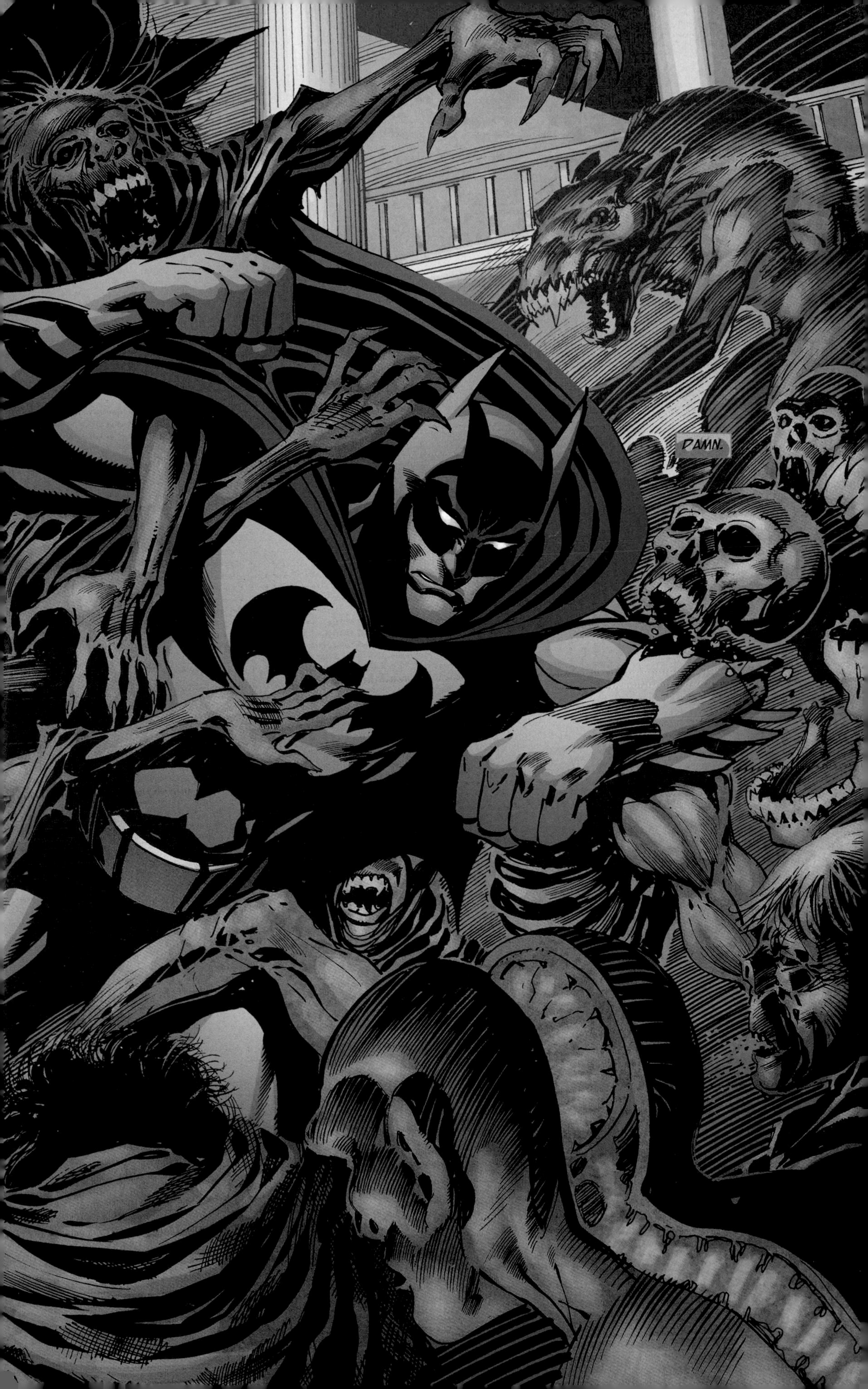
DAMN.

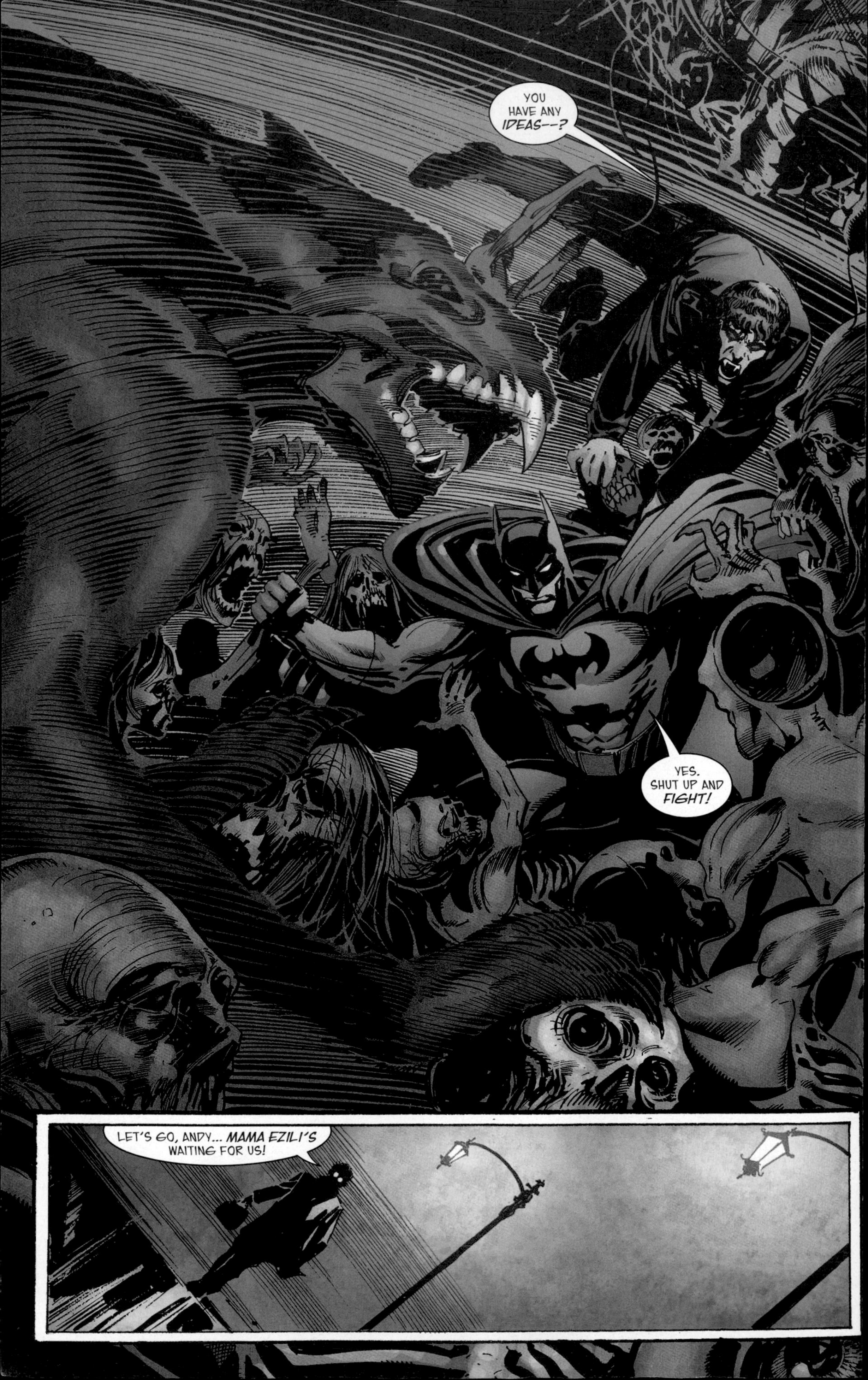
YOU HAVE ANY IDEAS--?
YES. SHUT UP AND FIGHT!
LET'S GO, ANDY... MAMA EZILI'S WAITING FOR US!

PART TWO: **DOWN IN THE BLACK BAYOU**

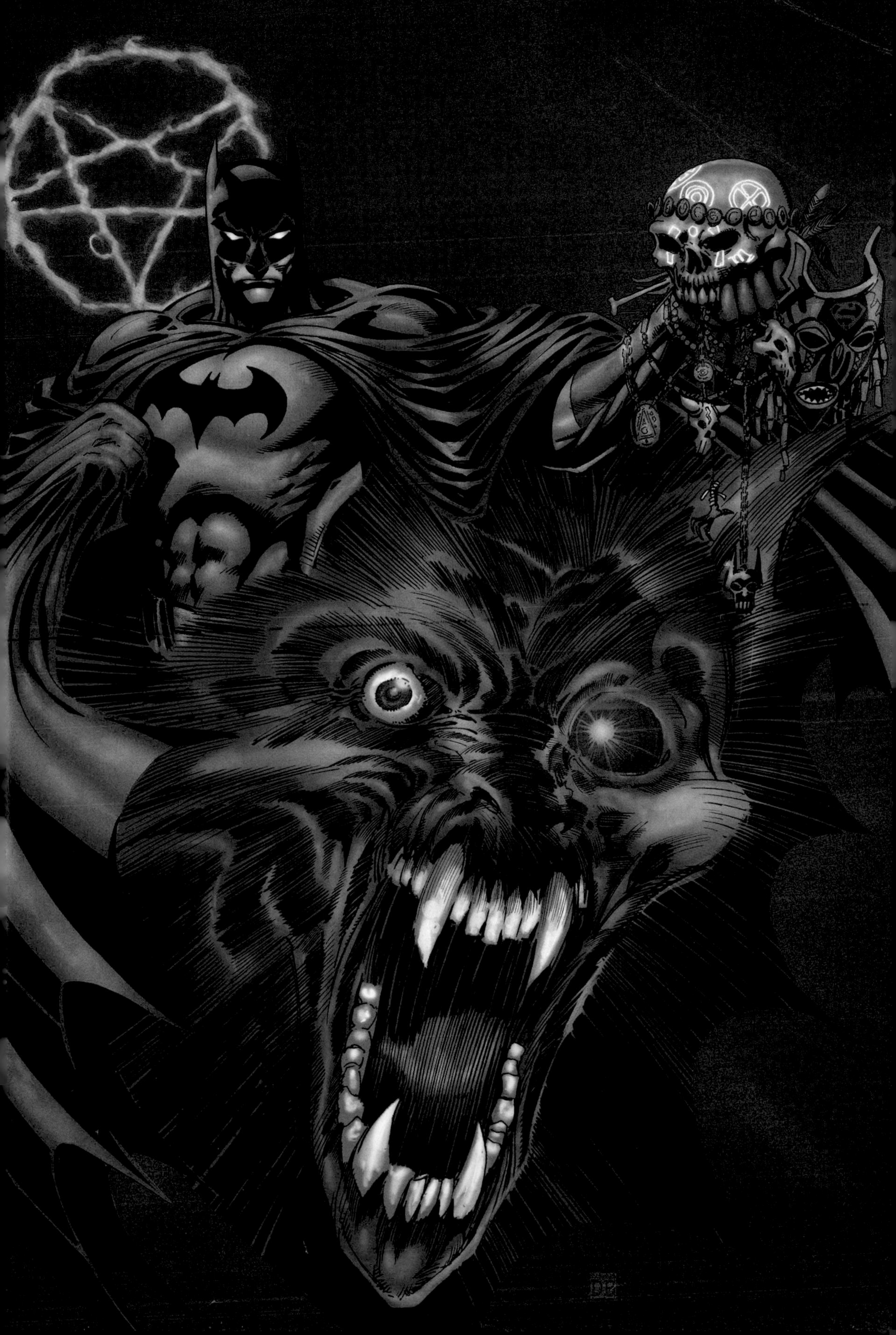

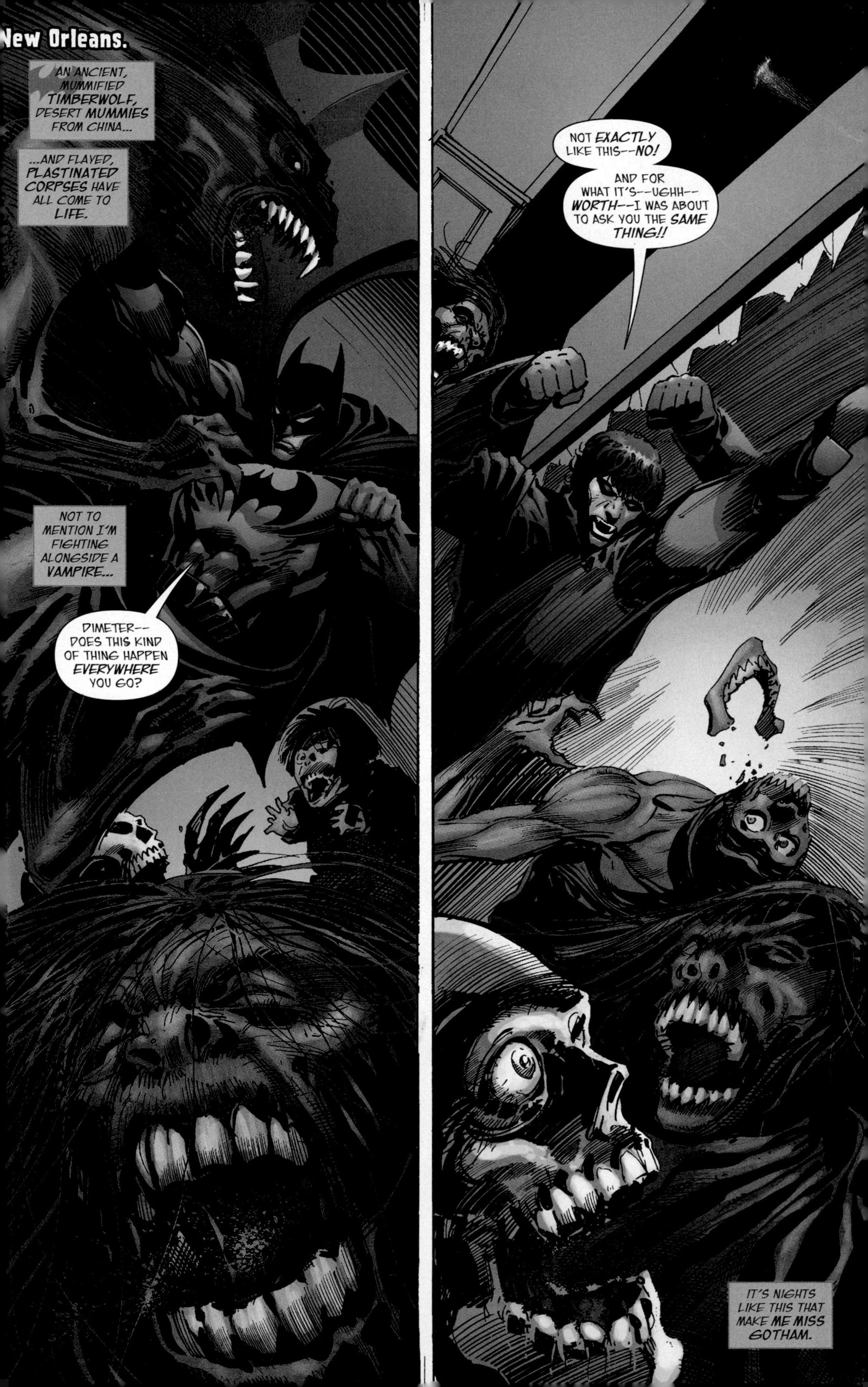
New Orleans.
AN ANCIENT, MUMMIFIED TIMBERWOLF, DESERT MUMMIES FROM CHINA...
...AND FLAYED, PLASTINATED CORPSES HAVE ALL COME TO LIFE.
NOT TO MENTION I'M FIGHTING ALONGSIDE A VAMPIRE...
DIMETER-- DOES THIS KIND OF THING HAPPEN EVERYWHERE YOU GO?
NOT EXACTLY LIKE THIS--NO!
AND FOR WHAT IT'S--UGHH--WORTH--I WAS ABOUT TO ASK YOU THE SAME THING!!
IT'S NIGHTS LIKE THIS THAT MAKE ME MISS GOTHAM.

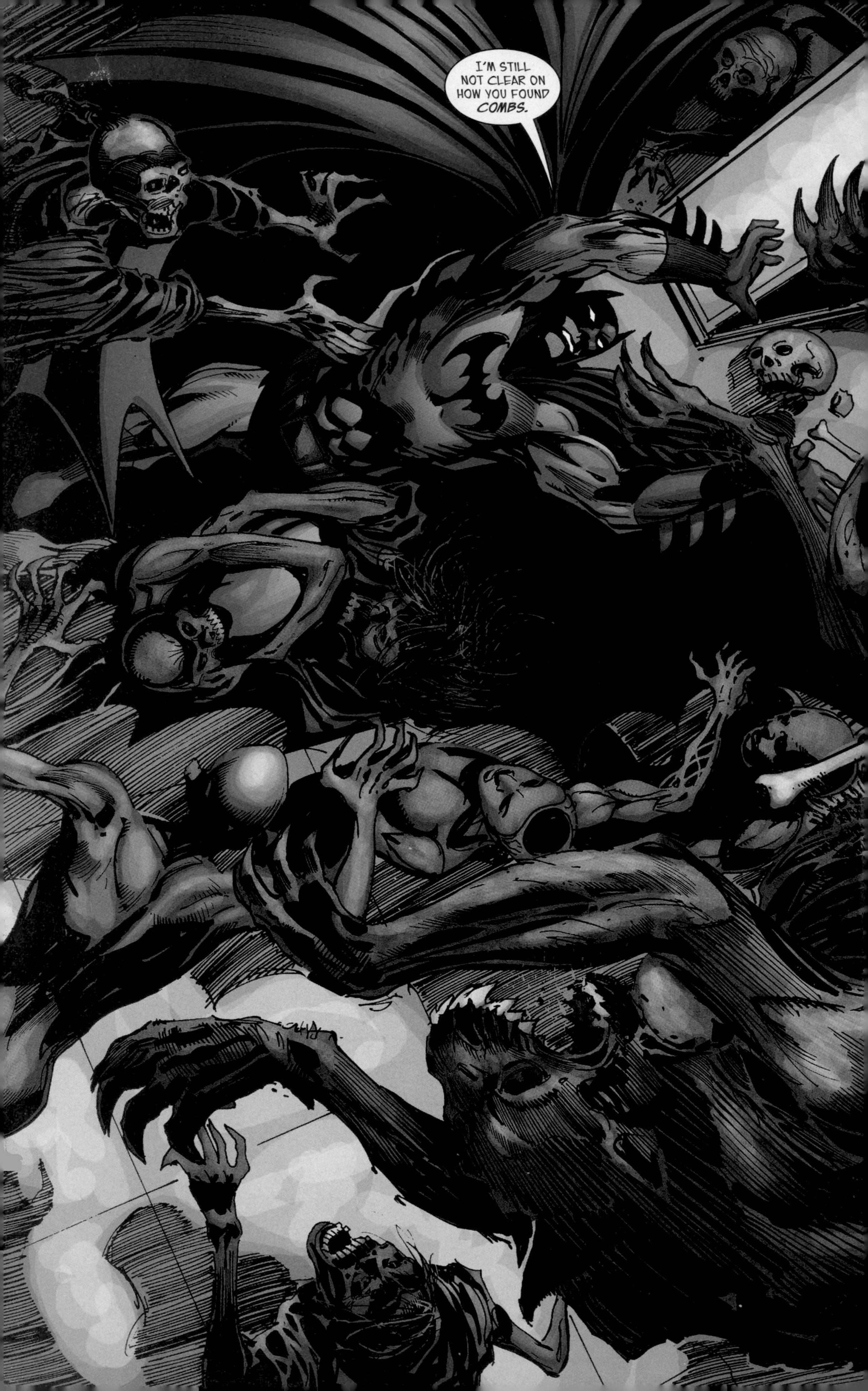
I'M STILL NOT CLEAR ON HOW YOU FOUND *COMBS*.

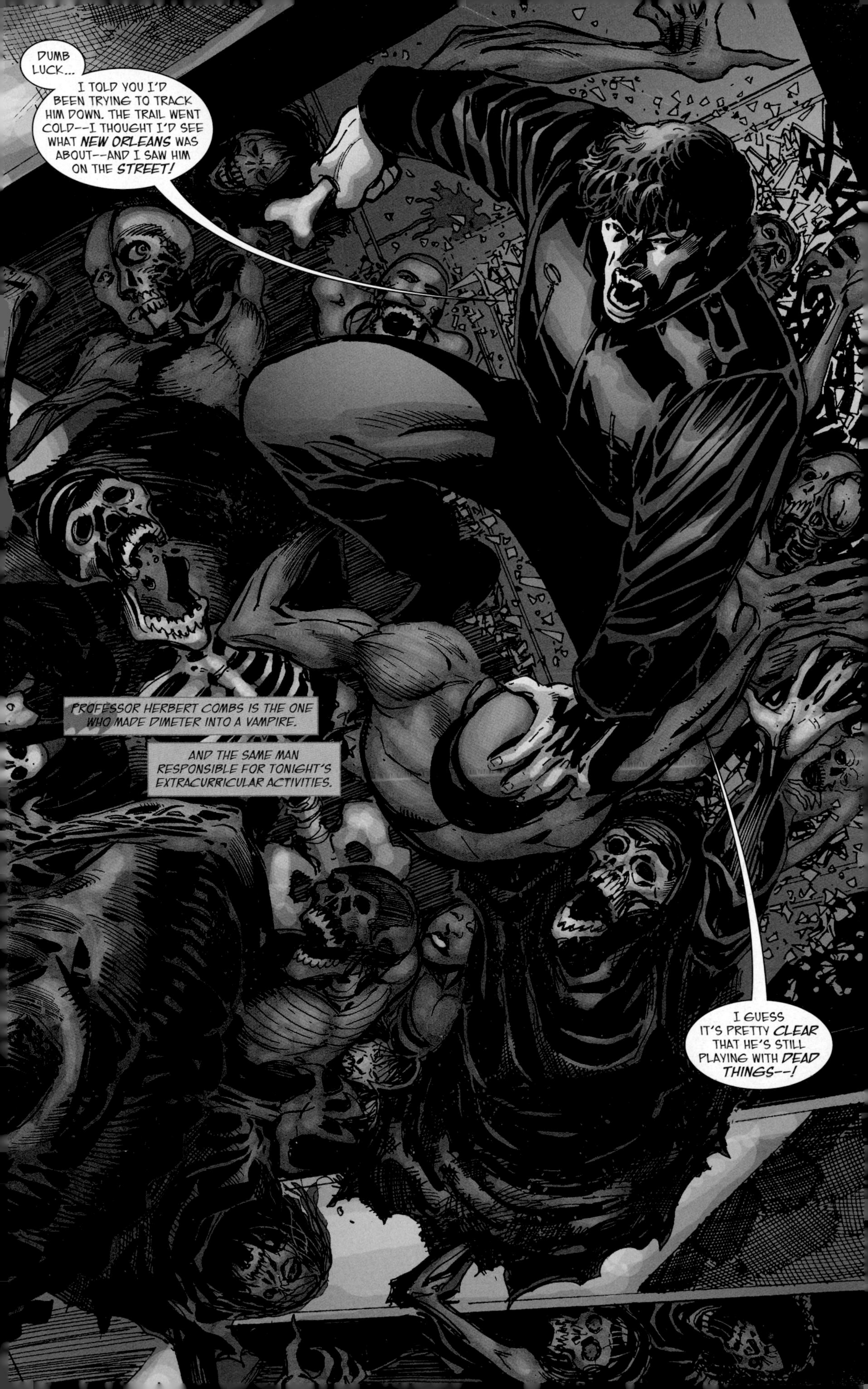
DUMB LUCK...
I TOLD YOU I'D BEEN TRYING TO TRACK HIM DOWN. THE TRAIL WENT COLD--I THOUGHT I'D SEE WHAT NEW ORLEANS WAS ABOUT--AND I SAW HIM ON THE STREET!
PROFESSOR HERBERT COMBS IS THE ONE WHO MADE DIMETER INTO A VAMPIRE.
AND THE SAME MAN RESPONSIBLE FOR TONIGHT'S EXTRACURRICULAR ACTIVITIES.
I GUESS IT'S PRETTY CLEAR THAT HE'S STILL PLAYING WITH DEAD THINGS--!

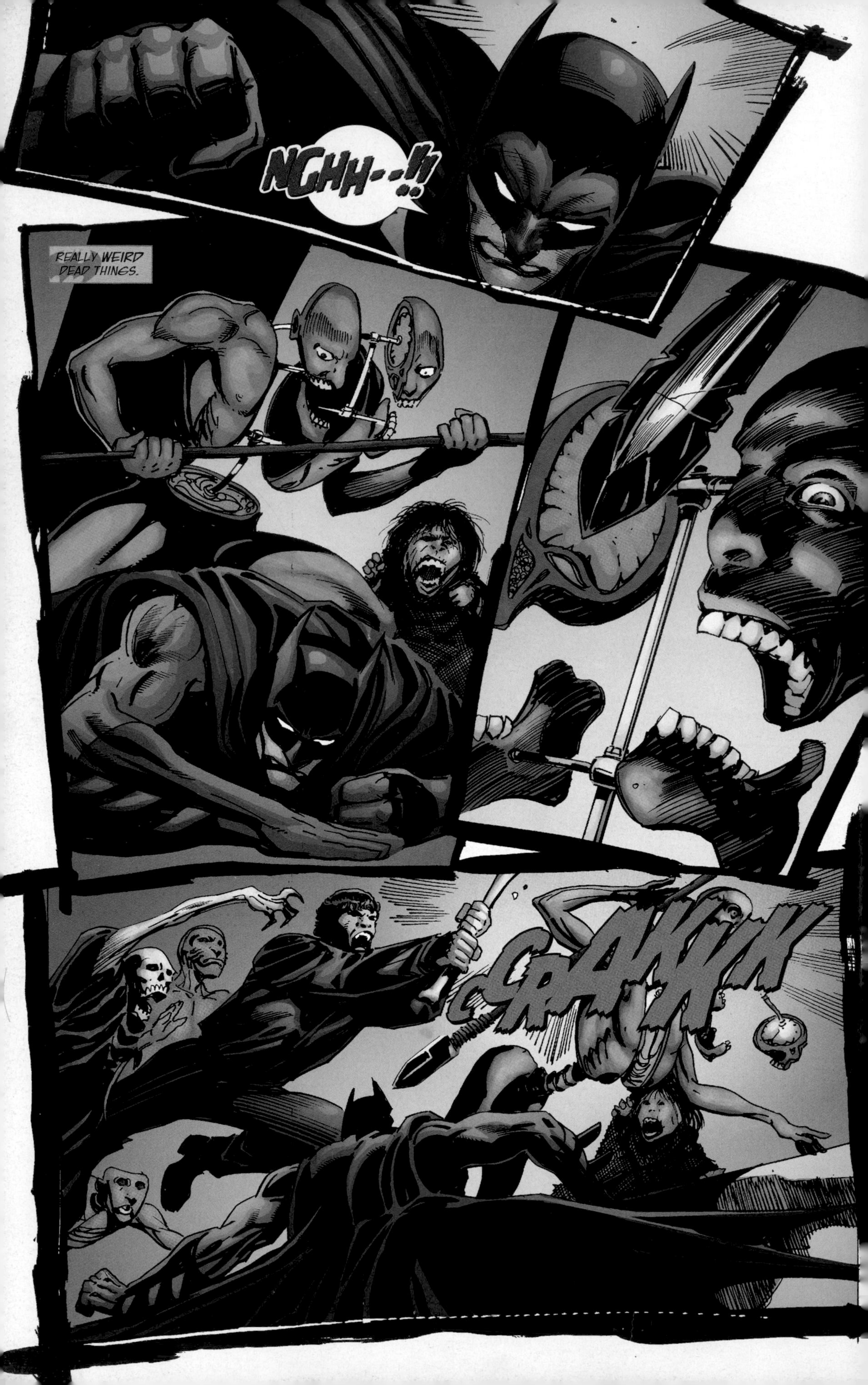
NGHH--!!
REALLY WEIRD DEAD THINGS.
CRAKKK

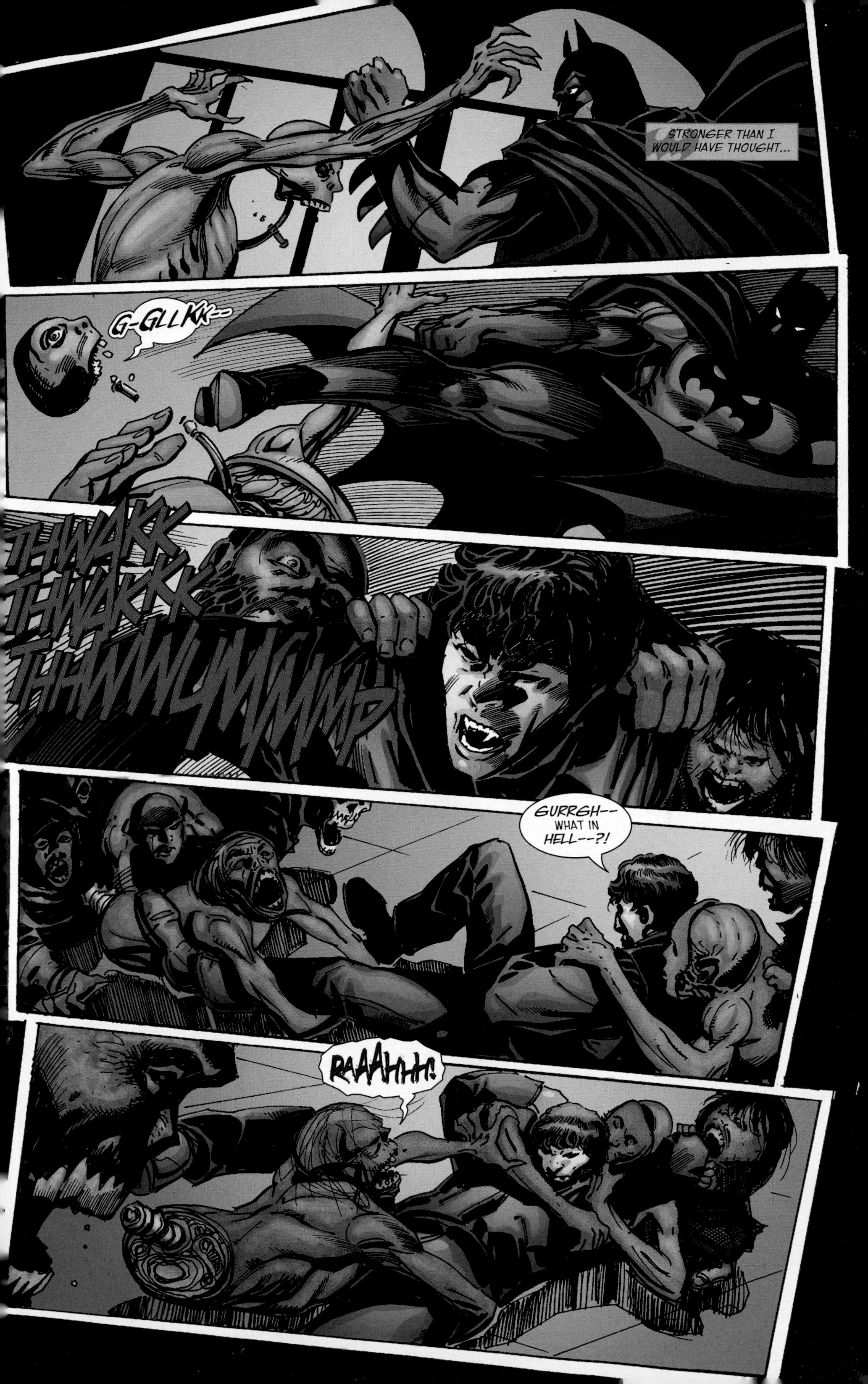
STRONGER THAN I WOULD HAVE THOUGHT...
G-GLLKK--
THWAKK
THWAKKK
THHWWUMMMMP
GURRGH-- WHAT IN HELL--?!
RAAAHHH!

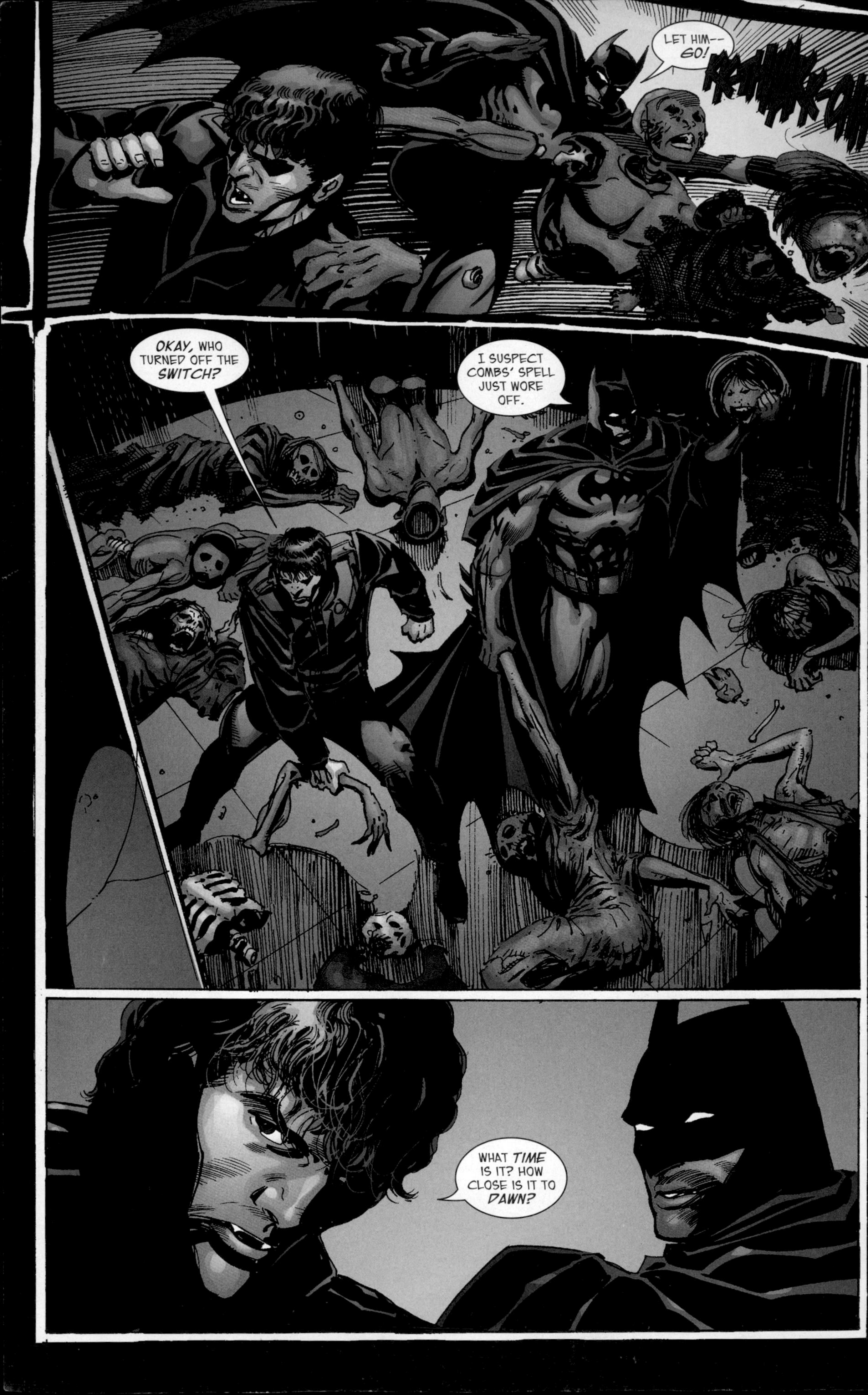

LET HIM-- GO!
KRAKK-OOM
OKAY, WHO TURNED OFF THE SWITCH?
I SUSPECT COMBS' SPELL JUST WORE OFF.
WHAT TIME IS IT? HOW CLOSE IS IT TO DAWN?

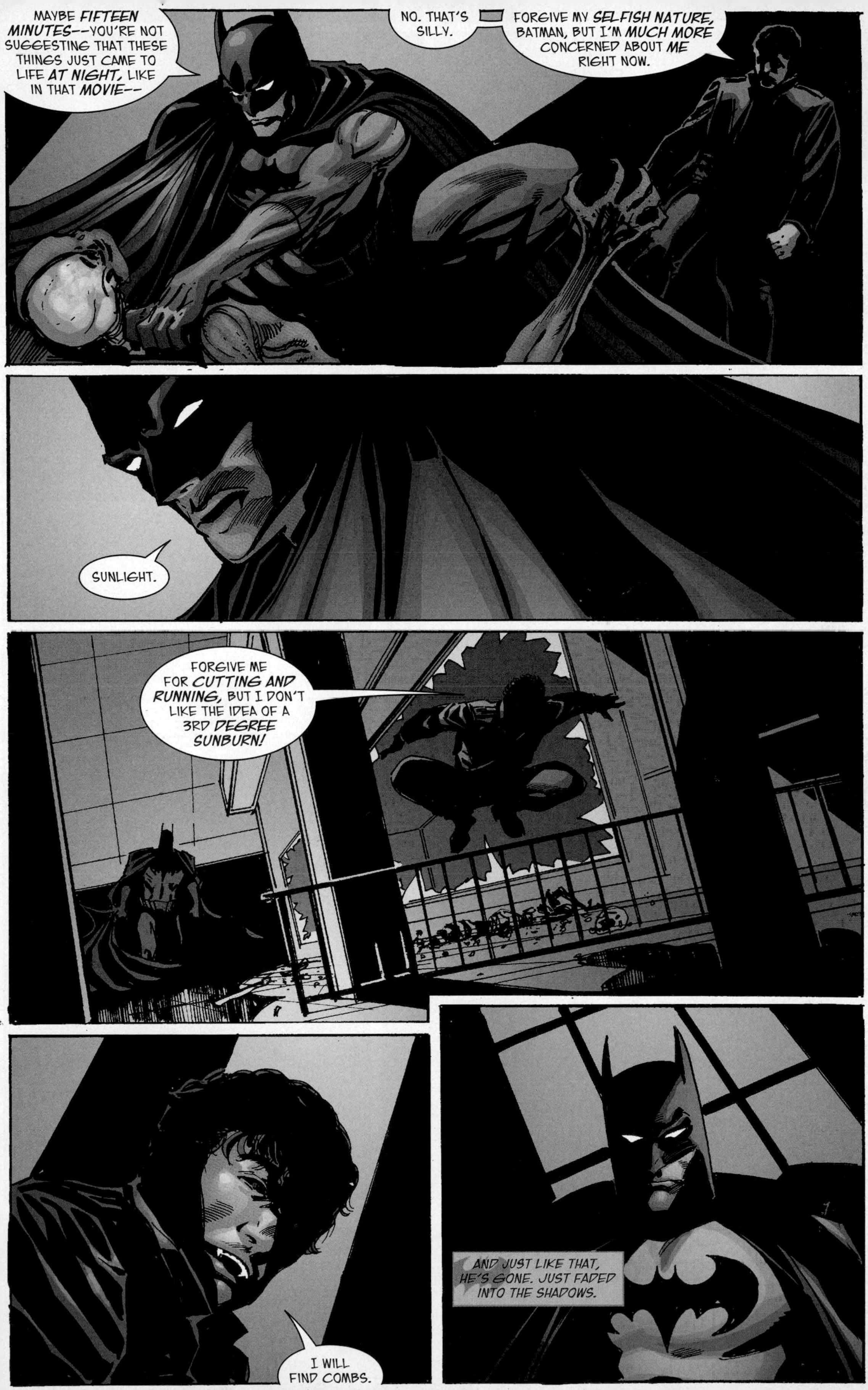
MAYBE FIFTEEN MINUTES--YOU'RE NOT SUGGESTING THAT THESE THINGS JUST CAME TO LIFE AT NIGHT, LIKE IN THAT MOVIE--
NO. THAT'S SILLY.
FORGIVE MY SELFISH NATURE, BATMAN, BUT I'M MUCH MORE CONCERNED ABOUT ME RIGHT NOW.
SUNLIGHT.
FORGIVE ME FOR CUTTING AND RUNNING, BUT I DON'T LIKE THE IDEA OF A 3RD DEGREE SUNBURN!
I WILL FIND COMBS.
AND JUST LIKE THAT, HE'S GONE. JUST FADED INTO THE SHADOWS.

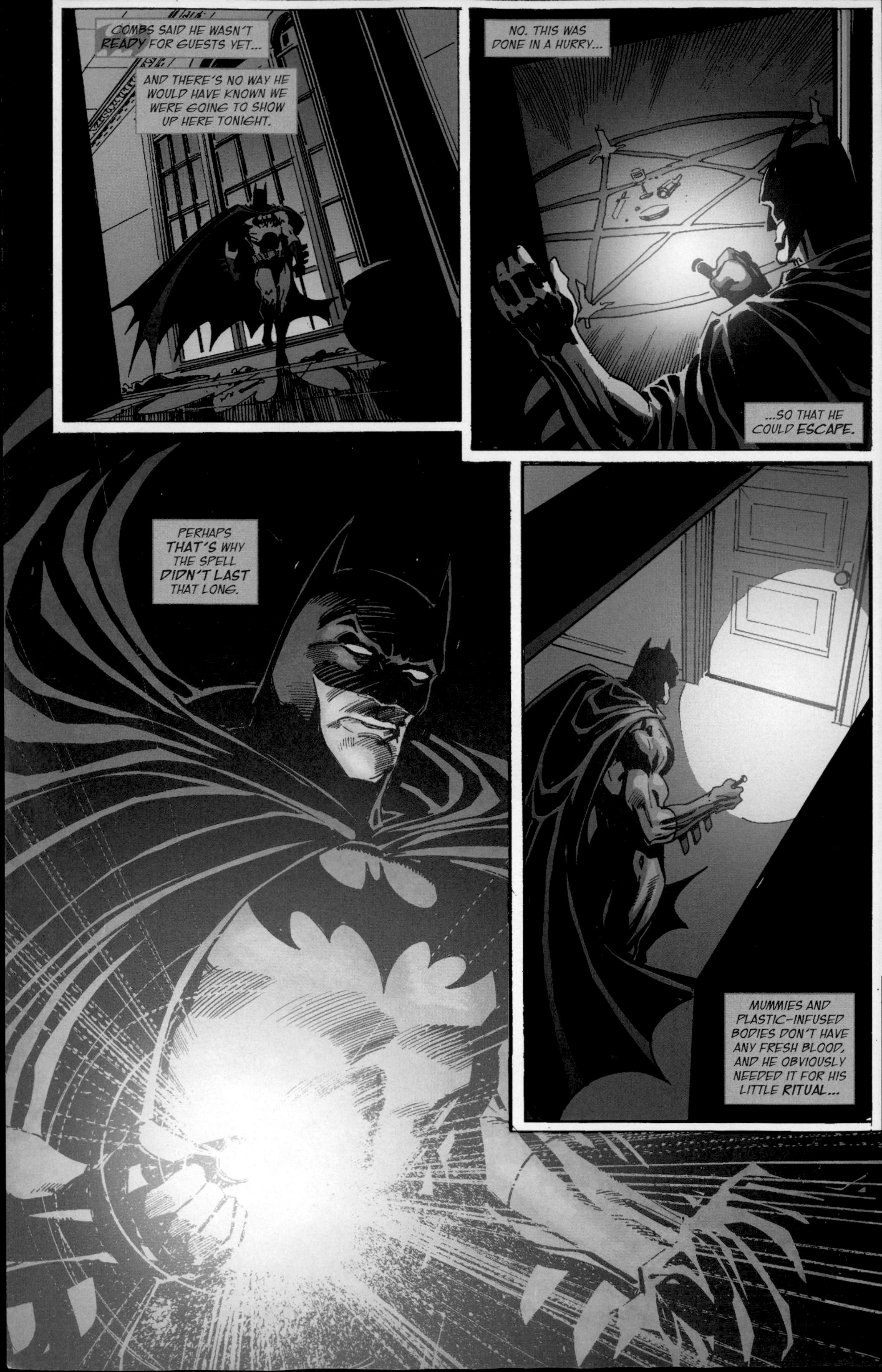
COMBS SAID HE WASN'T READY FOR GUESTS YET...
AND THERE'S NO WAY HE WOULD HAVE KNOWN WE WERE GOING TO SHOW UP HERE TONIGHT.
NO. THIS WAS DONE IN A HURRY...
...SO THAT HE COULD ESCAPE.
PERHAPS THAT'S WHY THE SPELL DIDN'T LAST THAT LONG.
MUMMIES AND PLASTIC-INFUSED BODIES DON'T HAVE ANY FRESH BLOOD, AND HE OBVIOUSLY NEEDED IT FOR HIS LITTLE RITUAL...

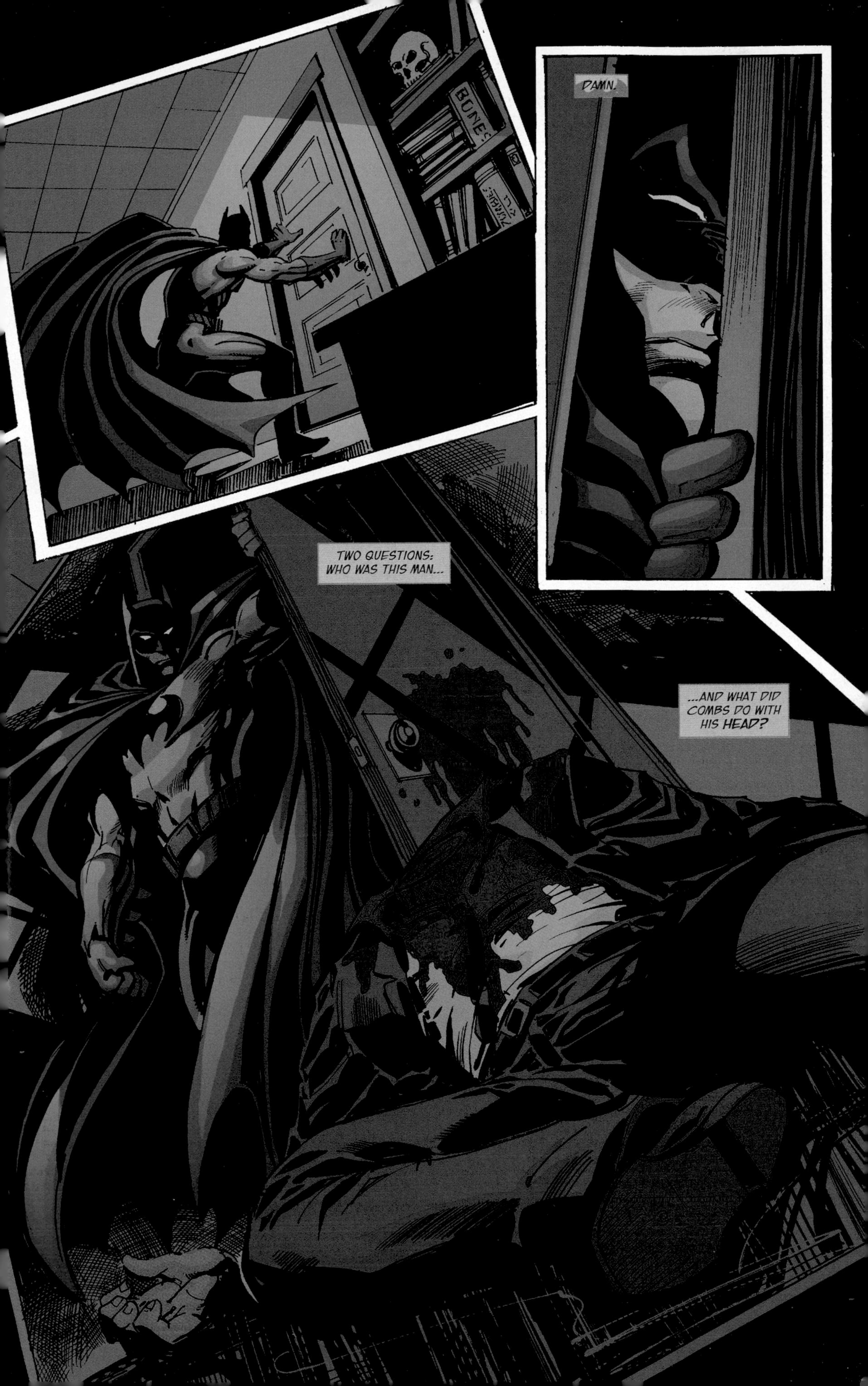
DAMN.
TWO QUESTIONS: WHO WAS THIS MAN...
...AND WHAT DID COMBS DO WITH HIS HEAD?
BONES

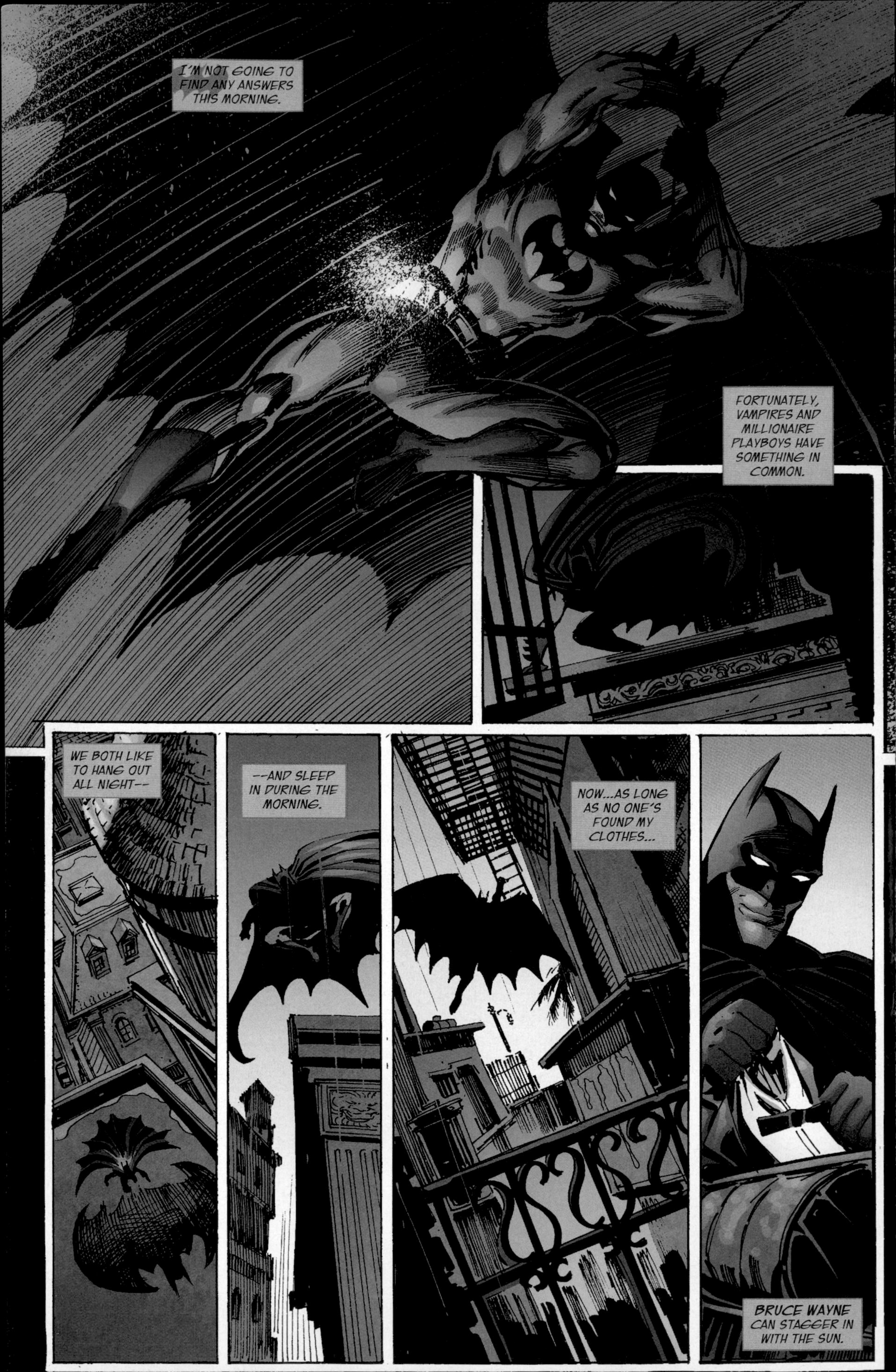
I'M NOT GOING TO FIND ANY ANSWERS THIS MORNING.
FORTUNATELY, VAMPIRES AND MILLIONAIRE PLAYBOYS HAVE SOMETHING IN COMMON.
WE BOTH LIKE TO HANG OUT ALL NIGHT--
--AND SLEEP IN DURING THE MORNING.
NOW...AS LONG AS NO ONE'S FOUND MY CLOTHES...
BRUCE WAYNE CAN STAGGER IN WITH THE SUN.

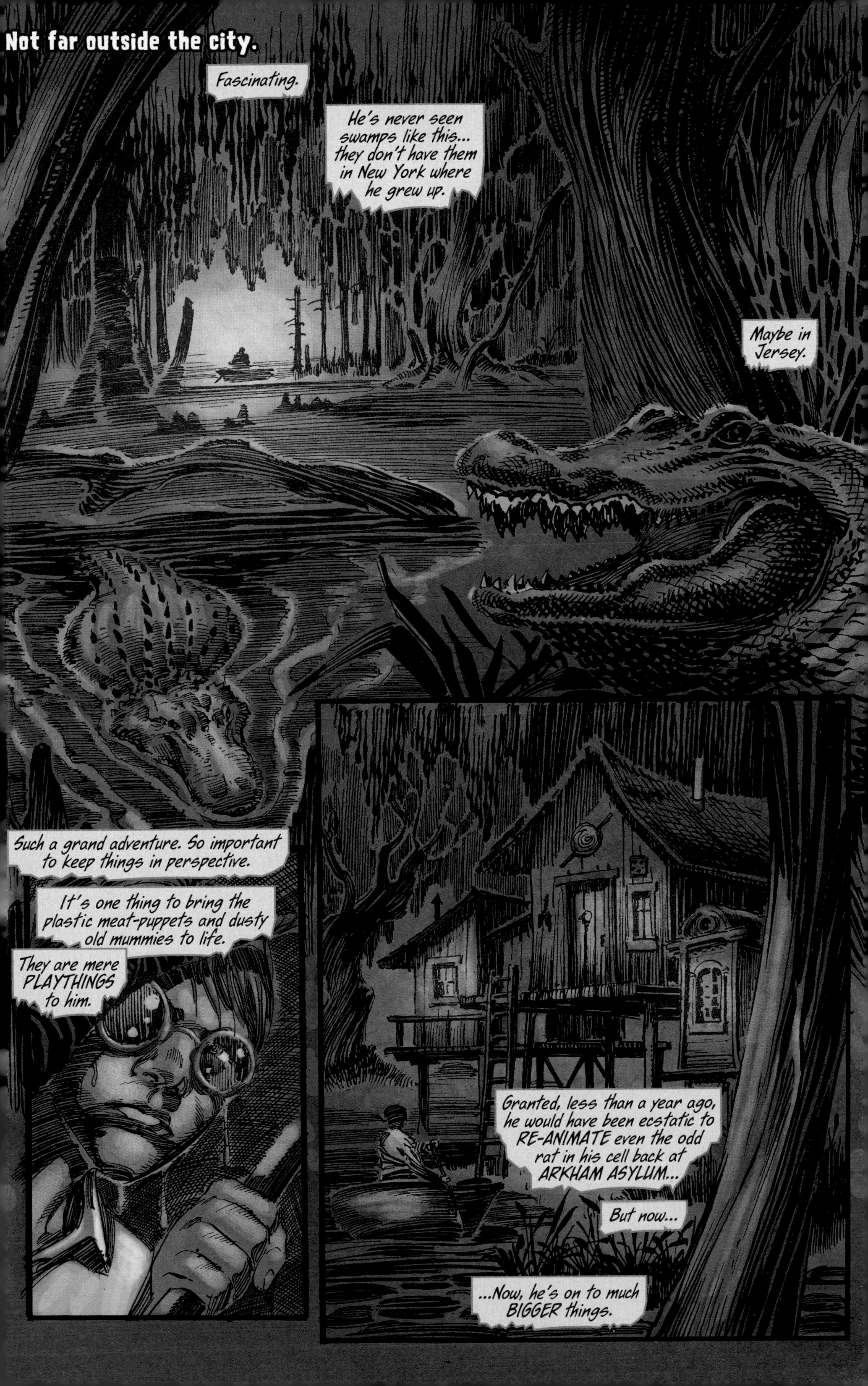
Not far outside the city.
Fascinating.
He's never seen swamps like this... they don't have them in New York where he grew up.
Maybe in Jersey.
Such a grand adventure. So important to keep things in perspective.
It's one thing to bring the plastic meat-puppets and dusty old mummies to life.
They are mere PLAYTHINGS to him.
Granted, less than a year ago, he would have been ecstatic to RE-ANIMATE even the odd rat in his cell back at ARKHAM ASYLUM...
But now...
...Now, he's on to much BIGGER things.

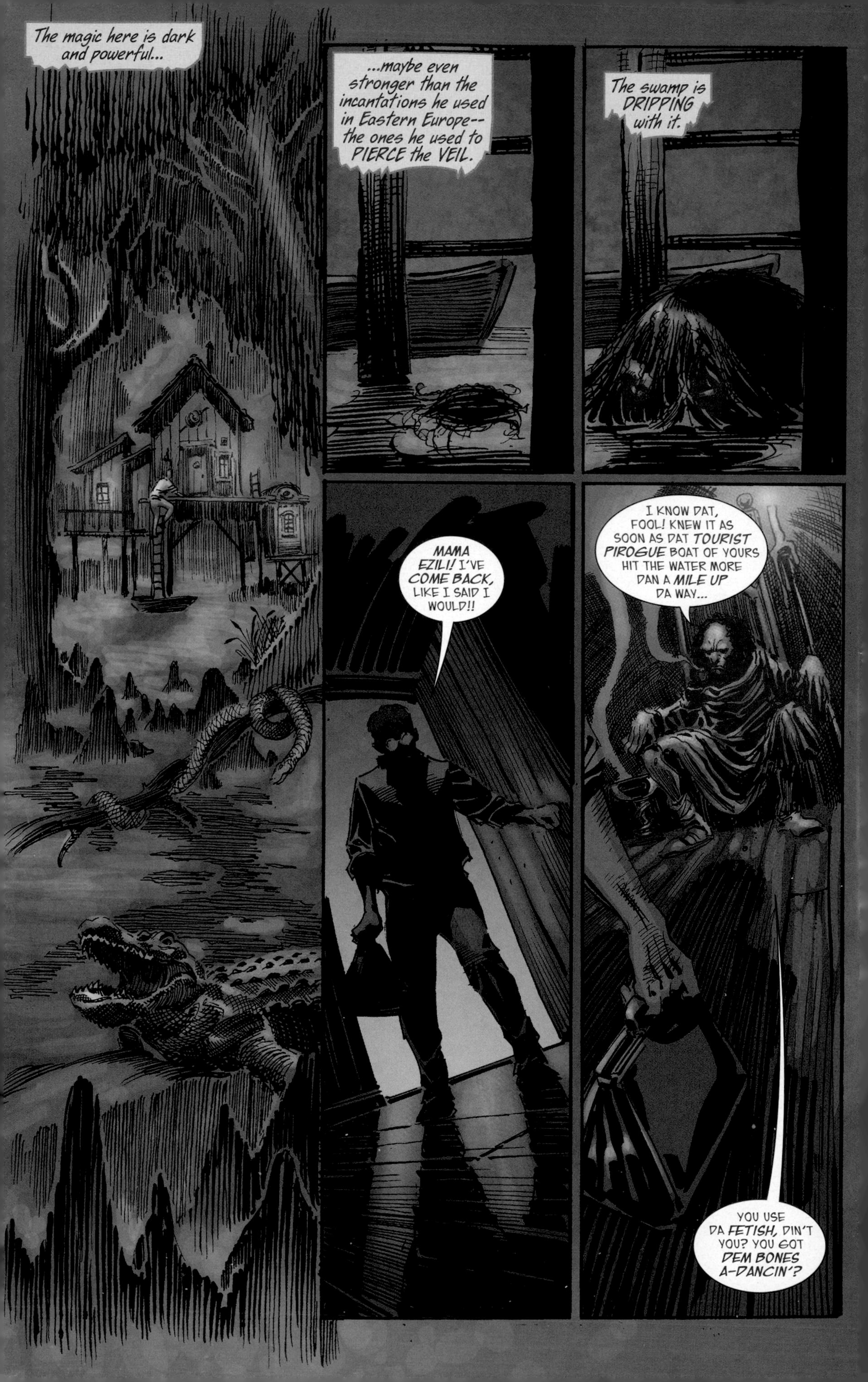
The magic here is dark and powerful...
...maybe even stronger than the incantations he used in Eastern Europe--the ones he used to PIERCE the VEIL.
The swamp is DRIPPING with it.
MAMA EZILI! I'VE COME BACK, LIKE I SAID I WOULD!!
I KNOW DAT, FOOL! KNEW IT AS SOON AS DAT TOURIST PIROGUE BOAT OF YOURS HIT THE WATER MORE DAN A MILE UP DA WAY...
YOU USE DA FETISH, DIN'T YOU? YOU GOT DEM BONES A-DANCIN'?

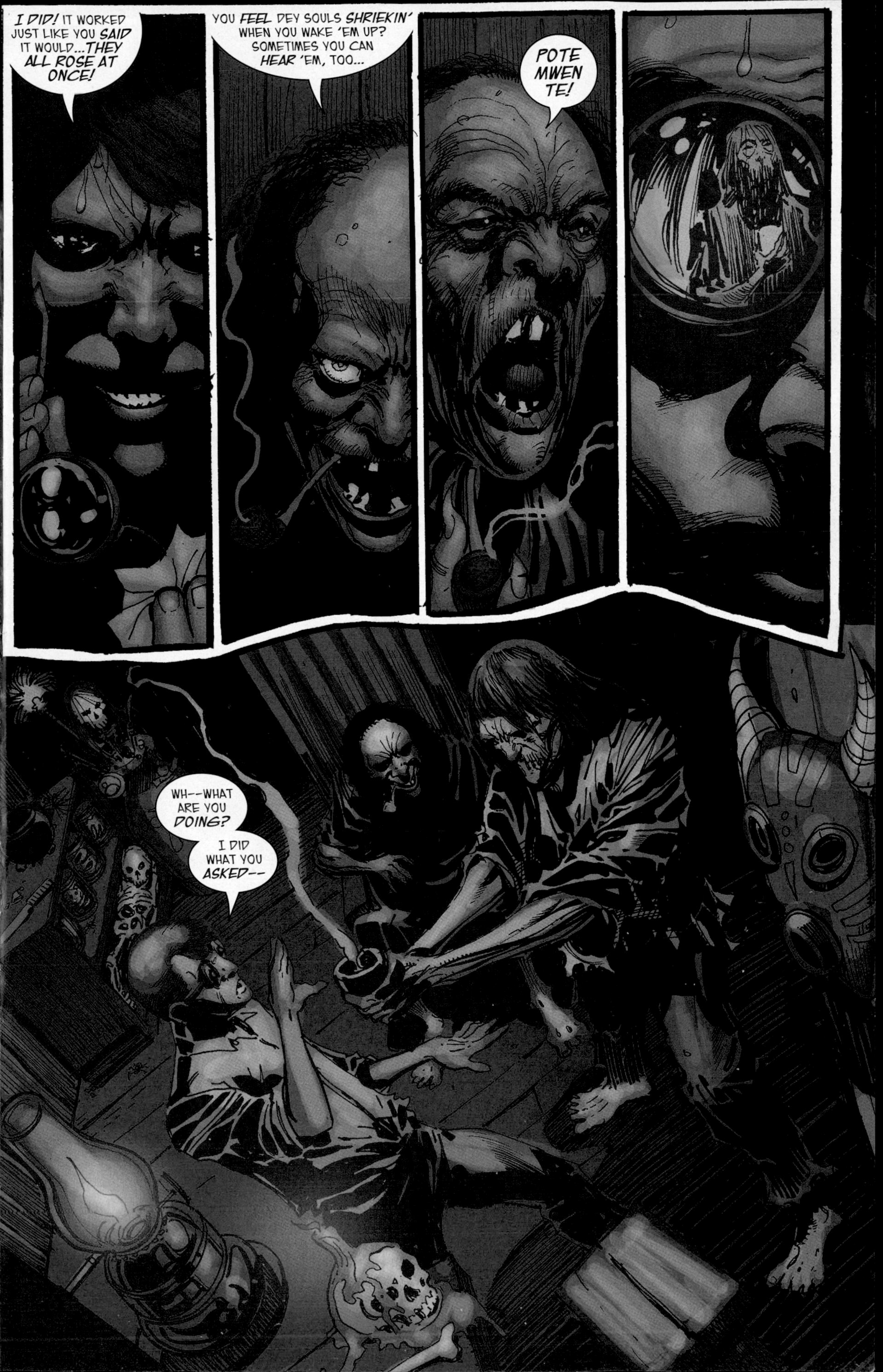
I DID! IT WORKED JUST LIKE YOU SAID IT WOULD...THEY ALL ROSE AT ONCE!
YOU FEEL DEY SOULS SHRIEKIN' WHEN YOU WAKE 'EM UP? SOMETIMES YOU CAN HEAR 'EM, TOO...
POTE MWEN TE!
WH--WHAT ARE YOU DOING?
I DID WHAT YOU ASKED--

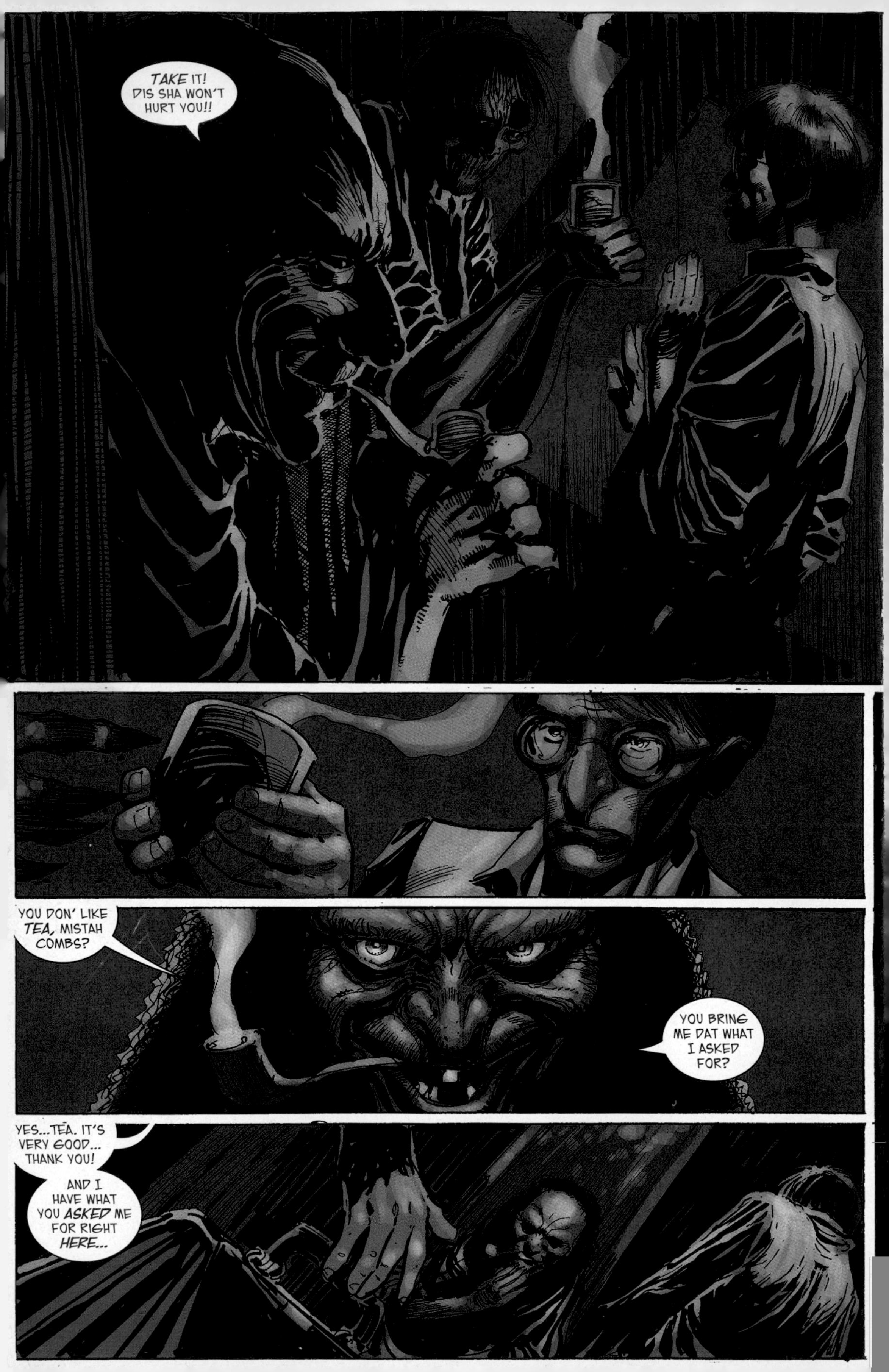
TAKE IT! DIS SHA WON'T HURT YOU!!
YOU DON' LIKE TEA, MISTAH COMBS?
YOU BRING ME DAT WHAT I ASKED FOR?
YES...TEA. IT'S VERY GOOD... THANK YOU!
AND I HAVE WHAT YOU ASKED ME FOR RIGHT HERE...

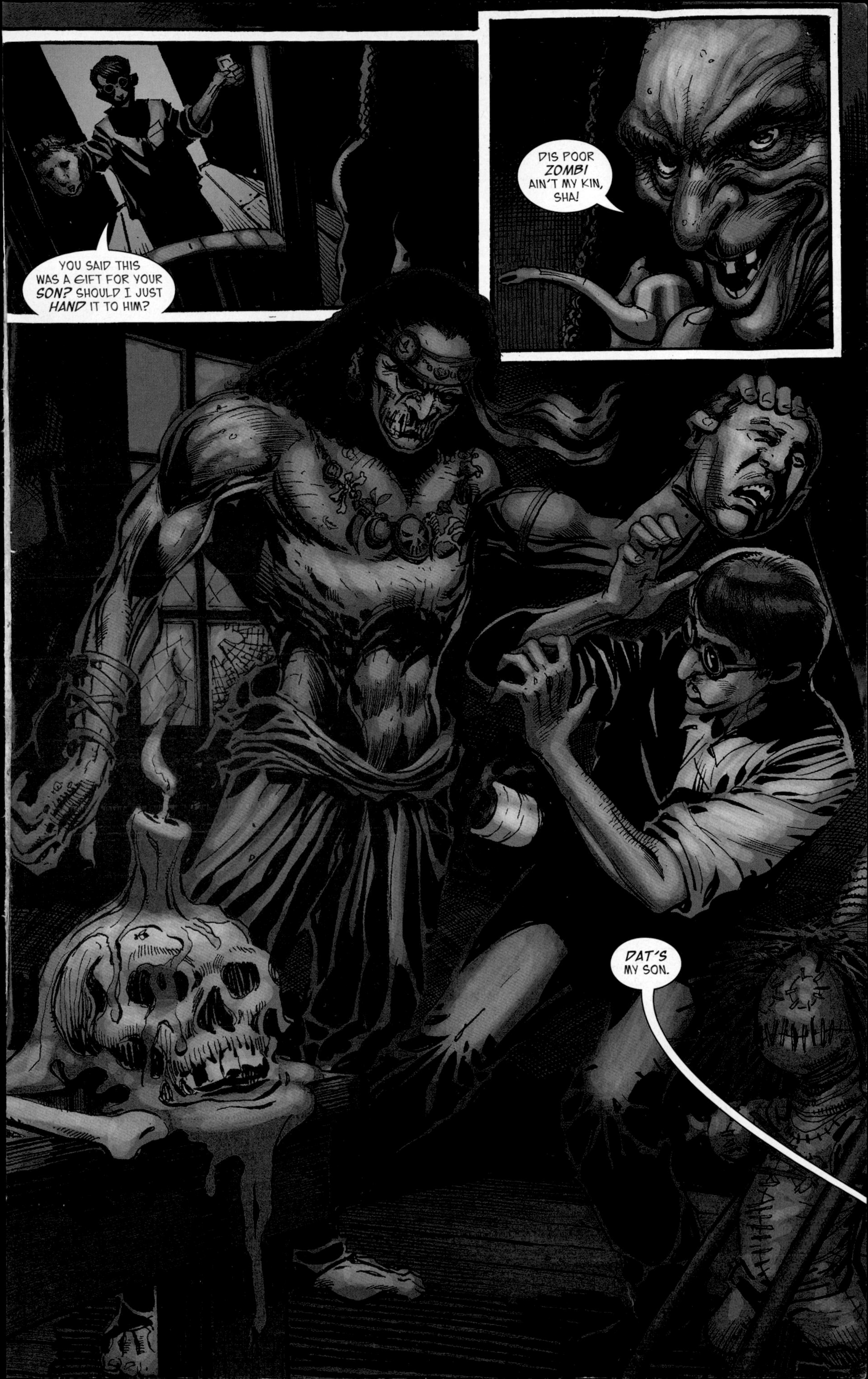
YOU SAID THIS WAS A GIFT FOR YOUR SON? SHOULD I JUST HAND IT TO HIM?
DIS POOR ZOMBI AIN'T MY KIN, SHA!
DAT'S MY SON.

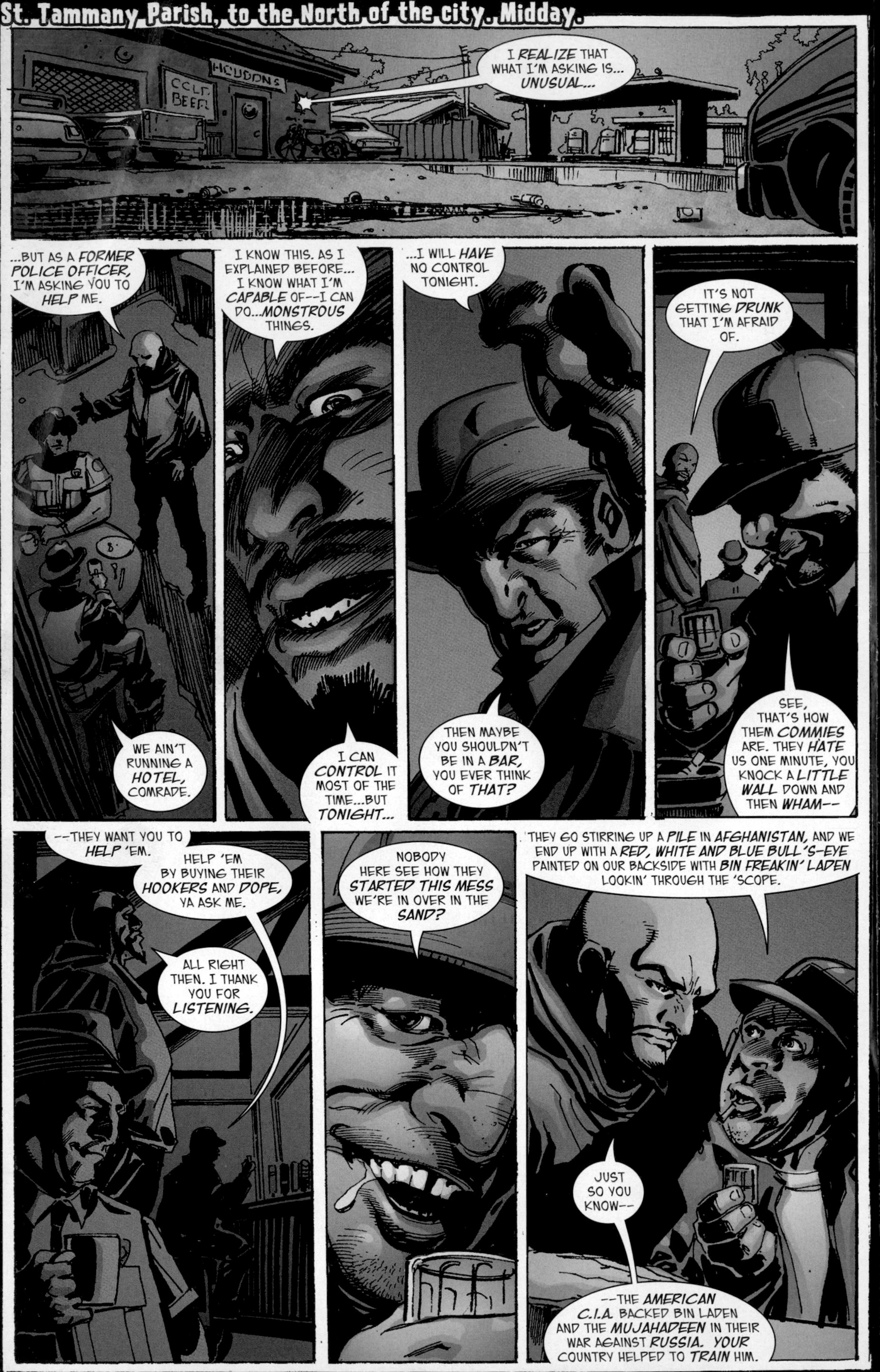
St. Tammany Parish, to the North of the city. Midday.
HOUDONS
COLD BEER
I REALIZE THAT WHAT I'M ASKING IS... UNUSUAL...
...BUT AS A FORMER POLICE OFFICER, I'M ASKING YOU TO HELP ME.
WE AIN'T RUNNING A HOTEL, COMRADE.
I KNOW THIS. AS I EXPLAINED BEFORE... I KNOW WHAT I'M CAPABLE OF--I CAN DO...MONSTROUS THINGS.
I CAN CONTROL IT MOST OF THE TIME...BUT TONIGHT...
...I WILL HAVE NO CONTROL TONIGHT.
THEN MAYBE YOU SHOULDN'T BE IN A BAR, YOU EVER THINK OF THAT?
IT'S NOT GETTING DRUNK THAT I'M AFRAID OF.
SEE, THAT'S HOW THEM COMMIES ARE. THEY HATE US ONE MINUTE, YOU KNOCK A LITTLE WALL DOWN AND THEN WHAM--
--THEY WANT YOU TO HELP 'EM.
HELP 'EM BY BUYING THEIR HOOKERS AND DOPE, YA ASK ME.
ALL RIGHT THEN. I THANK YOU FOR LISTENING.
NOBODY HERE SEE HOW THEY STARTED THIS MESS WE'RE IN OVER IN THE SAND?
THEY GO STIRRING UP A PILE IN AFGHANISTAN, AND WE END UP WITH A RED, WHITE AND BLUE BULL'S-EYE PAINTED ON OUR BACKSIDE WITH BIN FREAKIN' LADEN LOOKIN' THROUGH THE 'SCOPE.
JUST SO YOU KNOW--
--THE AMERICAN C.I.A. BACKED BIN LADEN AND THE MUJAHADEEN IN THEIR WAR AGAINST RUSSIA. YOUR COUNTRY HELPED TO TRAIN HIM.

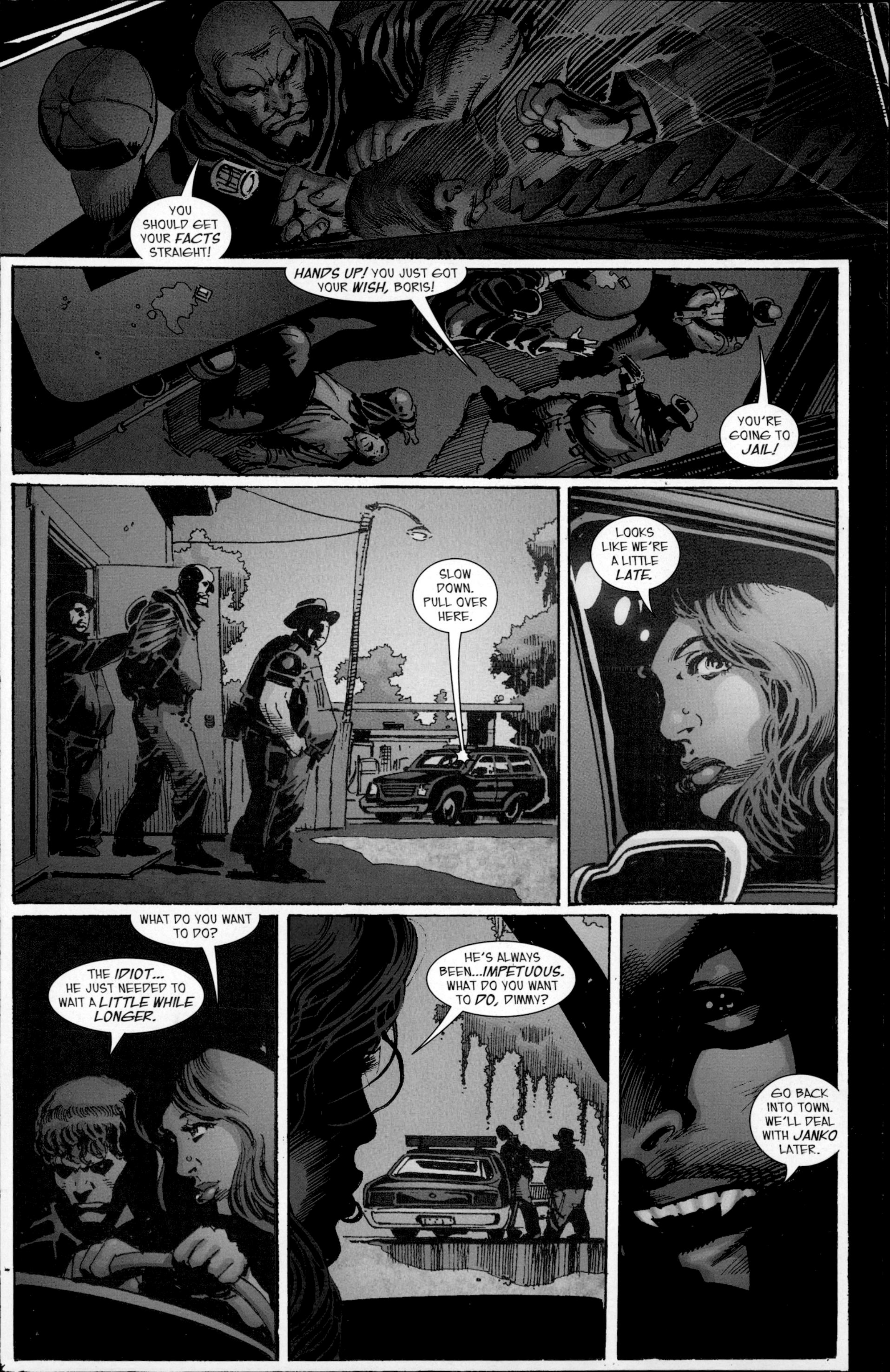
YOU SHOULD GET YOUR FACTS STRAIGHT!
HANDS UP! YOU JUST GOT YOUR WISH, BORIS!
YOU'RE GOING TO JAIL!
SLOW DOWN. PULL OVER HERE.
LOOKS LIKE WE'RE A LITTLE LATE.
WHAT DO YOU WANT TO DO?
THE IDIOT... HE JUST NEEDED TO WAIT A LITTLE WHILE LONGER.
HE'S ALWAYS BEEN...IMPETUOUS. WHAT DO YOU WANT TO DO, DIMMY?
GO BACK INTO TOWN. WE'LL DEAL WITH JANKO LATER.

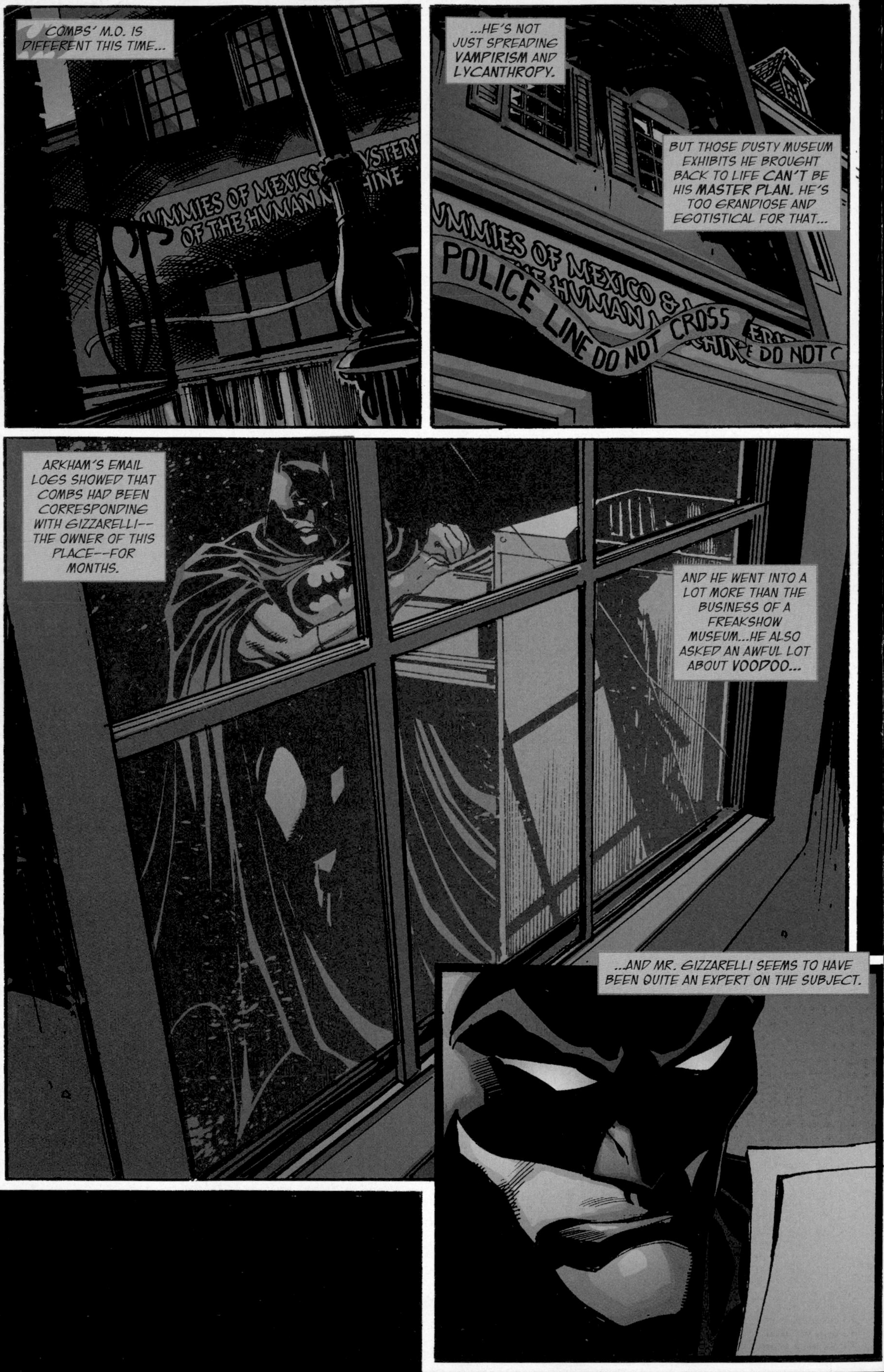
COMBS' M.O. IS DIFFERENT THIS TIME...
...HE'S NOT JUST SPREADING VAMPIRISM AND LYCANTHROPY.
BUT THOSE DUSTY MUSEUM EXHIBITS HE BROUGHT BACK TO LIFE CAN'T BE HIS MASTER PLAN. HE'S TOO GRANDIOSE AND EGOTISTICAL FOR THAT...
POLICE LINE DO NOT CROSS
ARKHAM'S EMAIL LOGS SHOWED THAT COMBS HAD BEEN CORRESPONDING WITH GIZZARELLI--THE OWNER OF THIS PLACE--FOR MONTHS.
AND HE WENT INTO A LOT MORE THAN THE BUSINESS OF A FREAKSHOW MUSEUM...HE ALSO ASKED AN AWFUL LOT ABOUT VOODOO...
...AND MR. GIZZARELLI SEEMS TO HAVE BEEN QUITE AN EXPERT ON THE SUBJECT.

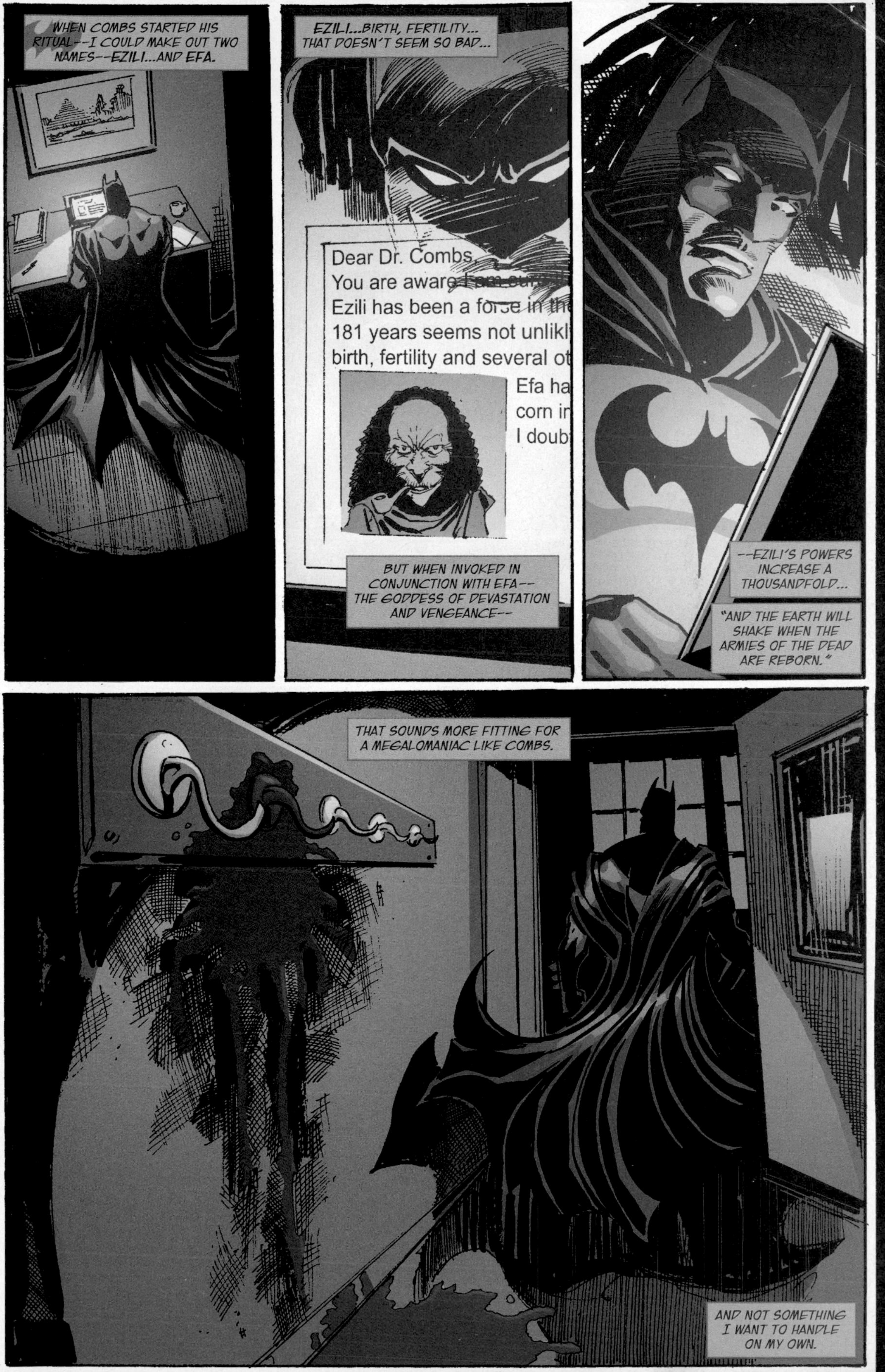

WHEN COMBS STARTED HIS RITUAL--I COULD MAKE OUT TWO NAMES--EZILI...AND EFA.
EZILI...BIRTH, FERTILITY... THAT DOESN'T SEEM SO BAD...
Dear Dr. Combs
You are aware
Ezili has been a
181 years seems not
birth, fertility and several
Efa
corn
I
BUT WHEN INVOKED IN CONJUNCTION WITH EFA-- THE GODDESS OF DEVASTATION AND VENGEANCE--
--EZILI'S POWERS INCREASE A THOUSANDFOLD...
"AND THE EARTH WILL SHAKE WHEN THE ARMIES OF THE DEAD ARE REBORN."
THAT SOUNDS MORE FITTING FOR A MEGALOMANIAC LIKE COMBS.
AND NOT SOMETHING I WANT TO HANDLE ON MY OWN.

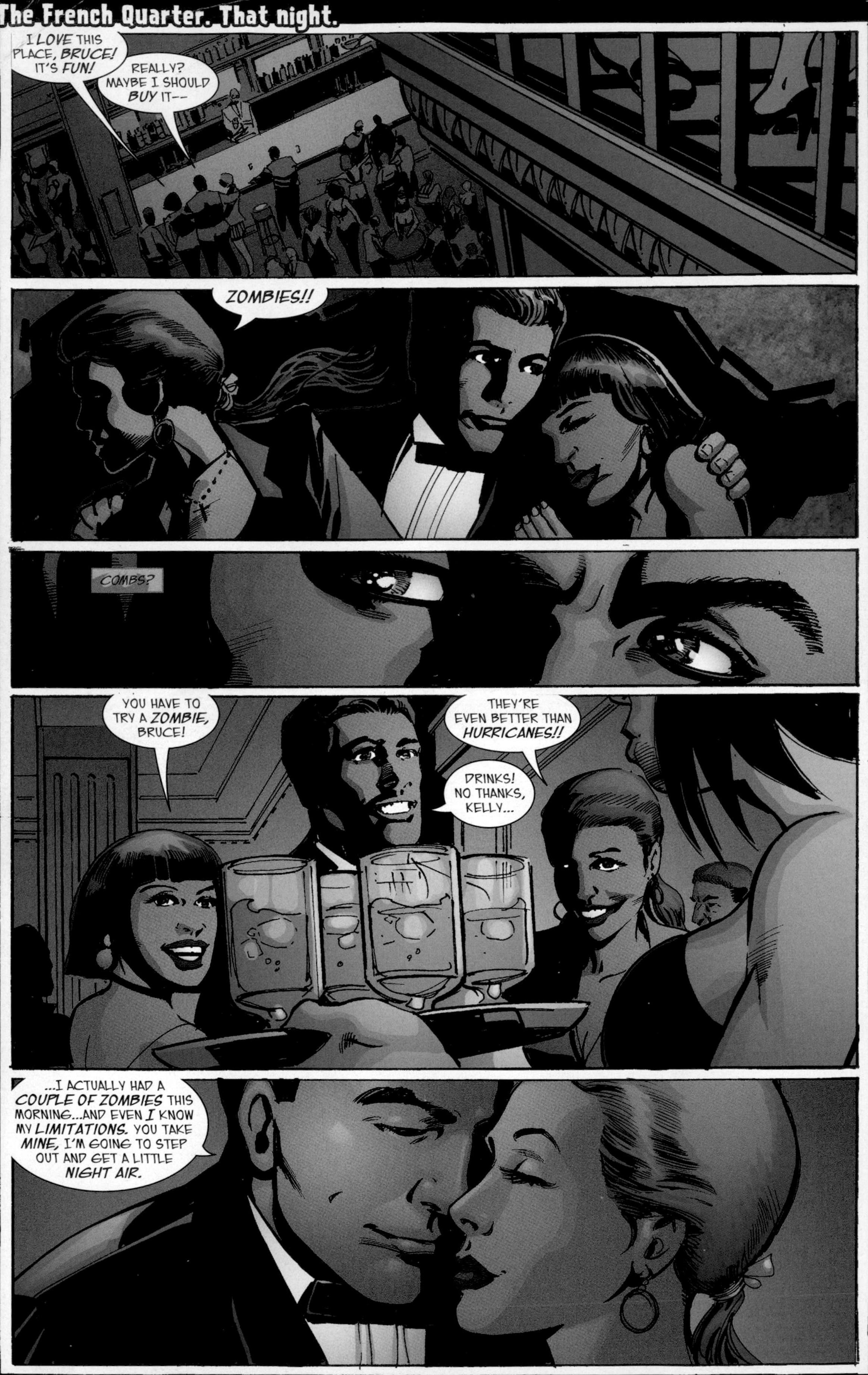

The French Quarter. That night.
I LOVE THIS PLACE, BRUCE! IT'S FUN!
REALLY? MAYBE I SHOULD BUY IT--
ZOMBIES!!
COMBS?
YOU HAVE TO TRY A ZOMBIE, BRUCE!
THEY'RE EVEN BETTER THAN HURRICANES!!
DRINKS! NO THANKS, KELLY...
...I ACTUALLY HAD A COUPLE OF ZOMBIES THIS MORNING...AND EVEN I KNOW MY LIMITATIONS. YOU TAKE MINE, I'M GOING TO STEP OUT AND GET A LITTLE NIGHT AIR.

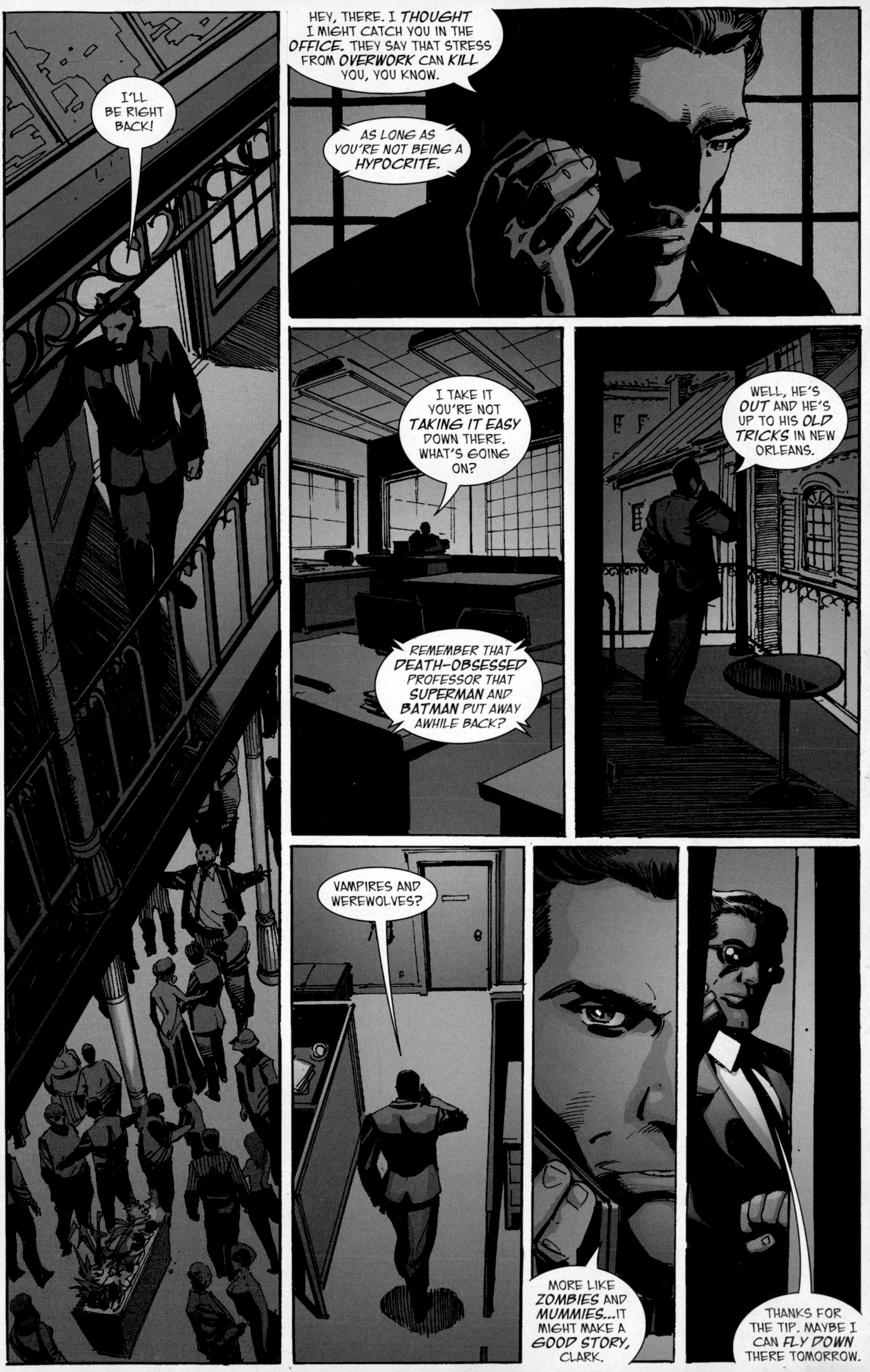
I'LL BE RIGHT BACK!
HEY, THERE. I THOUGHT I MIGHT CATCH YOU IN THE OFFICE. THEY SAY THAT STRESS FROM OVERWORK CAN KILL YOU, YOU KNOW.
AS LONG AS YOU'RE NOT BEING A HYPOCRITE.
I TAKE IT YOU'RE NOT TAKING IT EASY DOWN THERE. WHAT'S GOING ON?
REMEMBER THAT DEATH-OBSESSED PROFESSOR THAT SUPERMAN AND BATMAN PUT AWAY AWHILE BACK?
WELL, HE'S OUT AND HE'S UP TO HIS OLD TRICKS IN NEW ORLEANS.
VAMPIRES AND WEREWOLVES?
MORE LIKE ZOMBIES AND MUMMIES...IT MIGHT MAKE A GOOD STORY, CLARK.
THANKS FOR THE TIP. MAYBE I CAN FLY DOWN THERE TOMORROW.

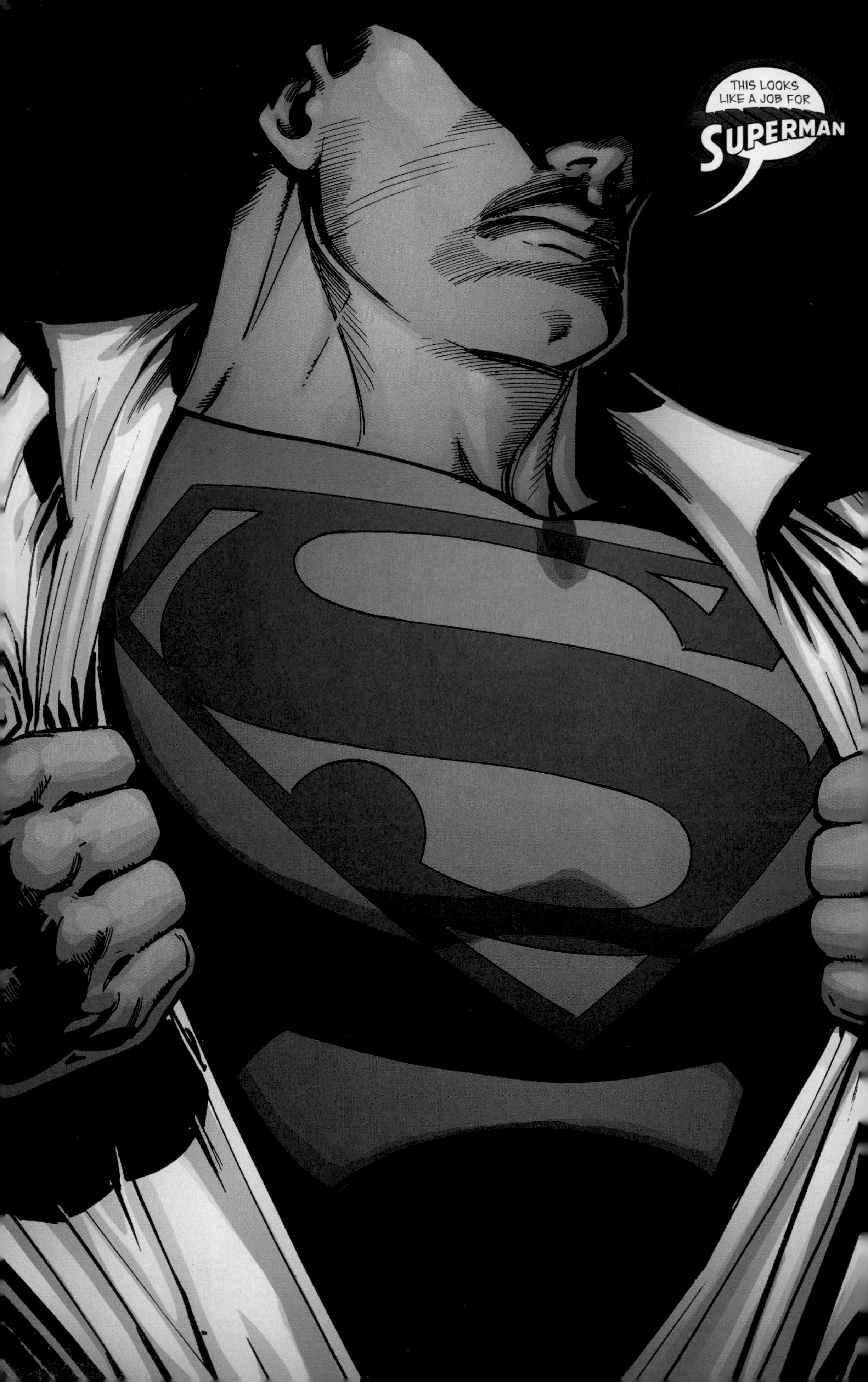
THIS LOOKS LIKE A JOB FOR
SUPERMAN

PART THREE: **FULL MOON**

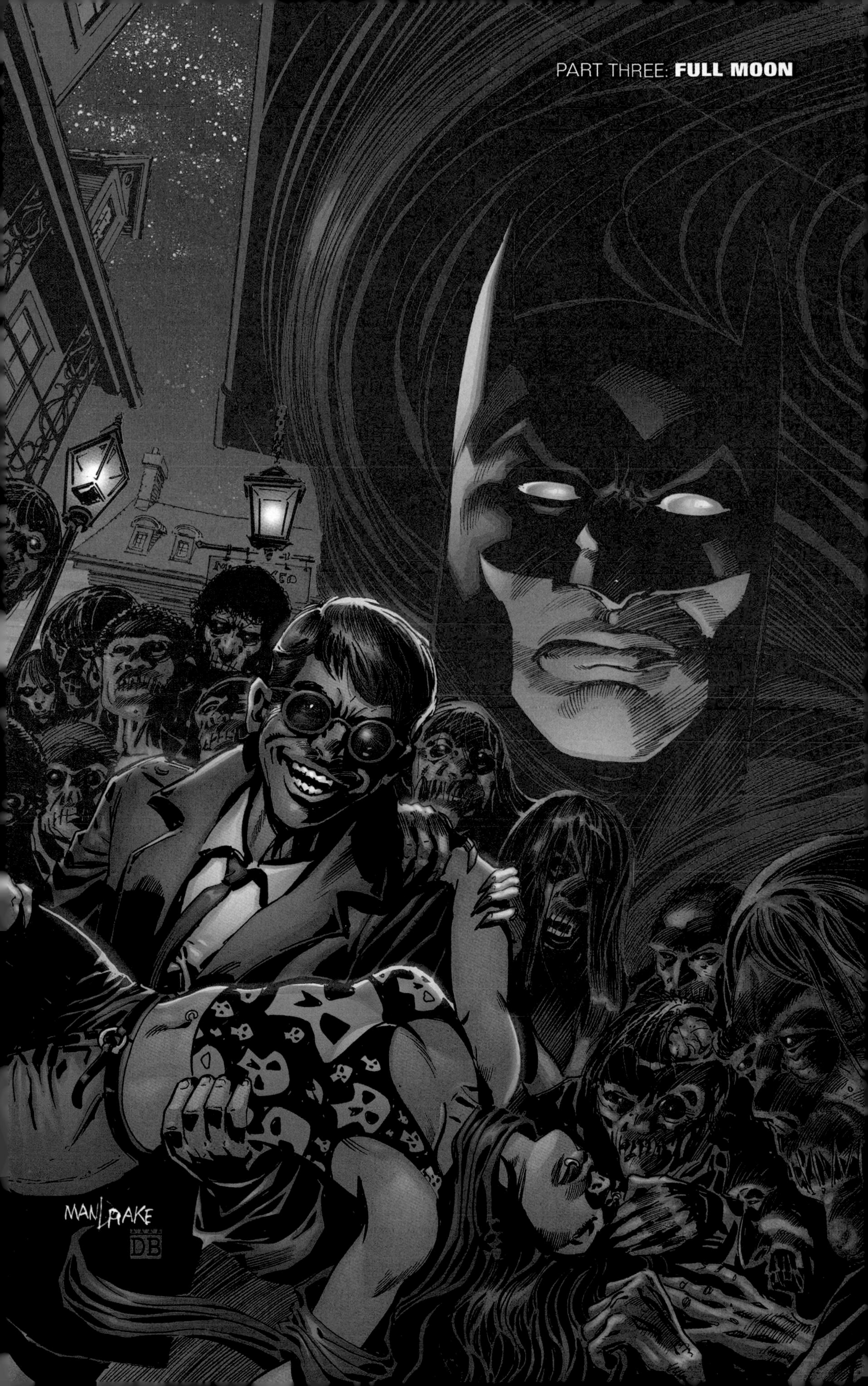

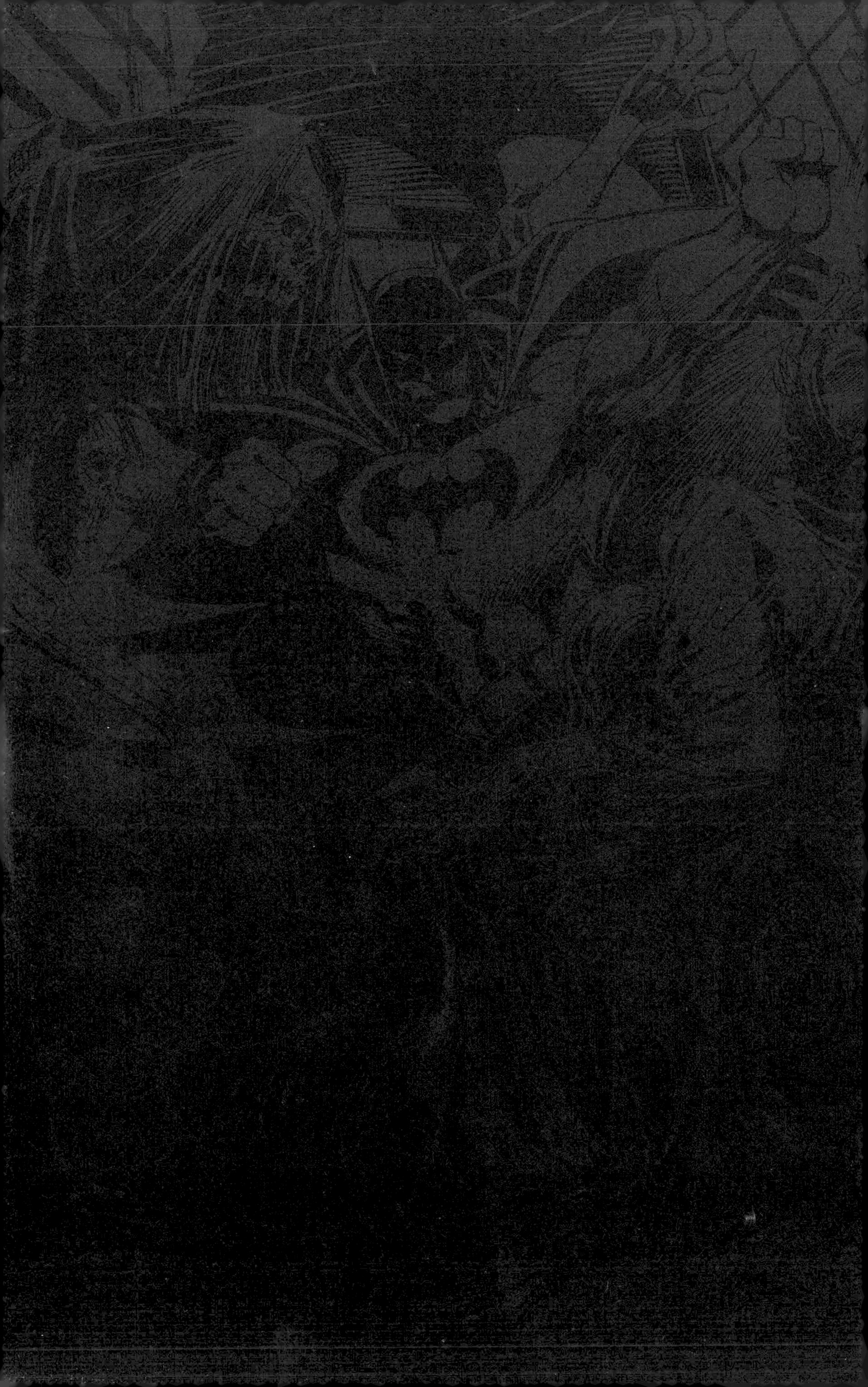

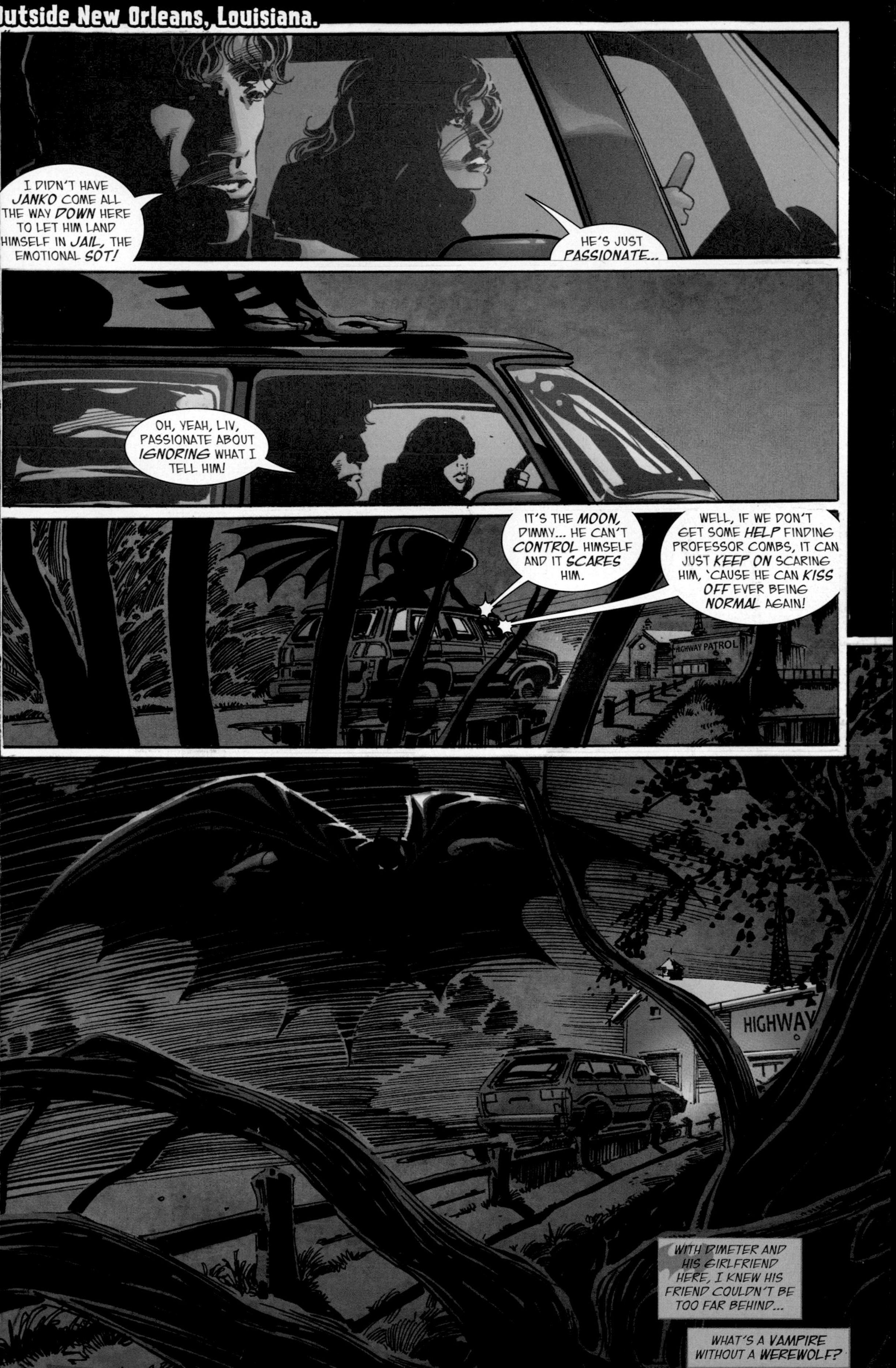
Outside New Orleans, Louisiana.
I DIDN'T HAVE JANKO COME ALL THE WAY DOWN HERE TO LET HIM LAND HIMSELF IN JAIL, THE EMOTIONAL SOT!
HE'S JUST PASSIONATE...
OH, YEAH, LIV, PASSIONATE ABOUT IGNORING WHAT I TELL HIM!
IT'S THE MOON, DIMMY... HE CAN'T CONTROL HIMSELF AND IT SCARES HIM.
WELL, IF WE DON'T GET SOME HELP FINDING PROFESSOR COMBS, IT CAN JUST KEEP ON SCARING HIM, 'CAUSE HE CAN KISS OFF EVER BEING NORMAL AGAIN!
HIGHWAY PATROL
HIGHWAY
WITH DIMETER AND HIS GIRLFRIEND HERE, I KNEW HIS FRIEND COULDN'T BE TOO FAR BEHIND...
WHAT'S A VAMPIRE WITHOUT A WEREWOLF?

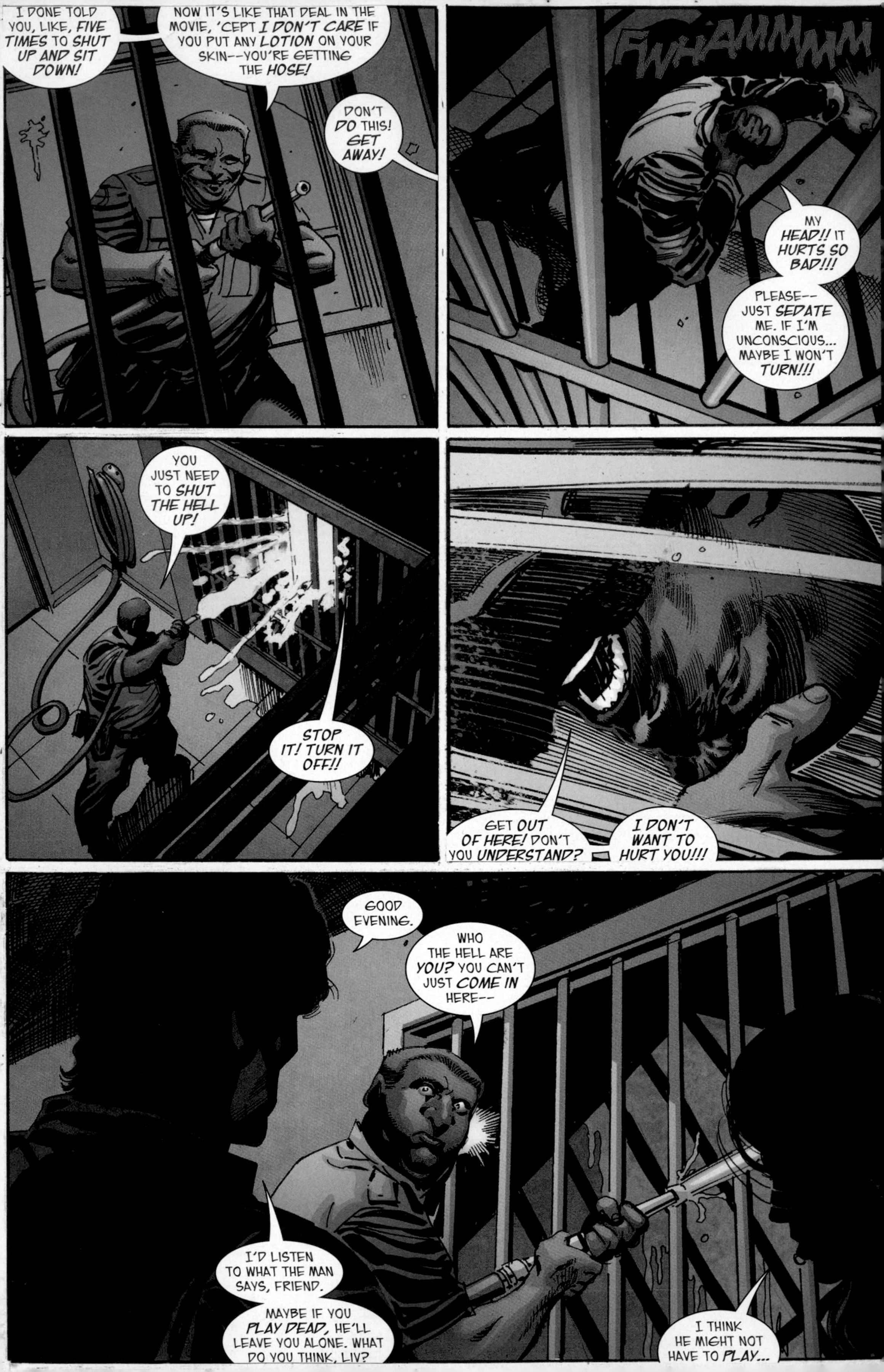
I DONE TOLD YOU, LIKE, FIVE TIMES TO SHUT UP AND SIT DOWN!
NOW IT'S LIKE THAT DEAL IN THE MOVIE, 'CEPT I DON'T CARE IF YOU PUT ANY LOTION ON YOUR SKIN--YOU'RE GETTING THE HOSE!
DON'T DO THIS! GET AWAY!
FWHAMMMM
MY HEAD!! IT HURTS SO BAD!!!
PLEASE-- JUST SEDATE ME. IF I'M UNCONSCIOUS... MAYBE I WON'T TURN!!!
YOU JUST NEED TO SHUT THE HELL UP!
STOP IT! TURN IT OFF!!
GET OUT OF HERE! DON'T YOU UNDERSTAND?
I DON'T WANT TO HURT YOU!!!
GOOD EVENING.
WHO THE HELL ARE YOU? YOU CAN'T JUST COME IN HERE--
I'D LISTEN TO WHAT THE MAN SAYS, FRIEND.
MAYBE IF YOU PLAY DEAD, HE'LL LEAVE YOU ALONE. WHAT DO YOU THINK, LIV?
I THINK HE MIGHT NOT HAVE TO PLAY...

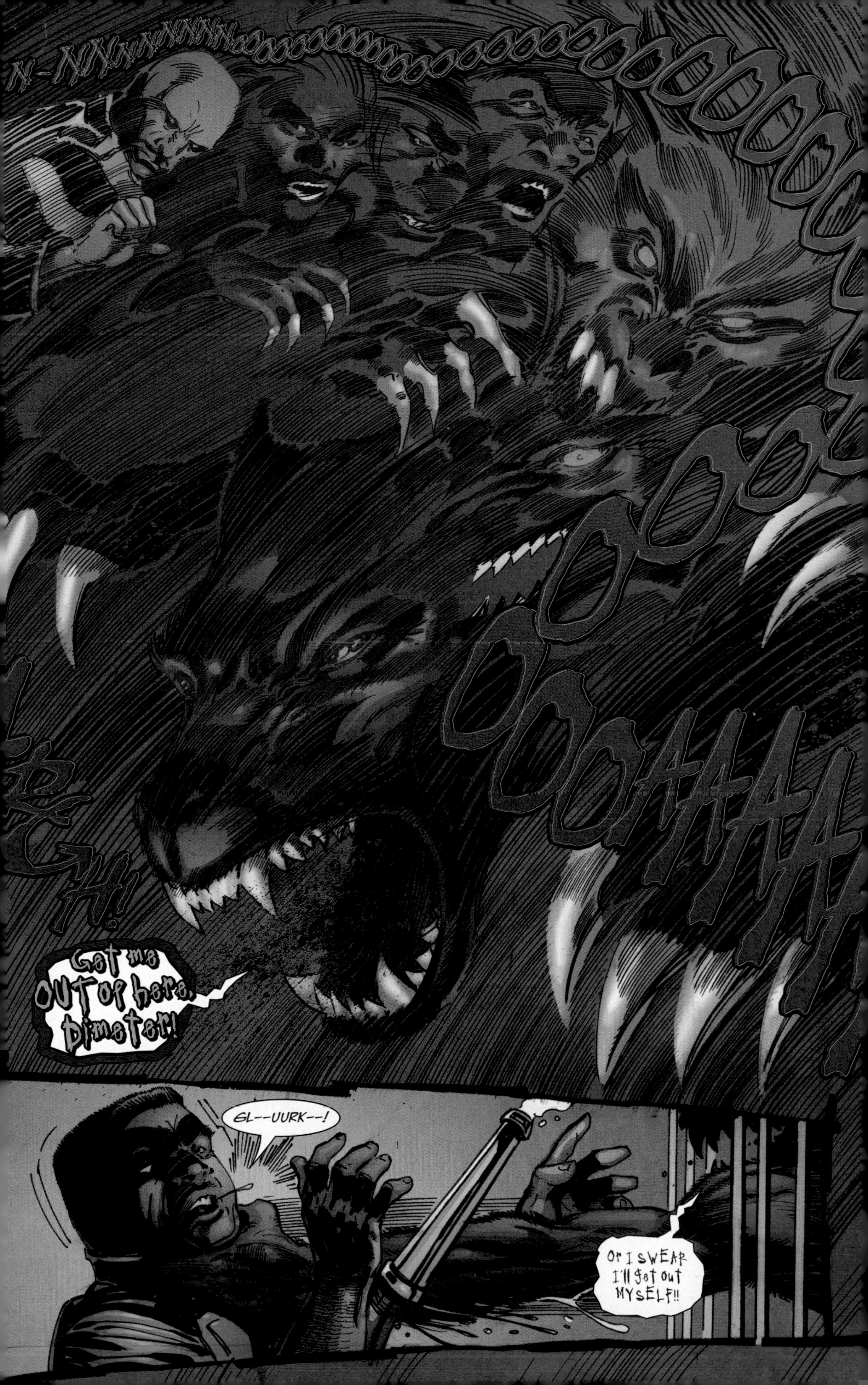
N-NNNNNNNNNNoooooooooooooooooooooOOOOOOOOOOOOOOOOOOAAAAA
Get me OUT of here, Dimeter!
GL--UURK--!
Or I SWEAR I'll get out MYSELF!!

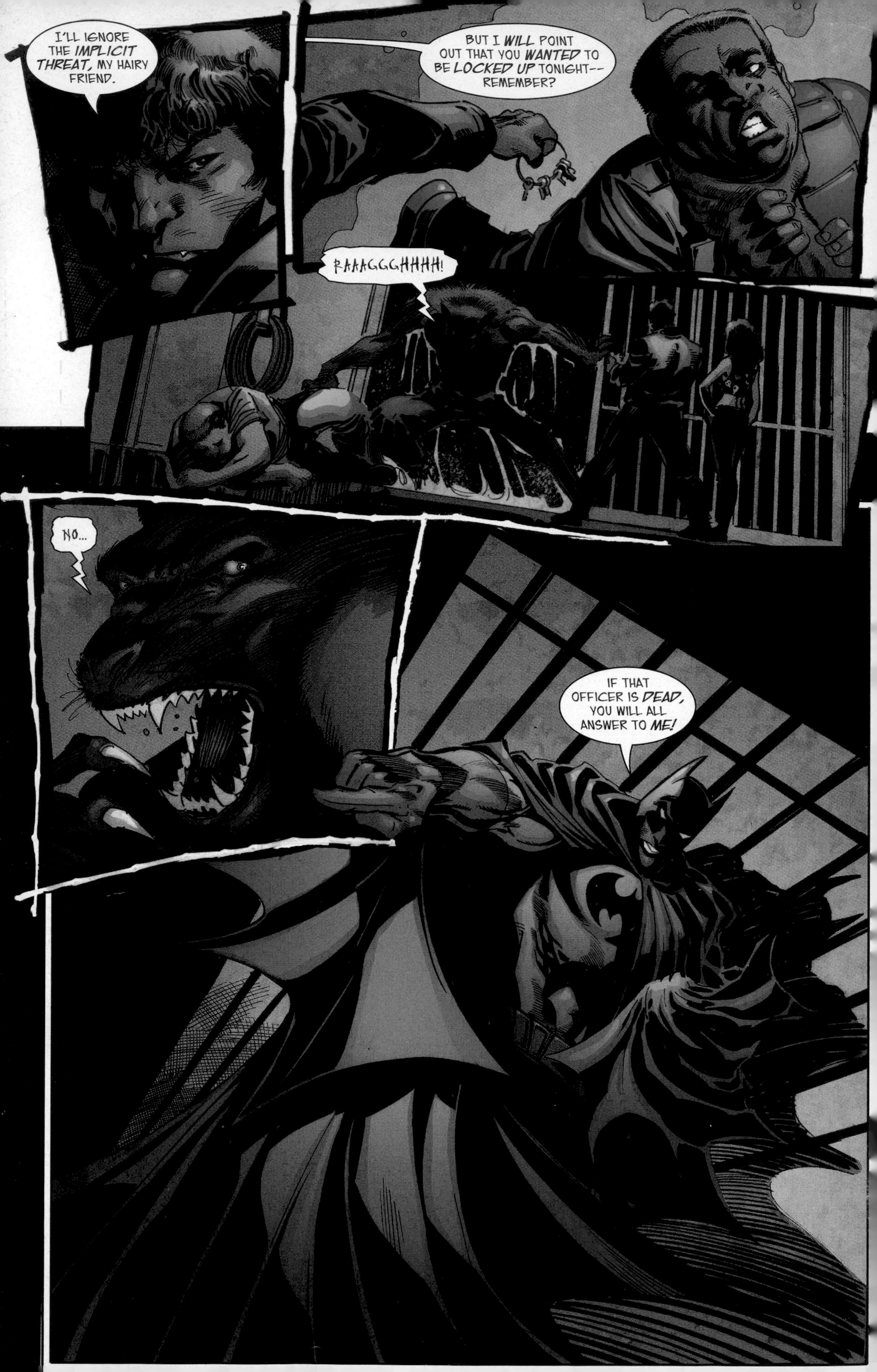
I'LL IGNORE THE IMPLICIT THREAT, MY HAIRY FRIEND.
BUT I WILL POINT OUT THAT YOU WANTED TO BE LOCKED UP TONIGHT-- REMEMBER?
RAAAGGGHHHH!
NO...
IF THAT OFFICER IS DEAD, YOU WILL ALL ANSWER TO ME!

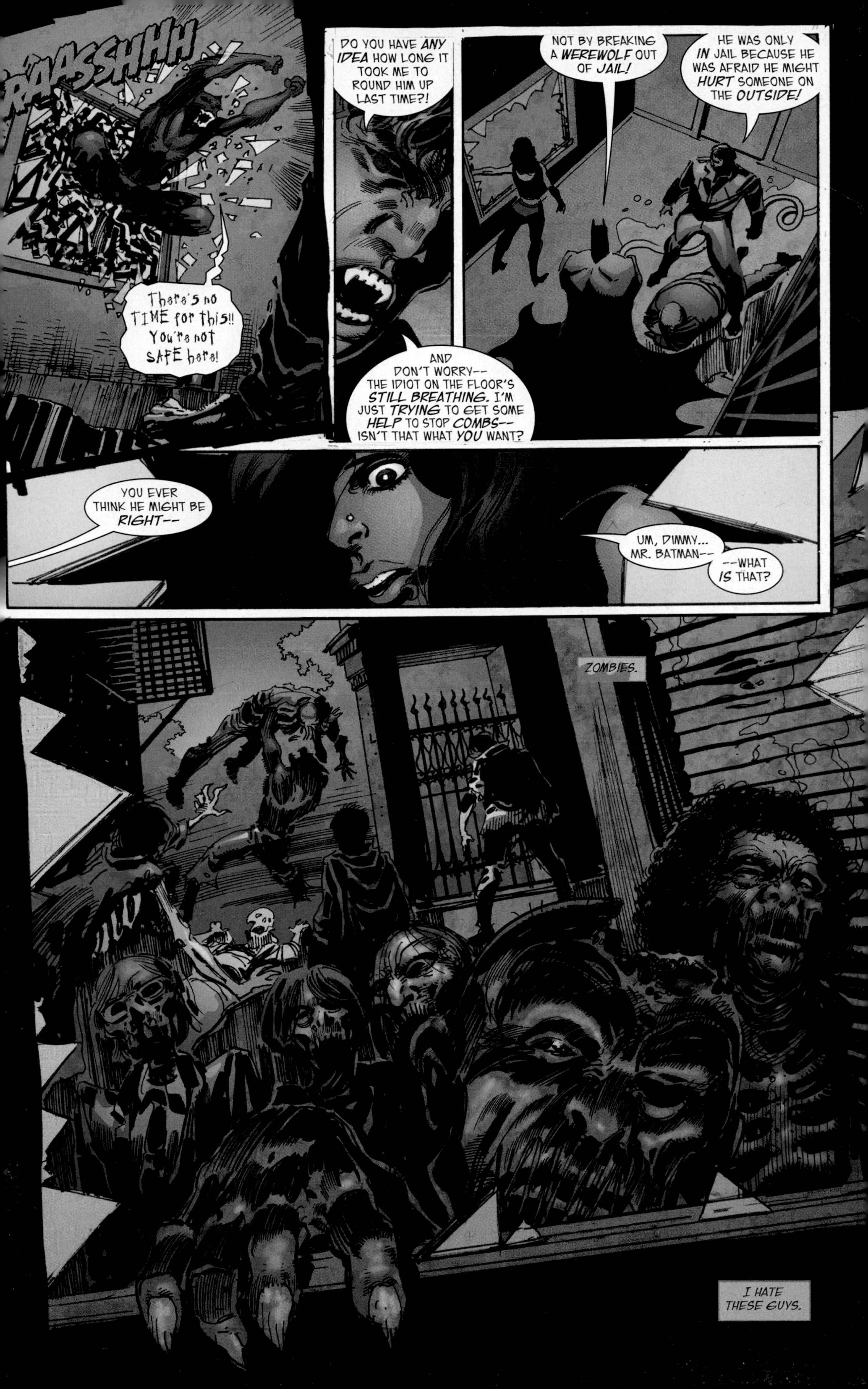
RAASSHHH
There's no TIME for this!! You're not SAFE here!
DO YOU HAVE ANY IDEA HOW LONG IT TOOK ME TO ROUND HIM UP LAST TIME?!
NOT BY BREAKING A WEREWOLF OUT OF JAIL!
HE WAS ONLY IN JAIL BECAUSE HE WAS AFRAID HE MIGHT HURT SOMEONE ON THE OUTSIDE!
AND DON'T WORRY-- THE IDIOT ON THE FLOOR'S STILL BREATHING. I'M JUST TRYING TO GET SOME HELP TO STOP COMBS-- ISN'T THAT WHAT YOU WANT?
YOU EVER THINK HE MIGHT BE RIGHT--
UM, DIMMY... MR. BATMAN--
--WHAT IS THAT?
ZOMBIES.
I HATE THESE GUYS.

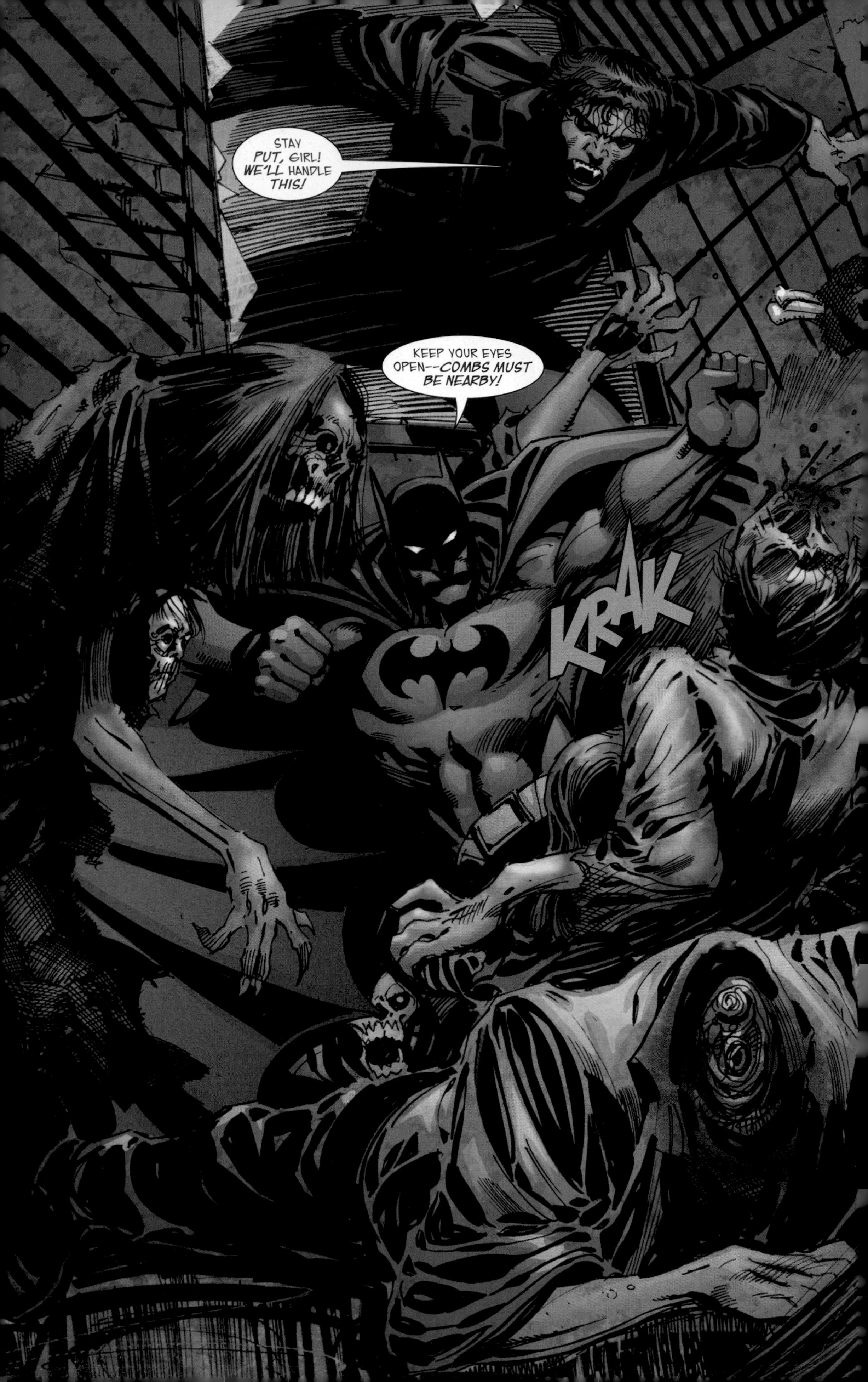
STAY PUT, GIRL! WE'LL HANDLE THIS!
KEEP YOUR EYES OPEN--COMBS MUST BE NEARBY!
KRAK

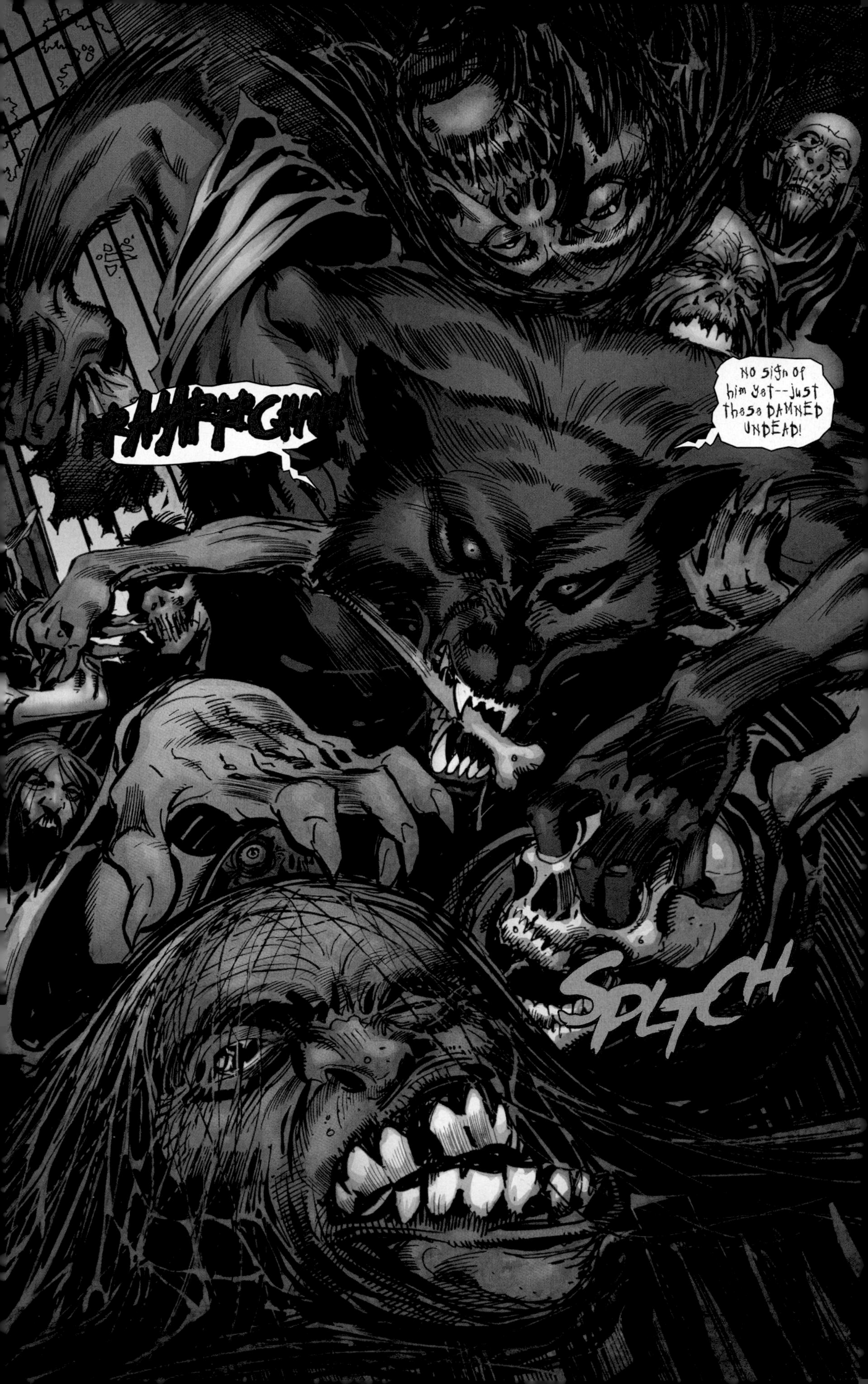
NO sign of him yet--just these DAMNED UNDEAD!
SPLTCH

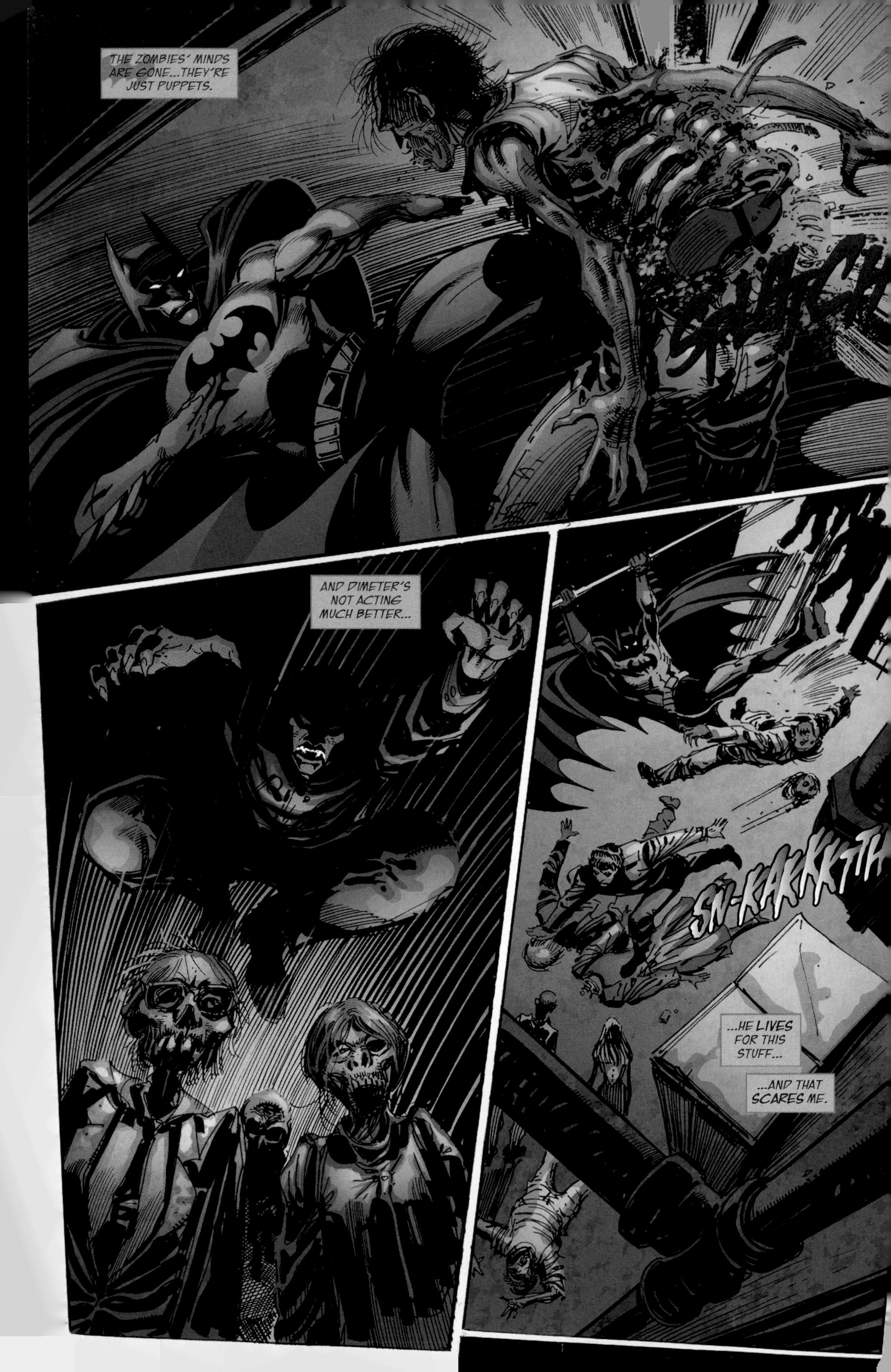
THE ZOMBIES' MINDS ARE GONE...THEY'RE JUST PUPPETS.
SPLUTCH
AND DIMETER'S NOT ACTING MUCH BETTER...
SN-KAKKKTTH
...HE LIVES FOR THIS STUFF...
...AND THAT SCARES ME.

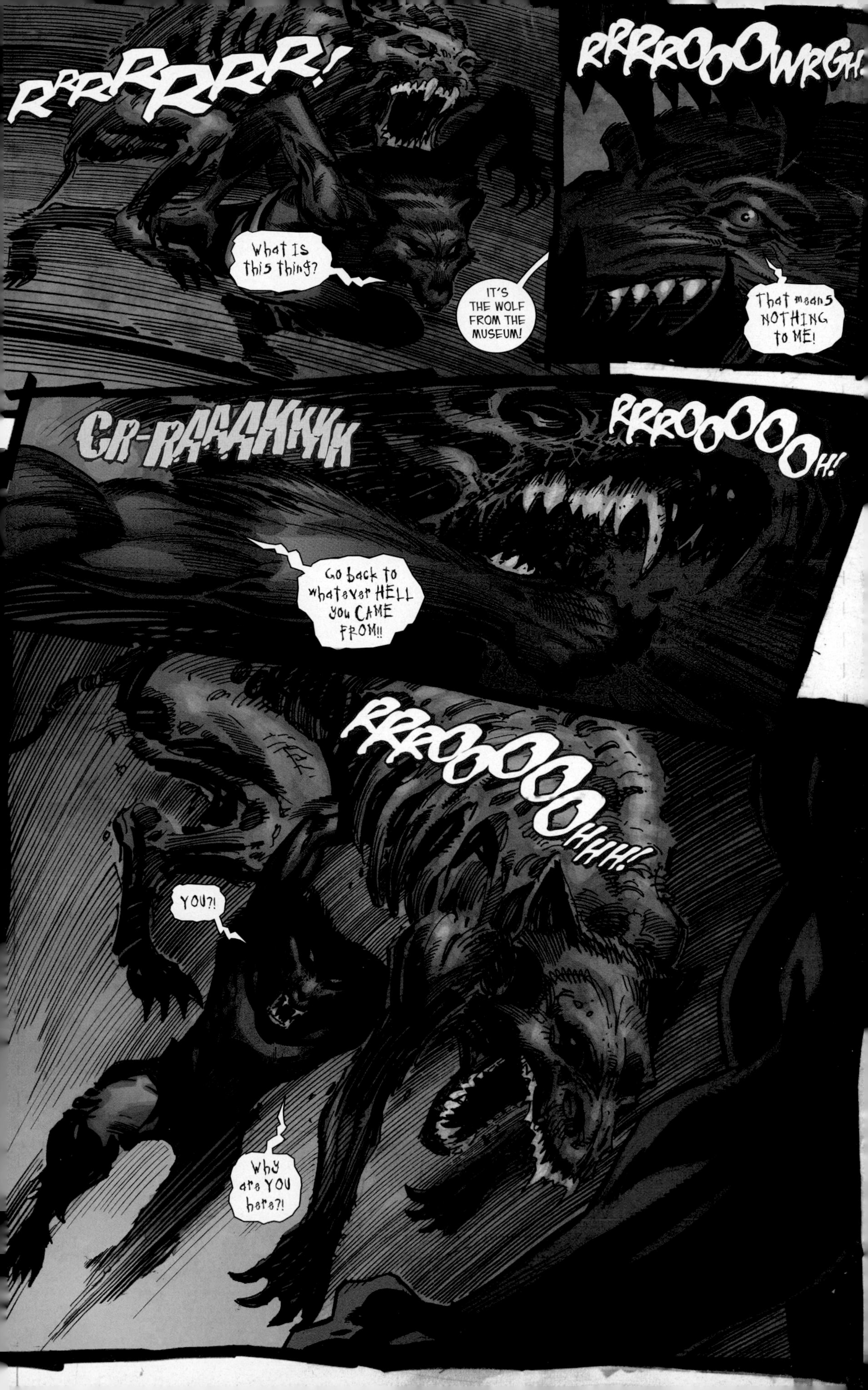
RRRRRRRR!
What is this thing?
RRRROOOOWRGH!
IT'S THE WOLF FROM THE MUSEUM!
That means NOTHING to ME!
CR-RAAAKKKK
RRROOOOOH!
Go back to whatever HELL you CAME FROM!!
RRROOOOOOHHH!
YOU?!
Why are YOU here?!

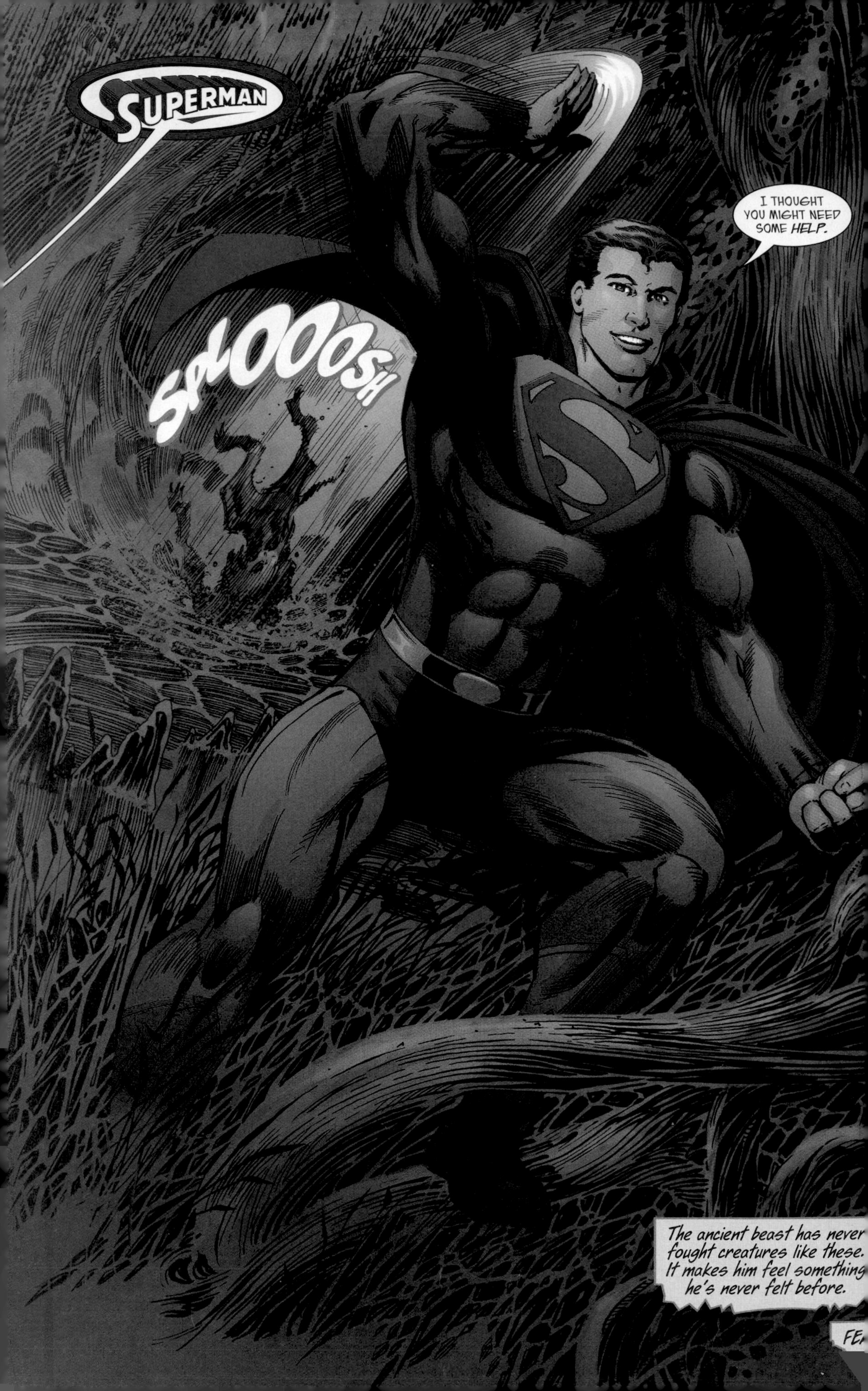
SUPERMAN
I THOUGHT YOU MIGHT NEED SOME *HELP*.
SPLOOOSH
The ancient beast has never fought creatures like these. It makes him feel something he's never felt before.
FE

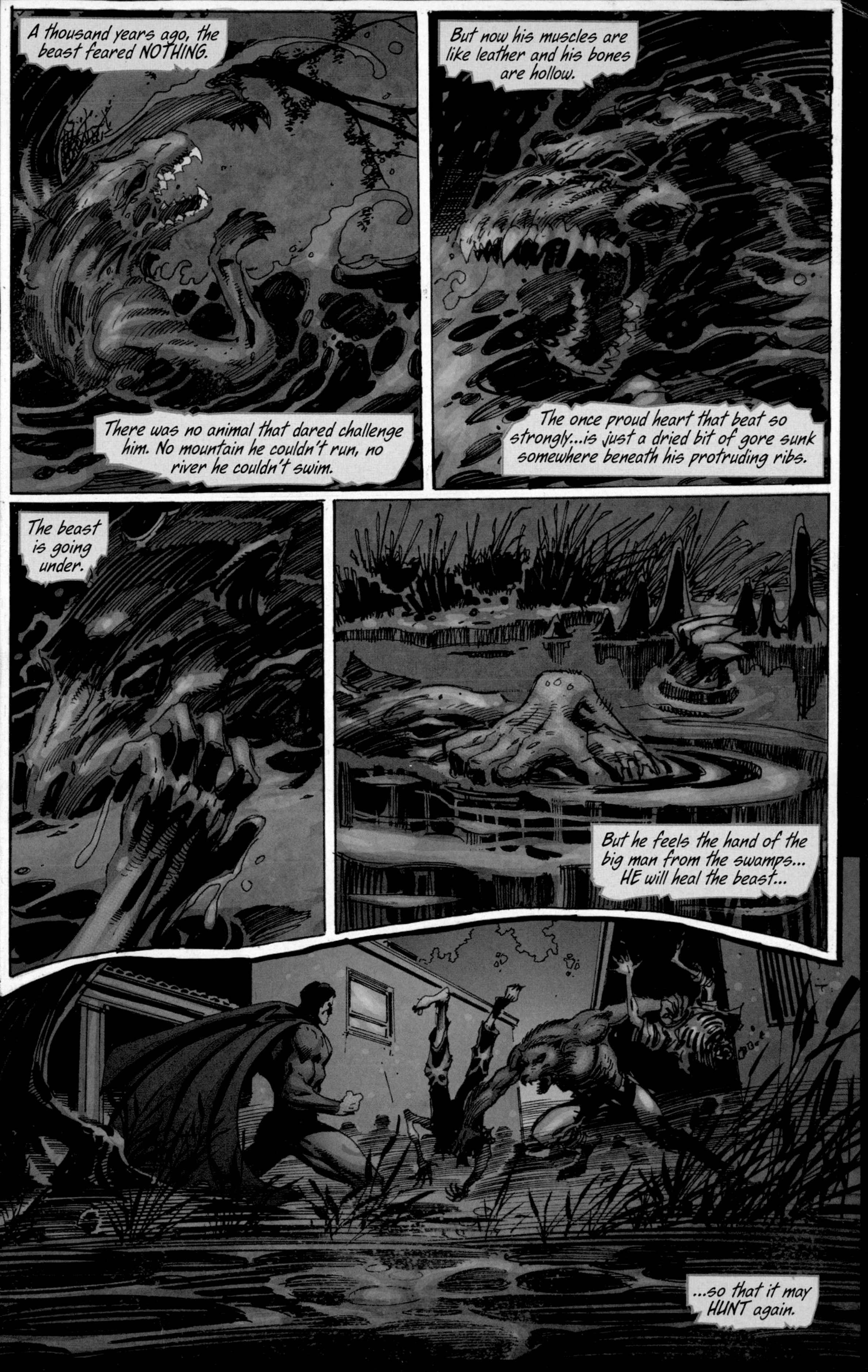
A thousand years ago, the beast feared NOTHING.
There was no animal that dared challenge him. No mountain he couldn't run, no river he couldn't swim.
But now his muscles are like leather and his bones are hollow.
The once proud heart that beat so strongly...is just a dried bit of gore sunk somewhere beneath his protruding ribs.
The beast is going under.
But he feels the hand of the big man from the swamps... HE will heal the beast...
...so that it may HUNT again.

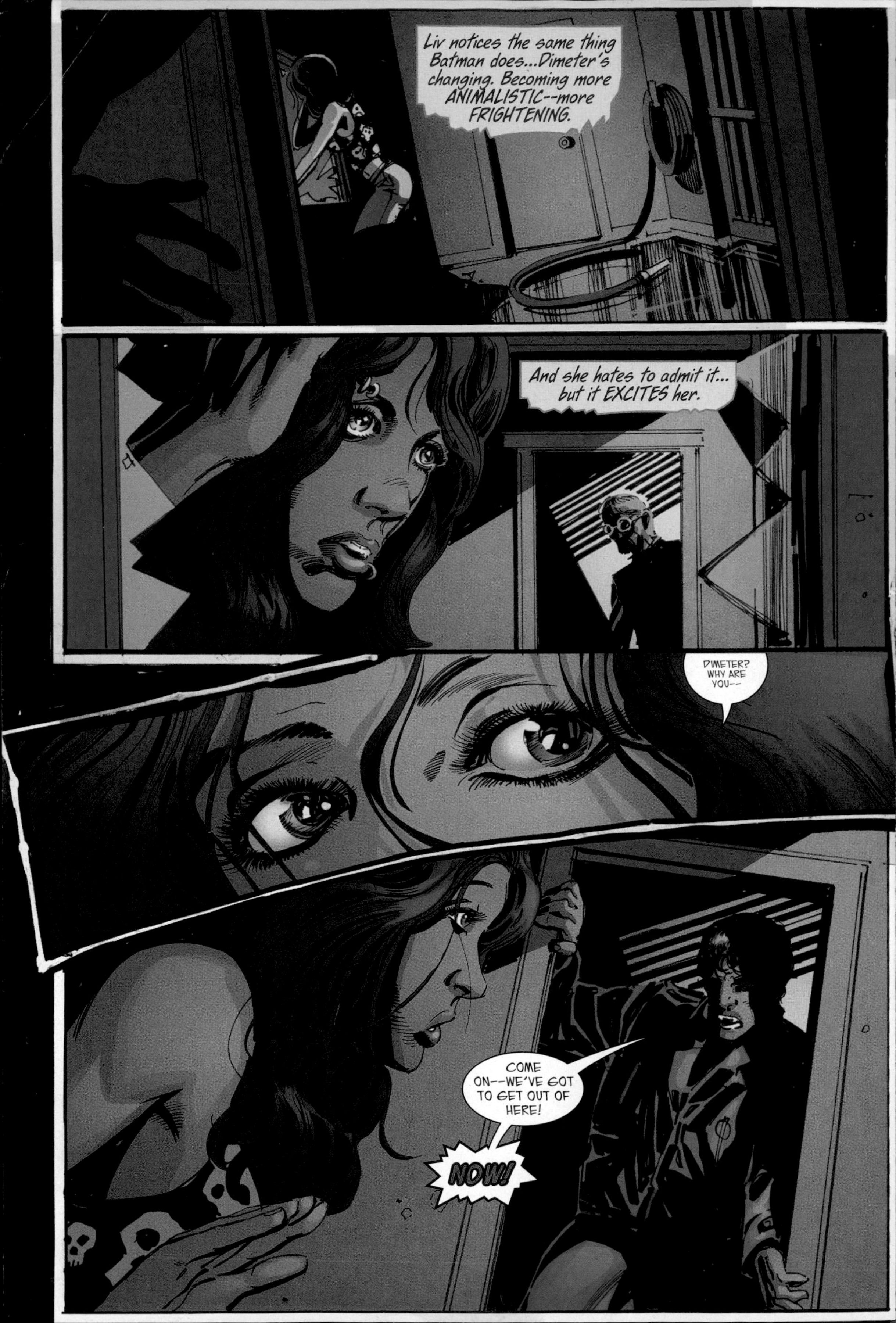
Liv notices the same thing Batman does...Dimeter's changing. Becoming more ANIMALISTIC--more FRIGHTENING.
And she hates to admit it... but it EXCITES her.
DIMETER? WHY ARE YOU--
COME ON--WE'VE GOT TO GET OUT OF HERE!
NOW!

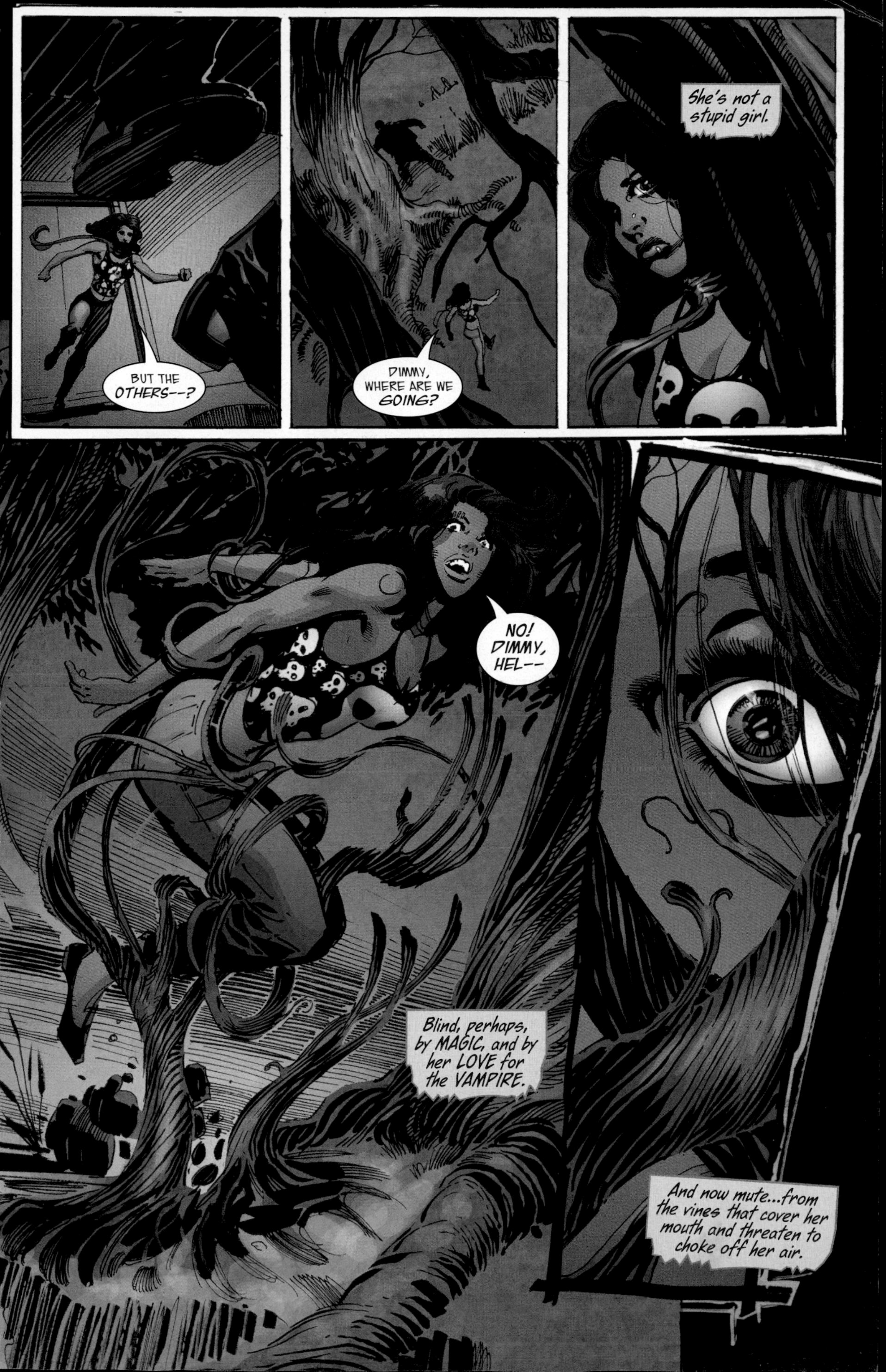
BUT THE OTHERS--?
DIMMY, WHERE ARE WE GOING?
She's not a stupid girl.
NO! DIMMY, HEL--
Blind, perhaps, by MAGIC, and by her LOVE for the VAMPIRE.
And now mute...from the vines that cover her mouth and threaten to choke off her air.

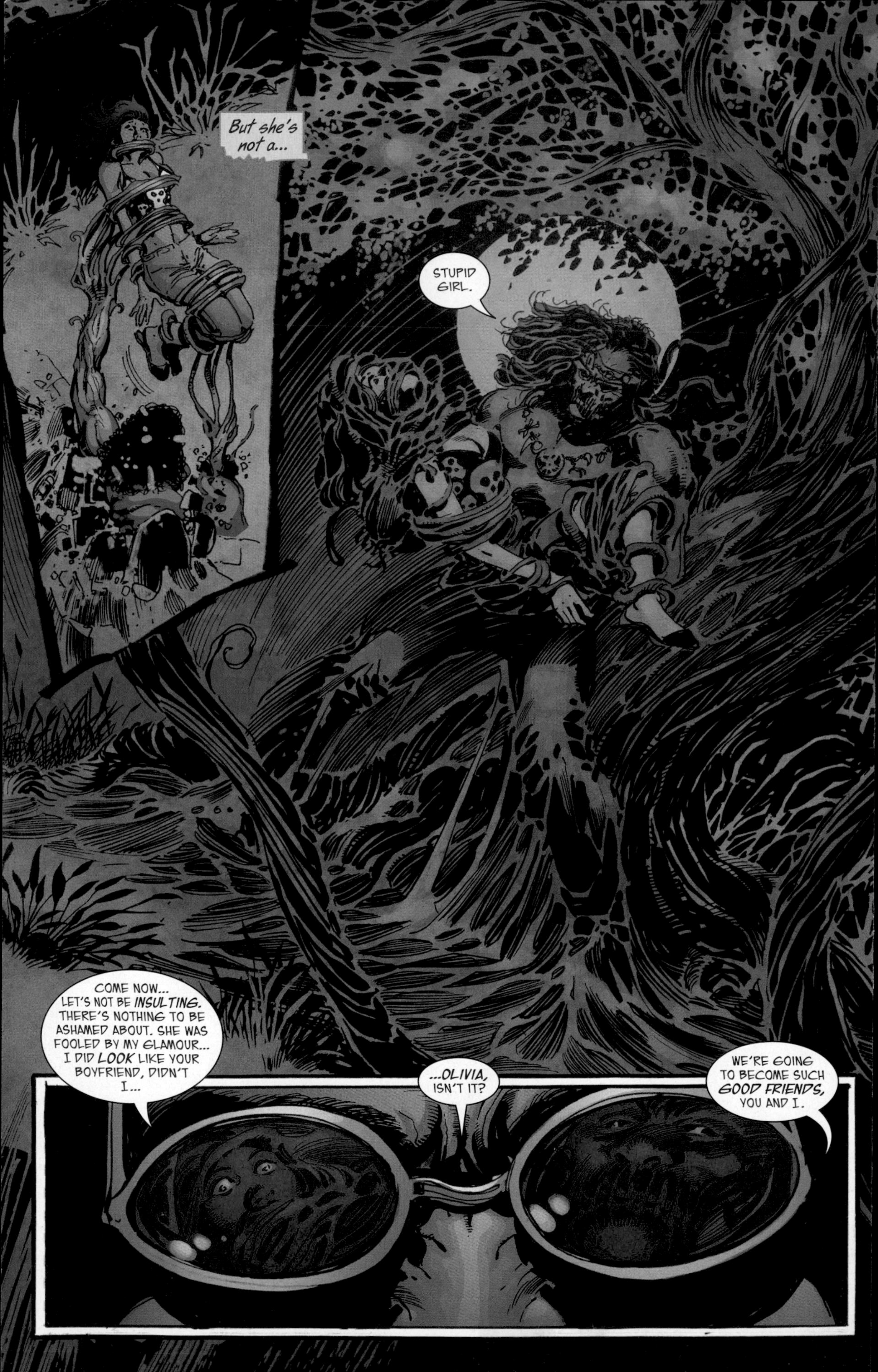
But she's not a...
STUPID GIRL.
COME NOW... LET'S NOT BE INSULTING. THERE'S NOTHING TO BE ASHAMED ABOUT. SHE WAS FOOLED BY MY GLAMOUR... I DID LOOK LIKE YOUR BOYFRIEND, DIDN'T I...
...OLIVIA, ISN'T IT?
WE'RE GOING TO BECOME SUCH GOOD FRIENDS, YOU AND I.

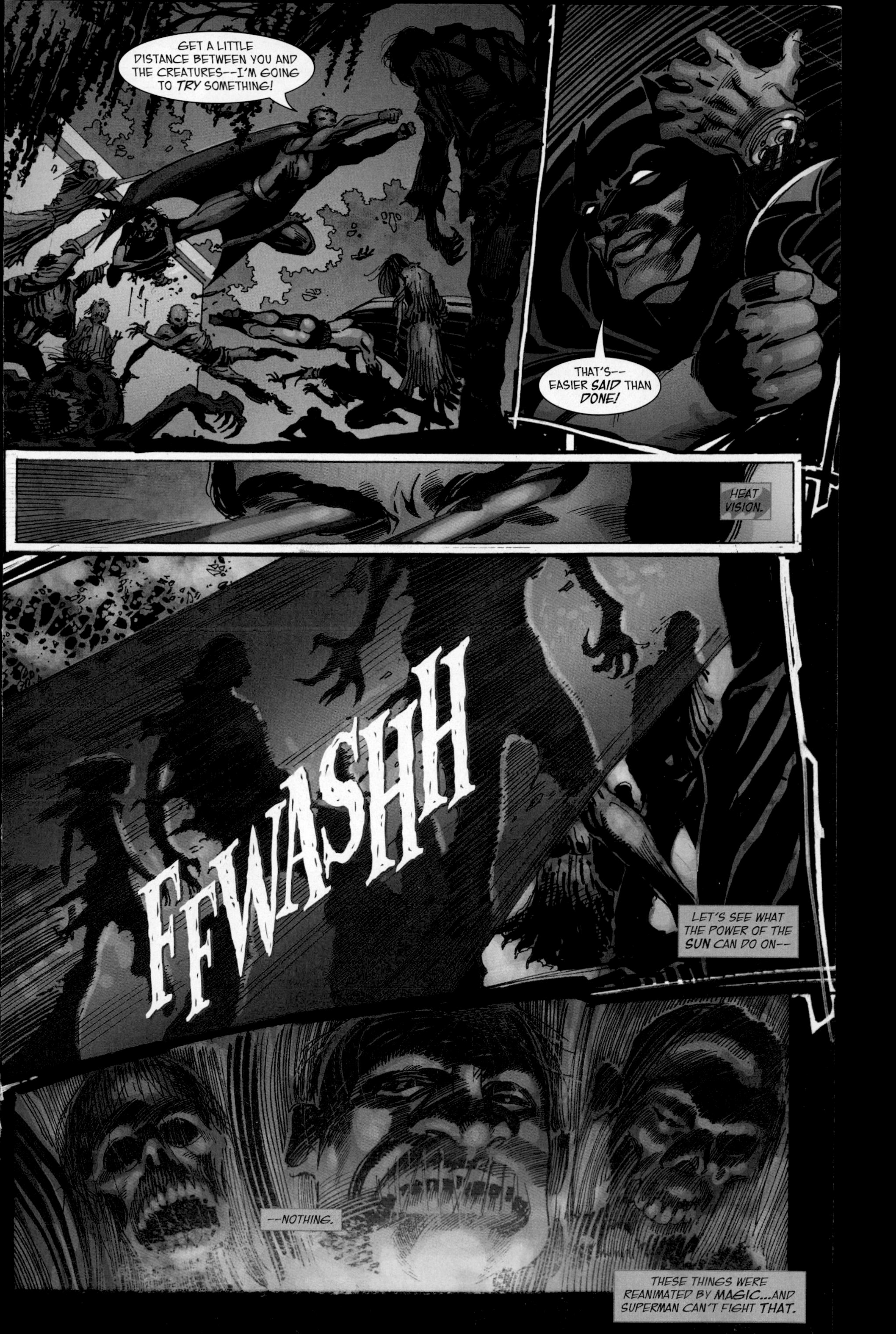
GET A LITTLE DISTANCE BETWEEN YOU AND THE CREATURES--I'M GOING TO *TRY* SOMETHING!
THAT'S-- EASIER *SAID* THAN *DONE!*
HEAT VISION.
FFWASHH
LET'S SEE WHAT THE POWER OF THE **SUN** CAN DO ON--
--NOTHING.
THESE THINGS WERE REANIMATED BY **MAGIC**... AND SUPERMAN CAN'T FIGHT **THAT**.

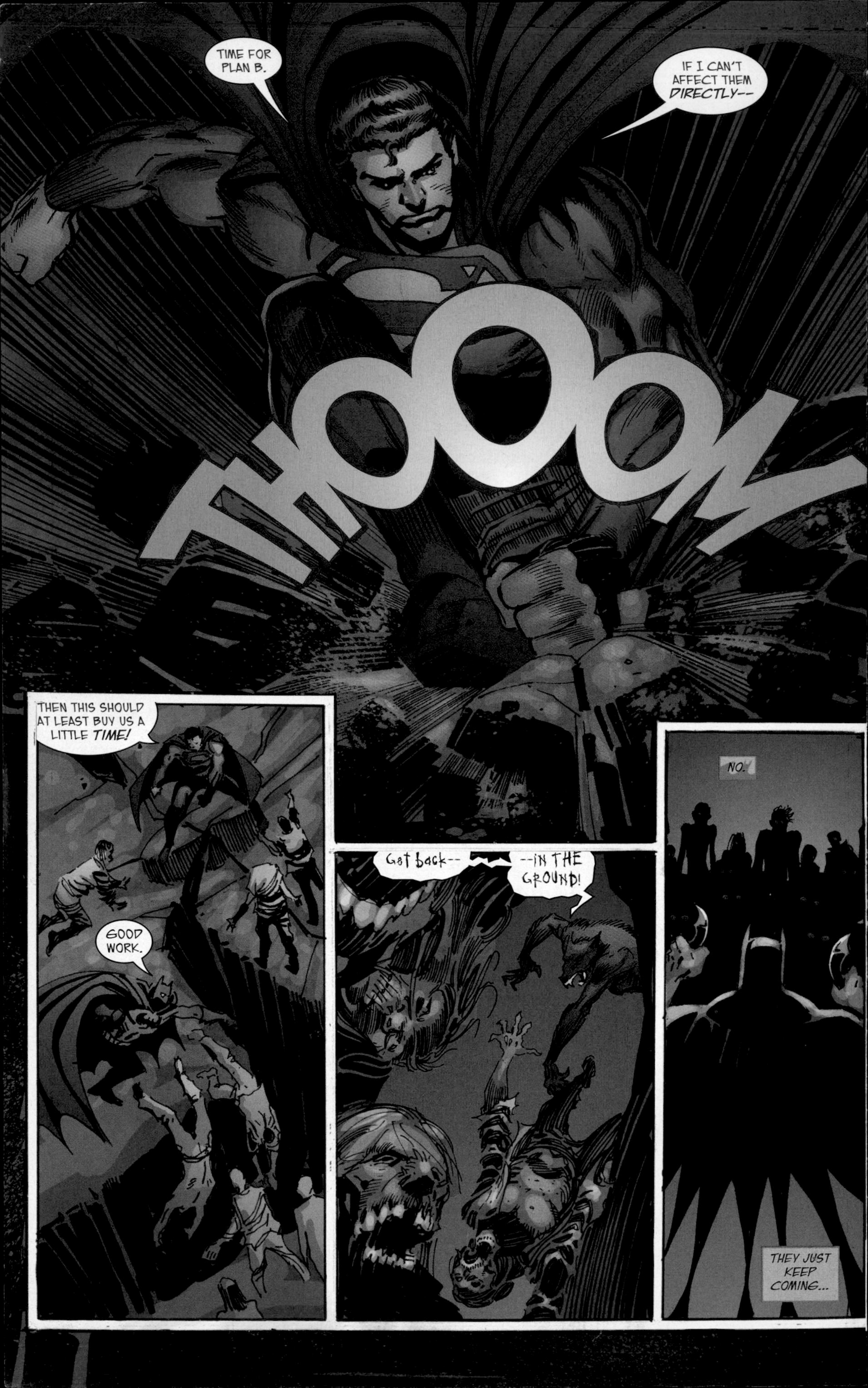
TIME FOR PLAN B.
IF I CAN'T AFFECT THEM DIRECTLY--
THOOOM
THEN THIS SHOULD AT LEAST BUY US A LITTLE TIME!
GOOD WORK.
Get back--
--IN THE GROUND!
NO.
THEY JUST KEEP COMING...

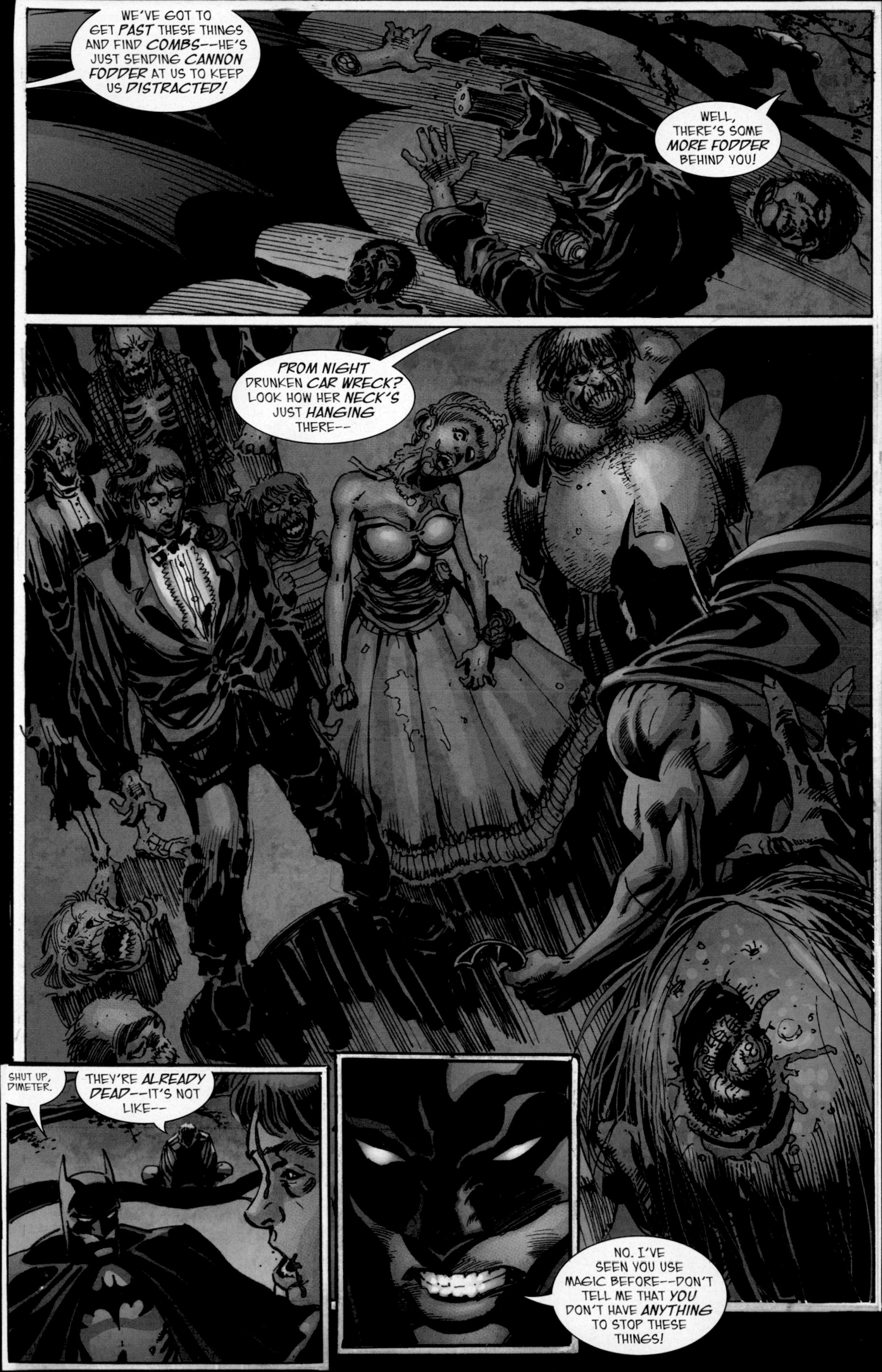
WE'VE GOT TO GET PAST THESE THINGS AND FIND COMBS--HE'S JUST SENDING CANNON FODDER AT US TO KEEP US DISTRACTED!
WELL, THERE'S SOME MORE FODDER BEHIND YOU!
PROM NIGHT DRUNKEN CAR WRECK? LOOK HOW HER NECK'S JUST HANGING THERE--
THEY'RE ALREADY DEAD--IT'S NOT LIKE--
SHUT UP, DIMETER.
NO. I'VE SEEN YOU USE MAGIC BEFORE--DON'T TELL ME THAT YOU DON'T HAVE ANYTHING TO STOP THESE THINGS!

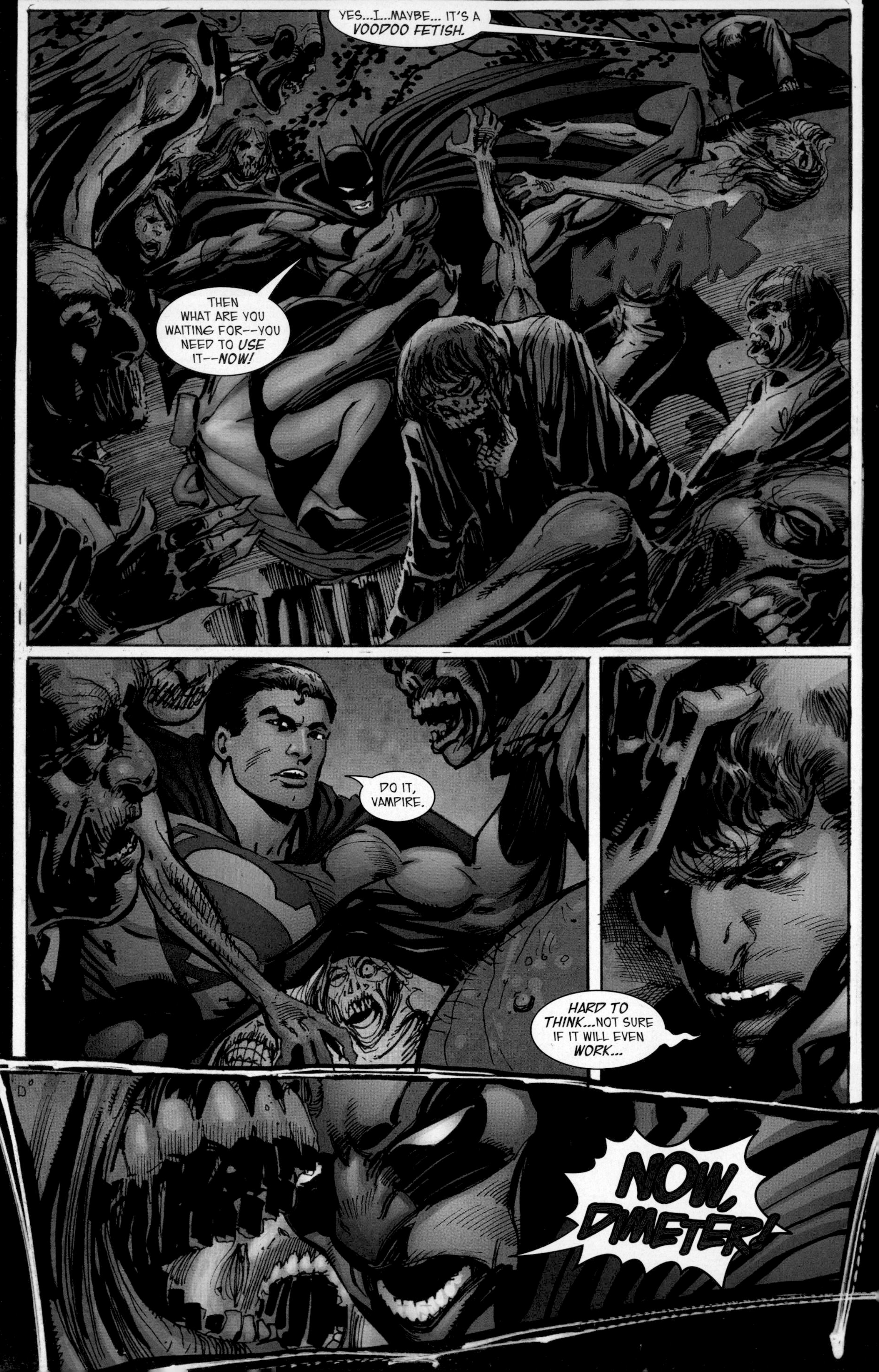
YES...I...MAYBE... IT'S A VOODOO FETISH.
KRAK
THEN WHAT ARE YOU WAITING FOR--YOU NEED TO USE IT--NOW!
DO IT, VAMPIRE.
HARD TO THINK...NOT SURE IF IT WILL EVEN WORK...
NOW, DIMETER!

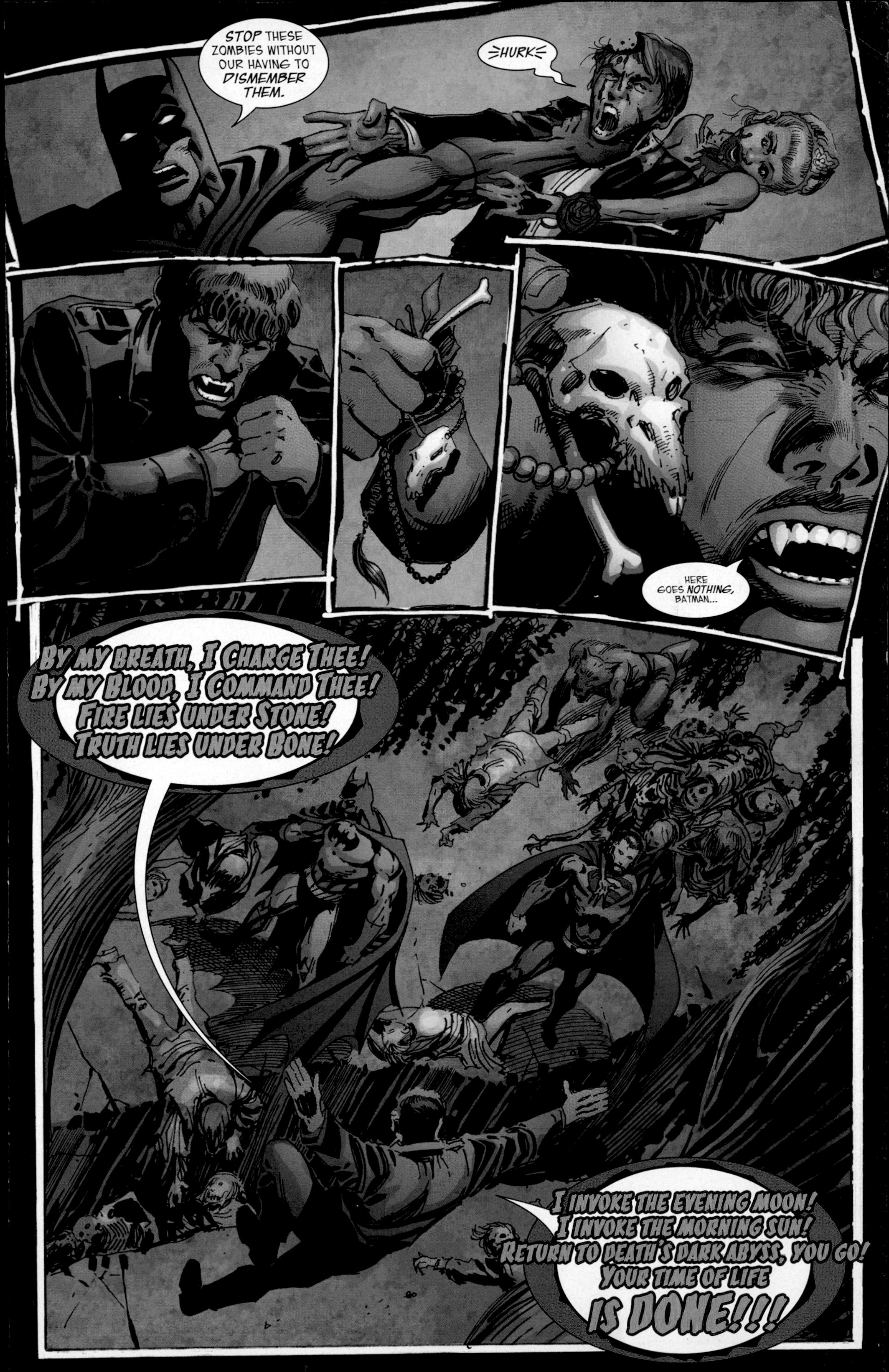
STOP THESE ZOMBIES WITHOUT OUR HAVING TO DISMEMBER THEM.
HURK
HERE GOES NOTHING, BATMAN...
By my Breath, I Charge Thee! By my Blood, I Command Thee! Fire lies under Stone! Truth lies under Bone!
I invoke the evening moon! I invoke the morning sun! Return to death's dark abyss, you go! Your time of life IS DONE!!!

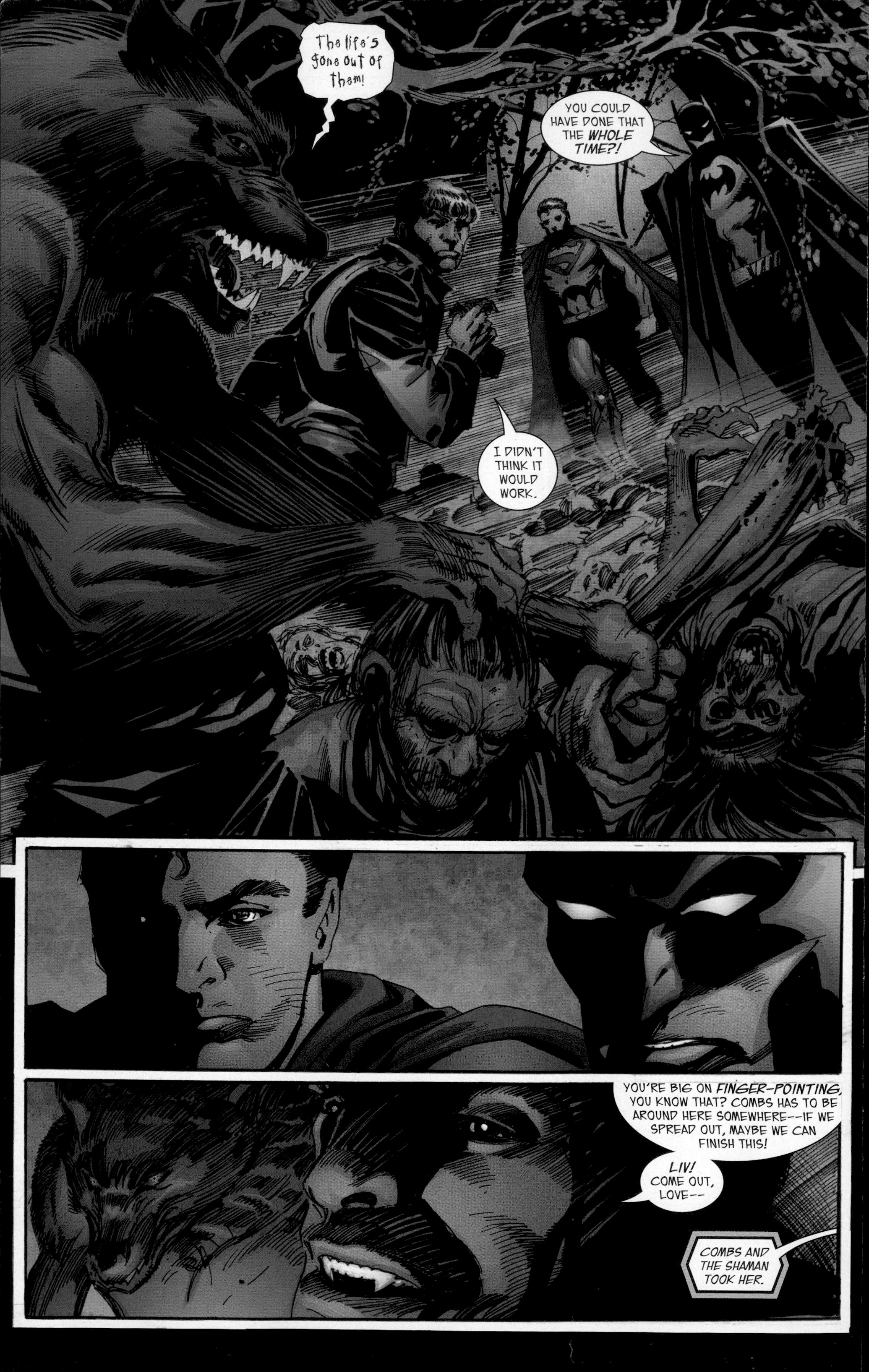
The life's gone out of them!
YOU COULD HAVE DONE THAT THE WHOLE TIME?!
I DIDN'T THINK IT WOULD WORK.
YOU'RE BIG ON FINGER-POINTING, YOU KNOW THAT? COMBS HAS TO BE AROUND HERE SOMEWHERE--IF WE SPREAD OUT, MAYBE WE CAN FINISH THIS!
LIV! COME OUT, LOVE--
COMBS AND THE SHAMAN TOOK HER.

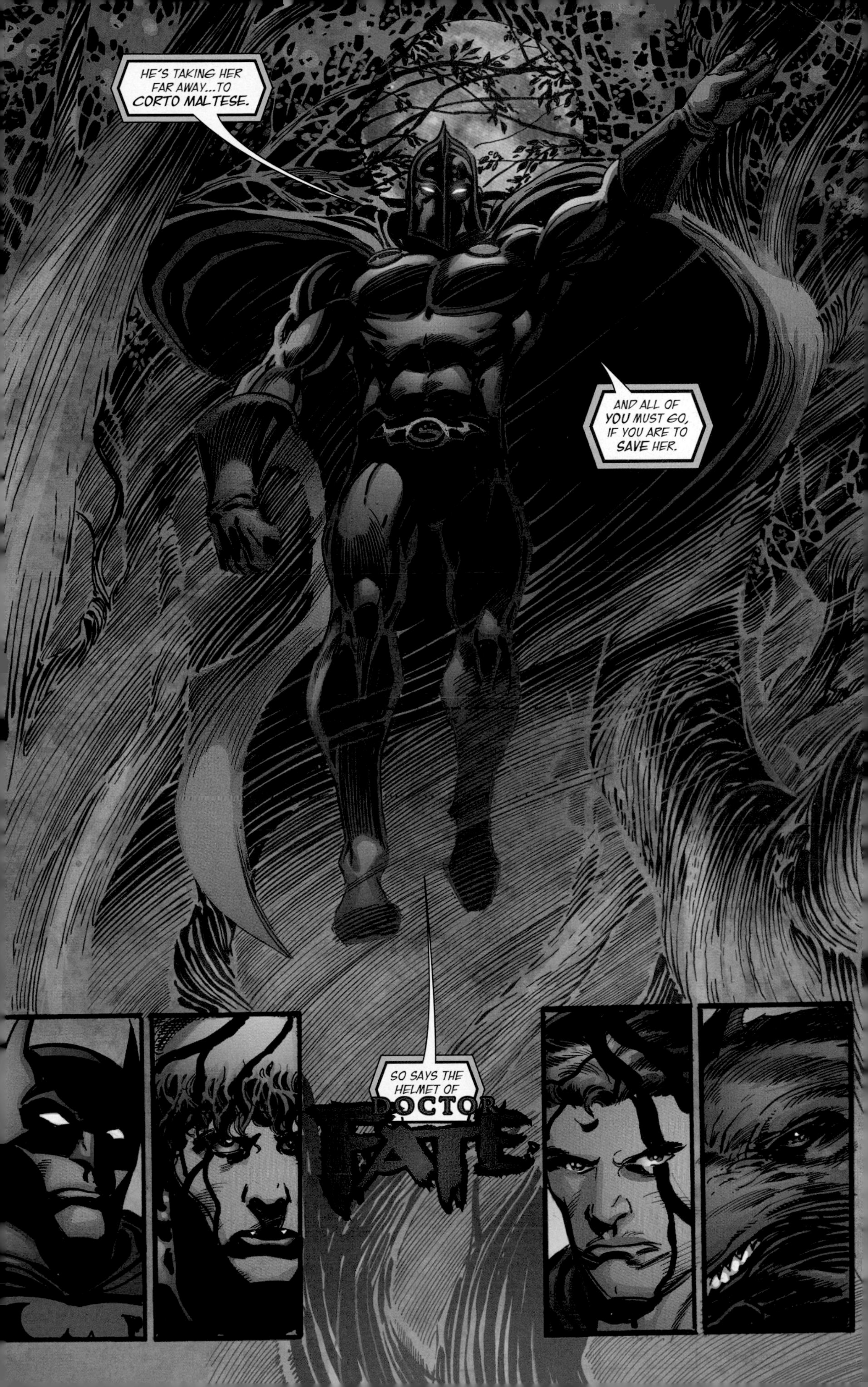
HE'S TAKING HER FAR AWAY...TO CORTO MALTESE.
AND ALL OF YOU MUST GO, IF YOU ARE TO SAVE HER.
SO SAYS THE HELMET OF
DOCTOR FATE.

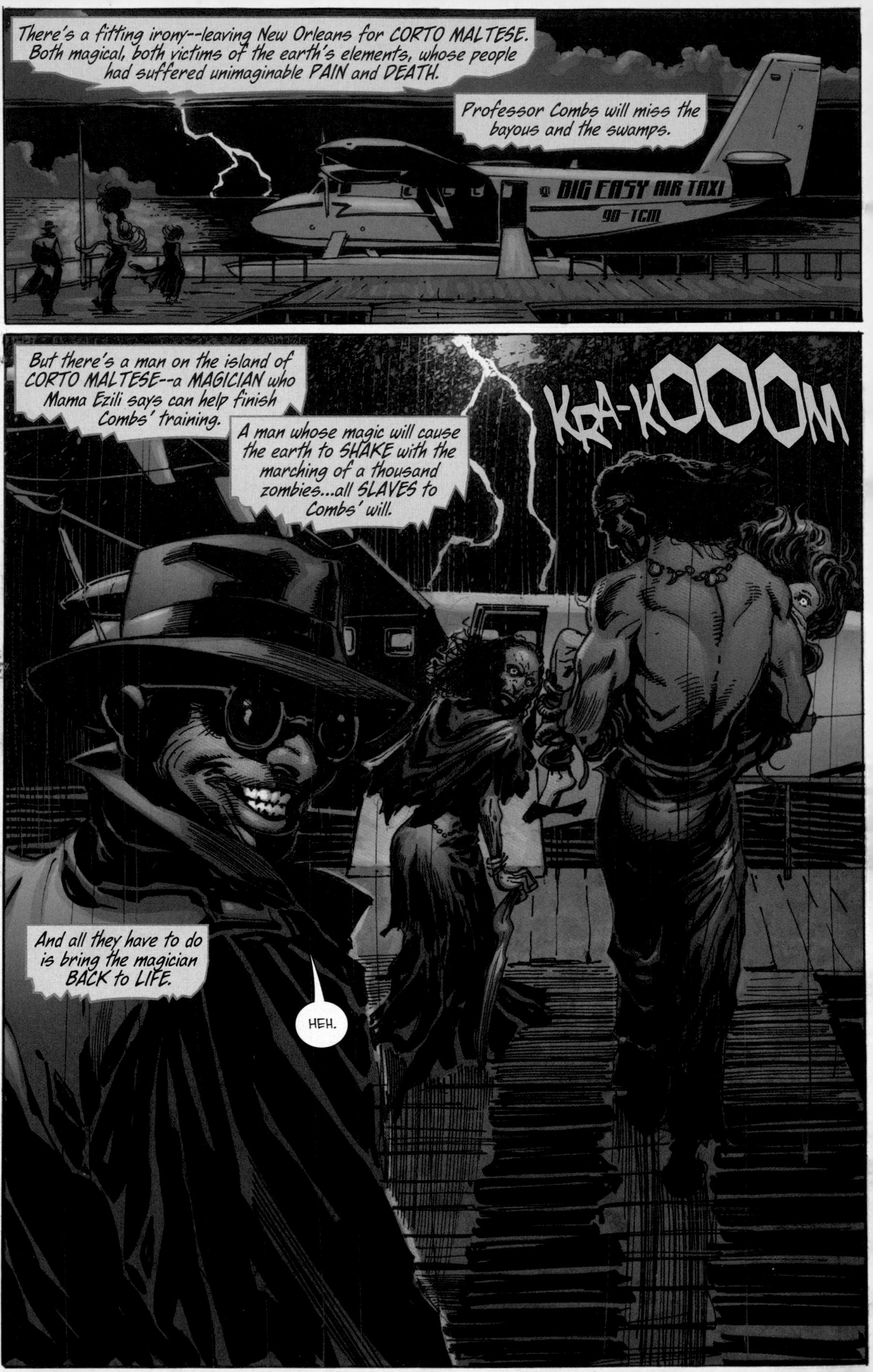
There's a fitting irony--leaving New Orleans for CORTO MALTESE. Both magical, both victims of the earth's elements, whose people had suffered unimaginable PAIN and DEATH.
Professor Combs will miss the bayous and the swamps.
BIG EASY AIR TAXI
9O-TCM
But there's a man on the island of CORTO MALTESE--a MAGICIAN who Mama Ezili says can help finish Combs' training.
A man whose magic will cause the earth to SHAKE with the marching of a thousand zombies...all SLAVES to Combs' will.
KRA-KOOOM
And all they have to do is bring the magician BACK to LIFE.
HEH.

PART FOUR: **THE CORPSES OF CORTO MALTESE**

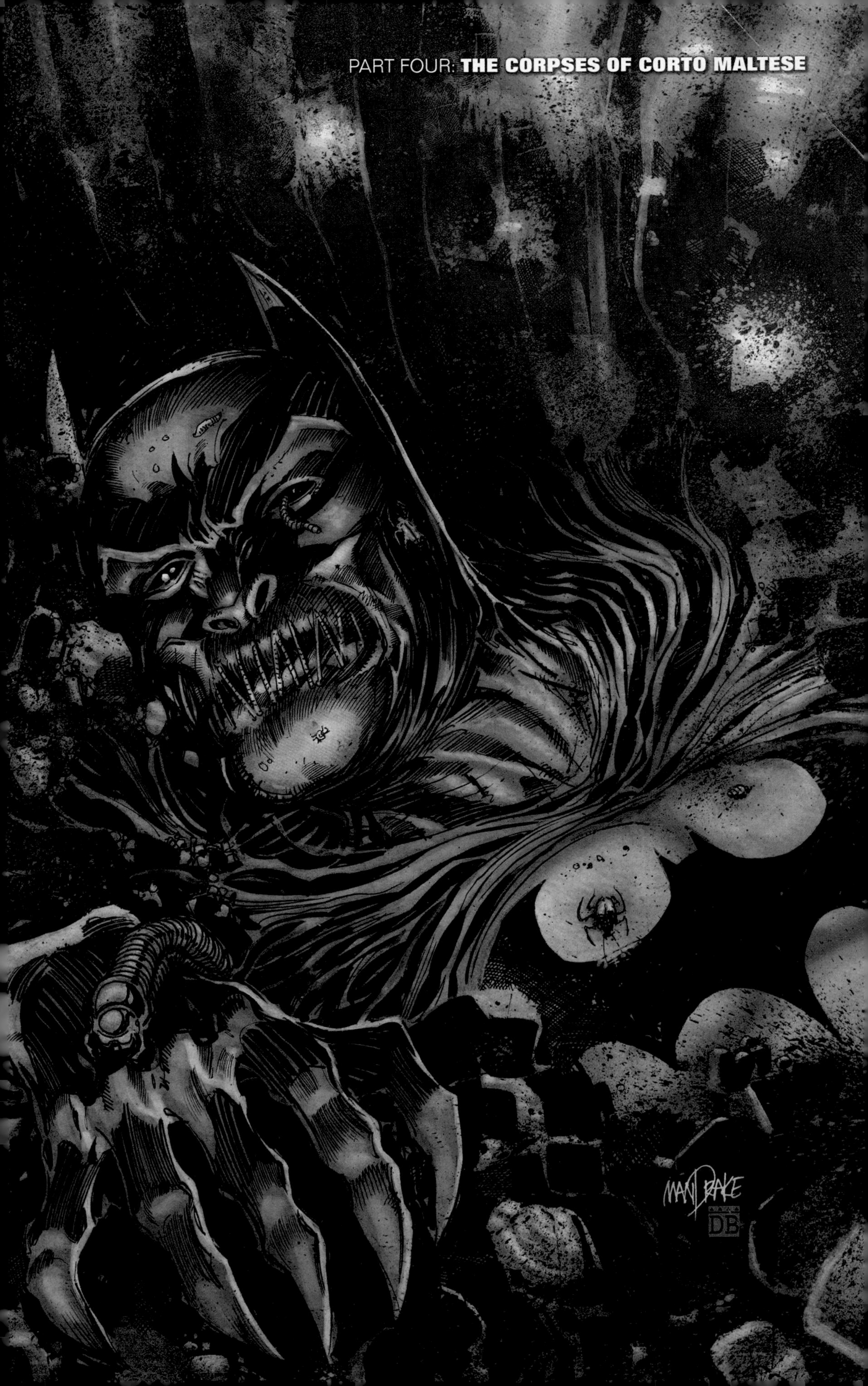

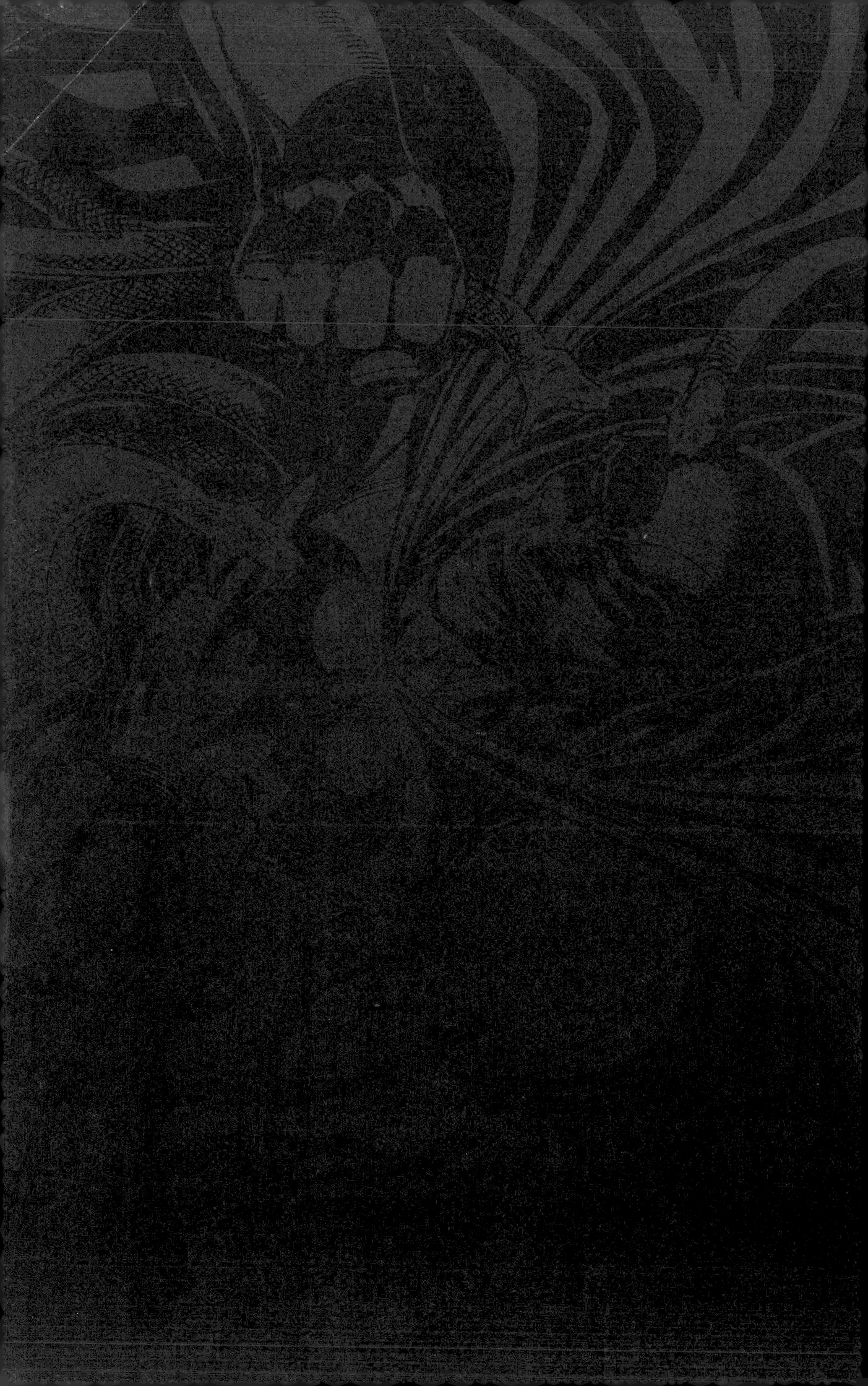

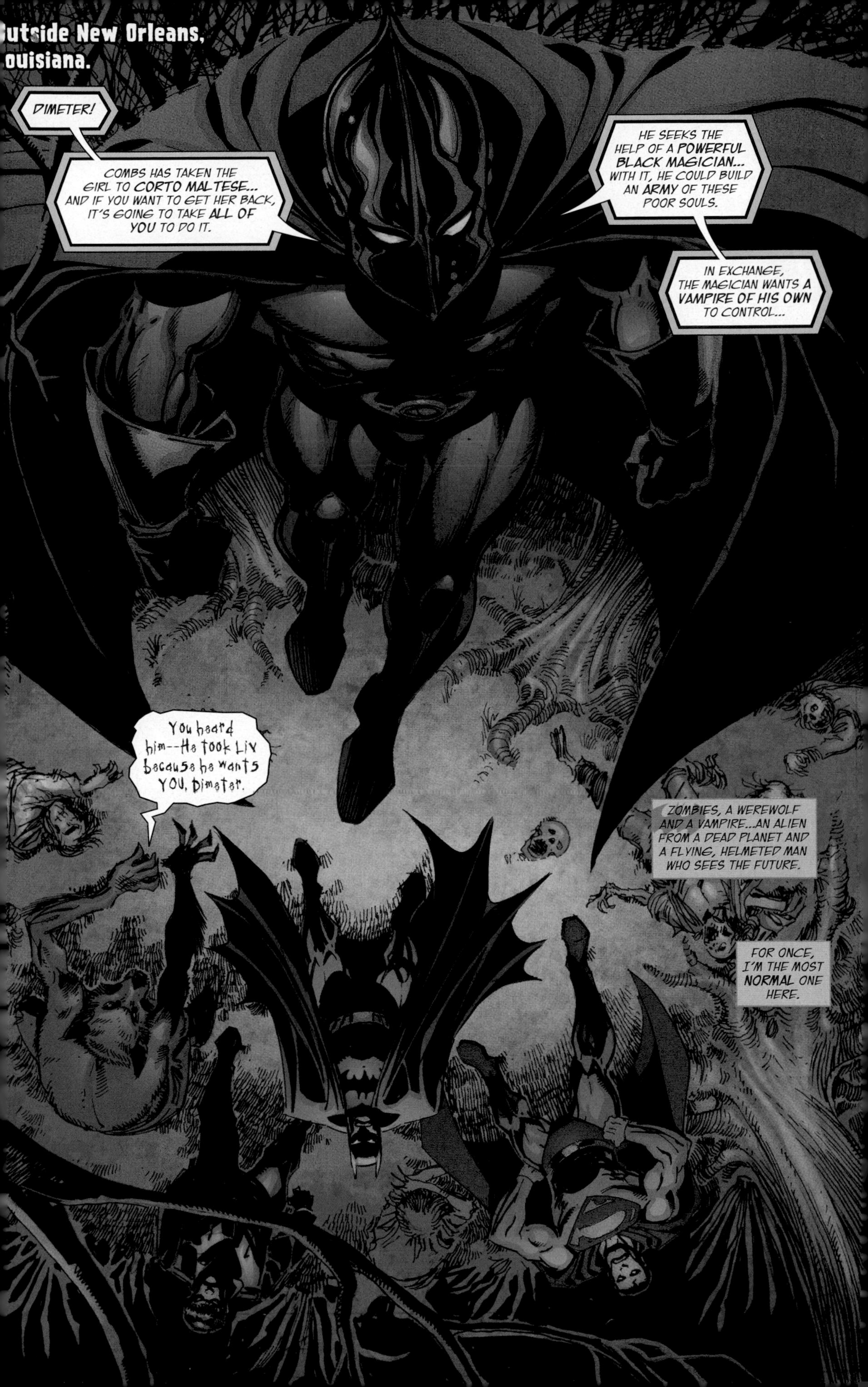
Outside New Orleans, Louisiana.
DIMETER!
COMBS HAS TAKEN THE GIRL TO CORTO MALTESE... AND IF YOU WANT TO GET HER BACK, IT'S GOING TO TAKE ALL OF YOU TO DO IT.
HE SEEKS THE HELP OF A POWERFUL BLACK MAGICIAN... WITH IT, HE COULD BUILD AN ARMY OF THESE POOR SOULS.
IN EXCHANGE, THE MAGICIAN WANTS A VAMPIRE OF HIS OWN TO CONTROL...
You heard him--He took Liv because he wants YOU, Dimeter.
ZOMBIES, A WEREWOLF AND A VAMPIRE...AN ALIEN FROM A DEAD PLANET AND A FLYING, HELMETED MAN WHO SEES THE FUTURE.
FOR ONCE, I'M THE MOST NORMAL ONE HERE.

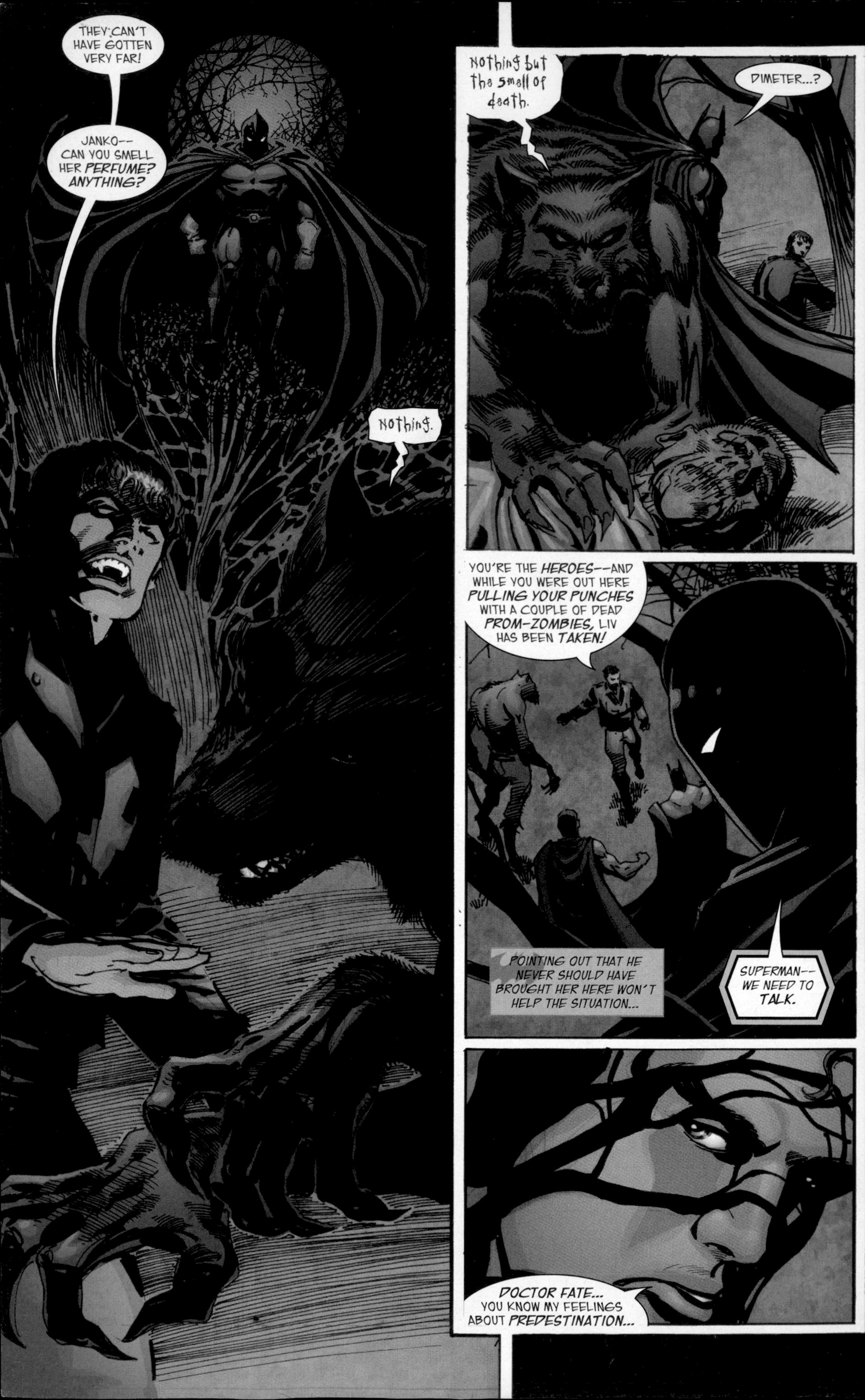

THEY CAN'T HAVE GOTTEN VERY FAR!
JANKO-- CAN YOU SMELL HER PERFUME? ANYTHING?
Nothing.
Nothing but the smell of death.
DIMETER...?
YOU'RE THE HEROES--AND WHILE YOU WERE OUT HERE PULLING YOUR PUNCHES WITH A COUPLE OF DEAD PROM-ZOMBIES, LIV HAS BEEN TAKEN!
POINTING OUT THAT HE NEVER SHOULD HAVE BROUGHT HER HERE WON'T HELP THE SITUATION...
SUPERMAN-- WE NEED TO TALK.
DOCTOR FATE... YOU KNOW MY FEELINGS ABOUT PREDESTINATION...

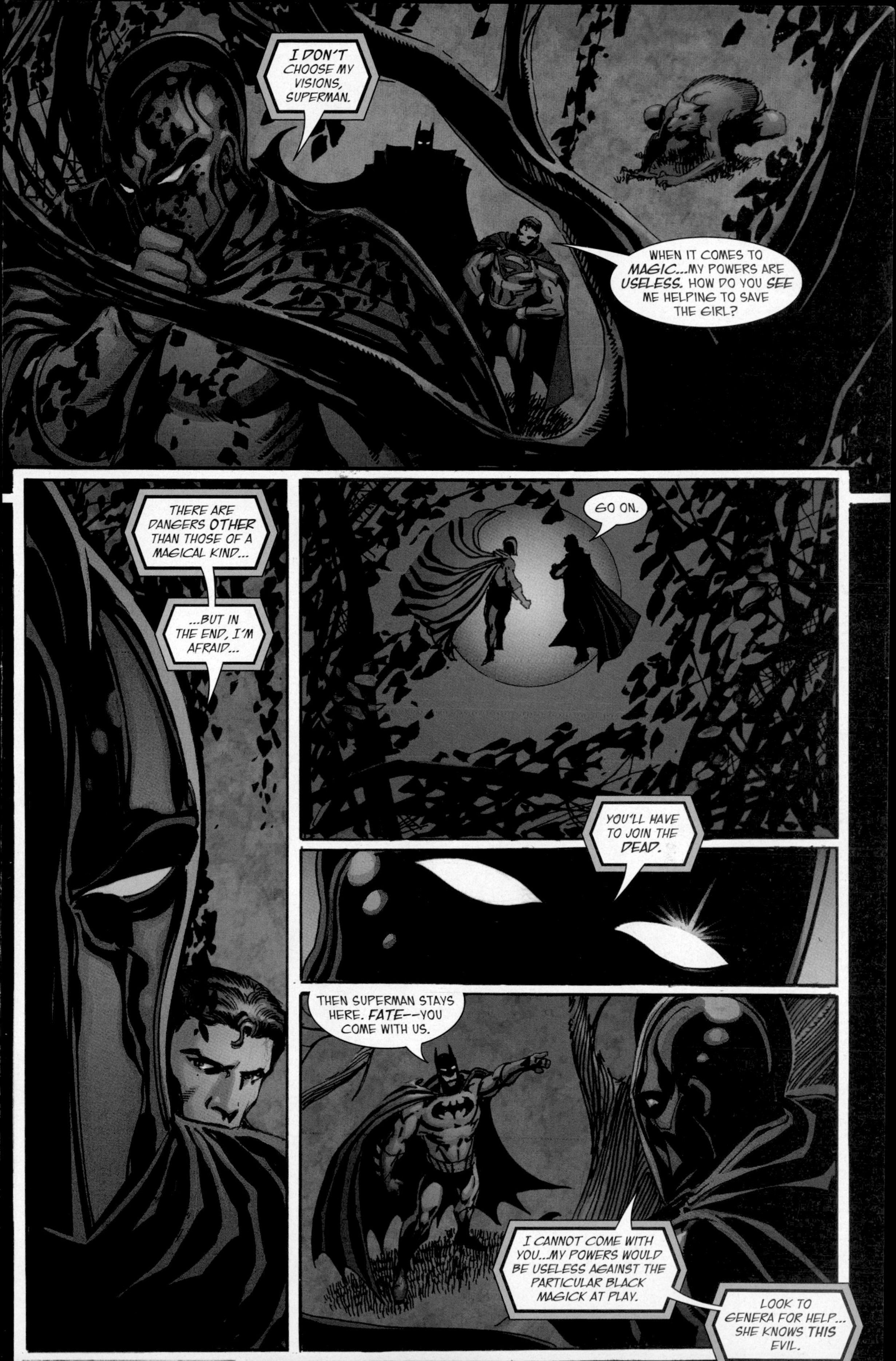
I DON'T CHOOSE MY VISIONS, SUPERMAN.
WHEN IT COMES TO MAGIC...MY POWERS ARE USELESS. HOW DO YOU SEE ME HELPING TO SAVE THE GIRL?
THERE ARE DANGERS OTHER THAN THOSE OF A MAGICAL KIND...
...BUT IN THE END, I'M AFRAID...
GO ON.
YOU'LL HAVE TO JOIN THE DEAD.
THEN SUPERMAN STAYS HERE. FATE--YOU COME WITH US.
I CANNOT COME WITH YOU...MY POWERS WOULD BE USELESS AGAINST THE PARTICULAR BLACK MAGICK AT PLAY.
LOOK TO GENERA FOR HELP... SHE KNOWS THIS EVIL.

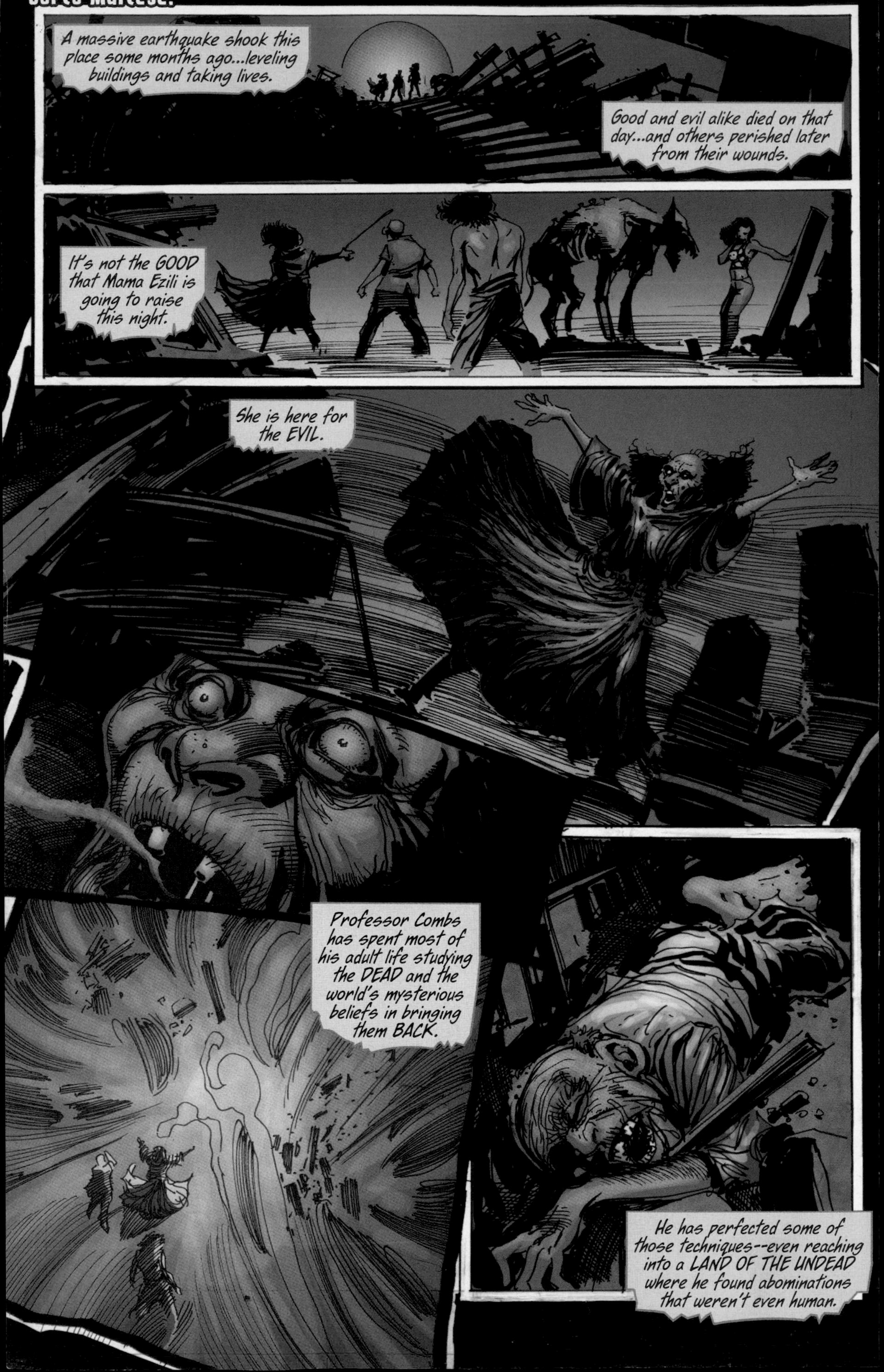
A massive earthquake shook this place some months ago...leveling buildings and taking lives.
Good and evil alike died on that day...and others perished later from their wounds.
It's not the GOOD that Mama Ezili is going to raise this night.
She is here for the EVIL.
Professor Combs has spent most of his adult life studying the DEAD and the world's mysterious beliefs in bringing them BACK.
He has perfected some of those techniques--even reaching into a LAND OF THE UNDEAD where he found abominations that weren't even human.

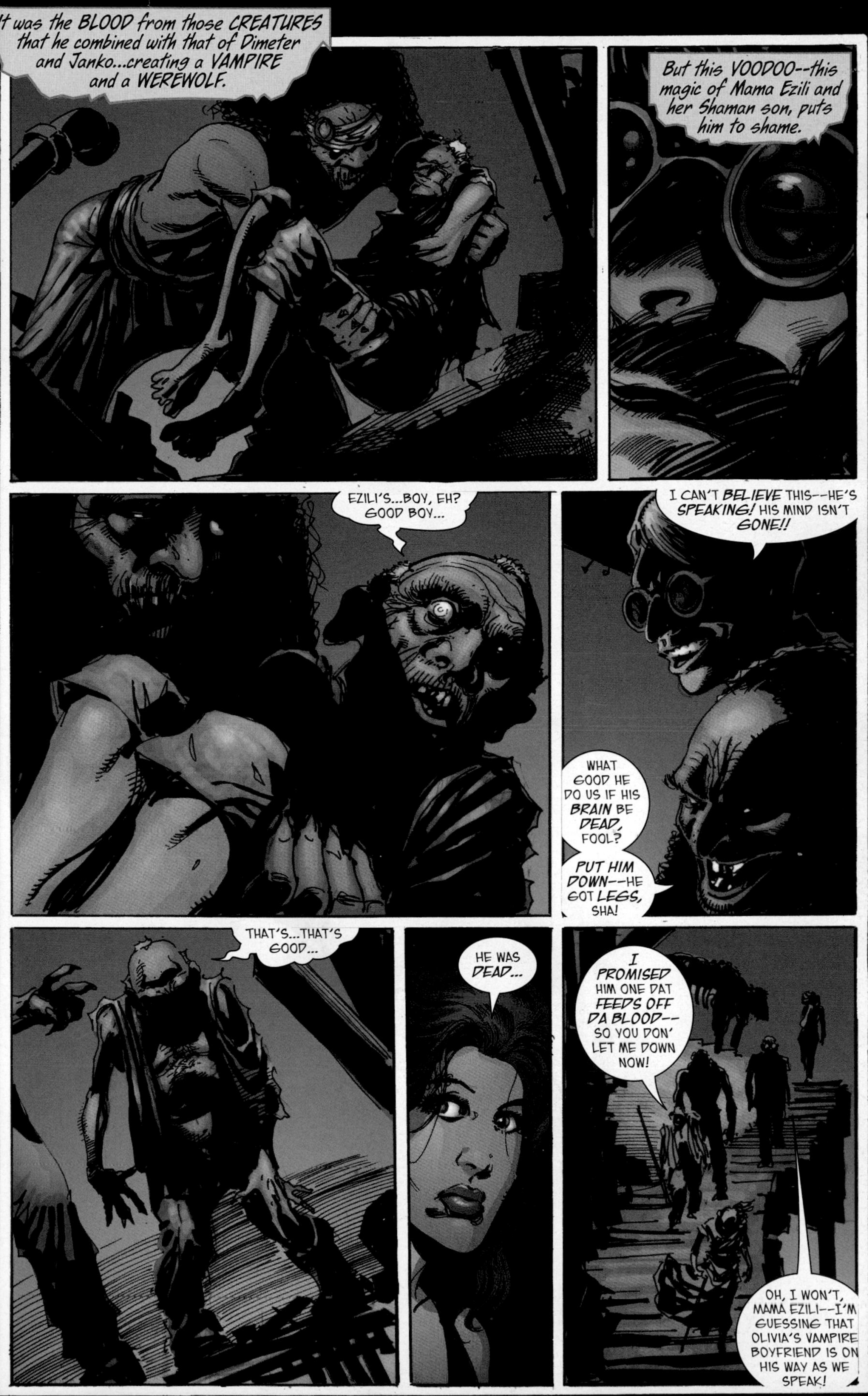
It was the BLOOD from those CREATURES that he combined with that of Dimeter and Janko...creating a VAMPIRE and a WEREWOLF.
But this VOODOO--this magic of Mama Ezili and her Shaman son, puts him to shame.
EZILI'S...BOY, EH? GOOD BOY...
I CAN'T BELIEVE THIS--HE'S SPEAKING! HIS MIND ISN'T GONE!!
WHAT GOOD HE DO US IF HIS BRAIN BE DEAD, FOOL?
PUT HIM DOWN--HE GOT LEGS, SHA!
THAT'S...THAT'S GOOD...
HE WAS DEAD...
I PROMISED HIM ONE DAT FEEDS OFF DA BLOOD-- SO YOU DON' LET ME DOWN NOW!
OH, I WON'T, MAMA EZILI--I'M GUESSING THAT OLIVIA'S VAMPIRE BOYFRIEND IS ON HIS WAY AS WE SPEAK!

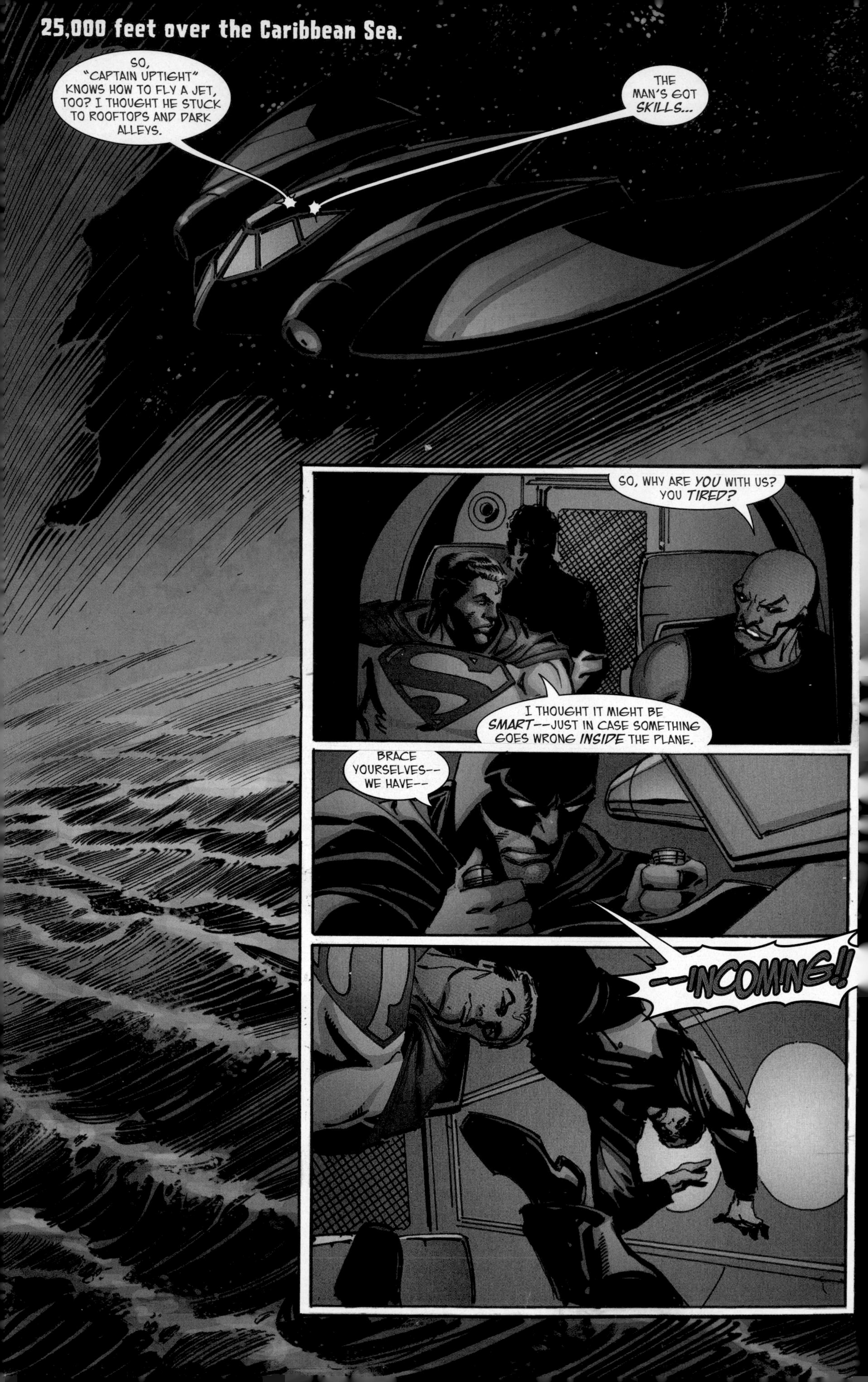
25,000 feet over the Caribbean Sea.
SO, "CAPTAIN UPTIGHT" KNOWS HOW TO FLY A JET, TOO? I THOUGHT HE STUCK TO ROOFTOPS AND DARK ALLEYS.
THE MAN'S GOT SKILLS...
SO, WHY ARE YOU WITH US? YOU TIRED?
I THOUGHT IT MIGHT BE SMART--JUST IN CASE SOMETHING GOES WRONG INSIDE THE PLANE.
BRACE YOURSELVES--WE HAVE--
--INCOMING!!

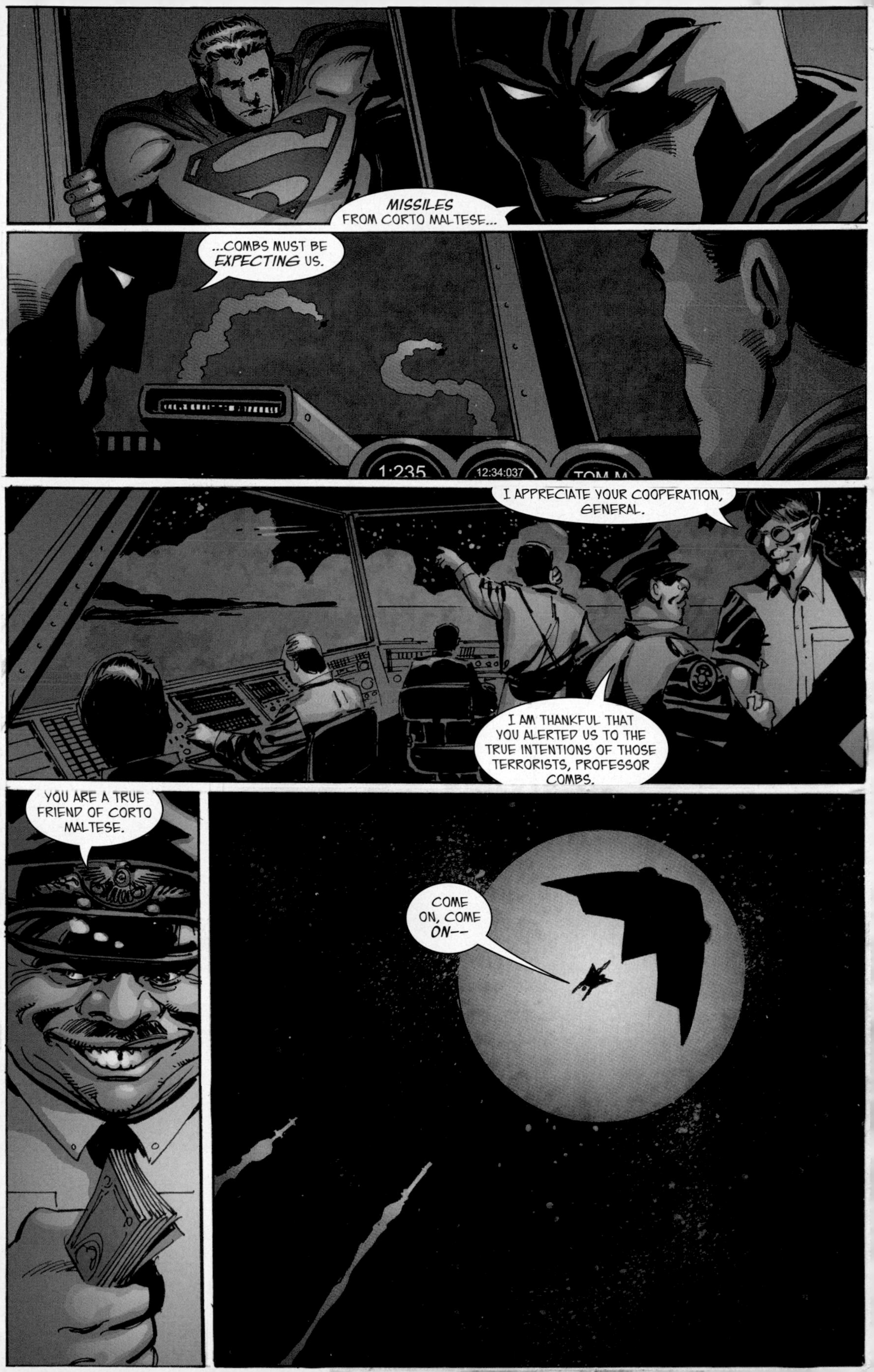

MISSILES FROM CORTO MALTESE...
...COMBS MUST BE EXPECTING US.
1:235
12:34:037
I APPRECIATE YOUR COOPERATION, GENERAL.
I AM THANKFUL THAT YOU ALERTED US TO THE TRUE INTENTIONS OF THOSE TERRORISTS, PROFESSOR COMBS.
YOU ARE A TRUE FRIEND OF CORTO MALTESE.
COME ON, COME ON--

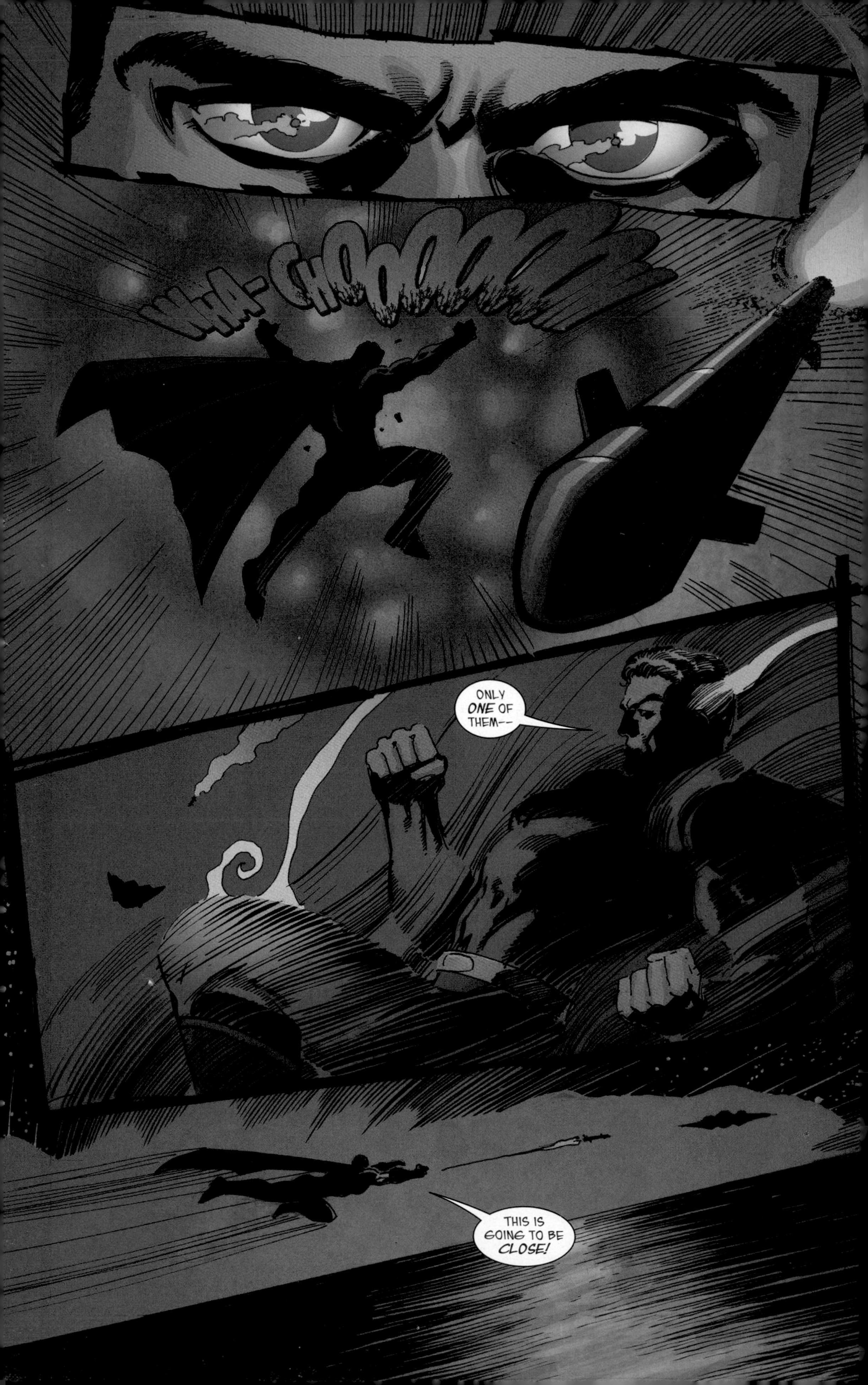
WHA-CHOOOOOM
ONLY ONE OF THEM--
THIS IS GOING TO BE CLOSE!

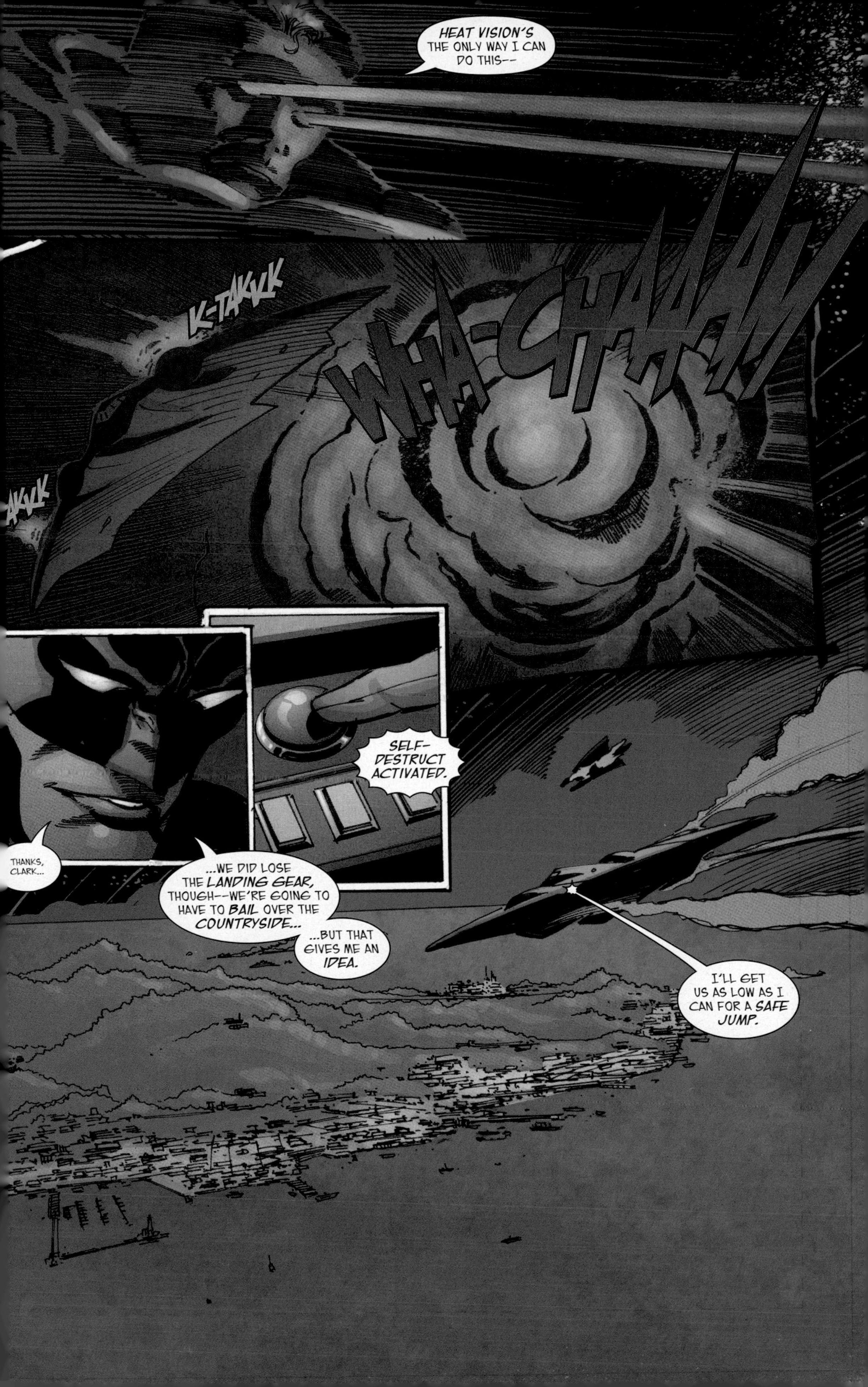
HEAT VISION'S THE ONLY WAY I CAN DO THIS--
K-TAKAK
AKAK
WHA-CHAAAAM
SELF-DESTRUCT ACTIVATED.
THANKS, CLARK...
...WE DID LOSE THE LANDING GEAR, THOUGH--WE'RE GOING TO HAVE TO BAIL OVER THE COUNTRYSIDE...
...BUT THAT GIVES ME AN IDEA.
I'LL GET US AS LOW AS I CAN FOR A SAFE JUMP.

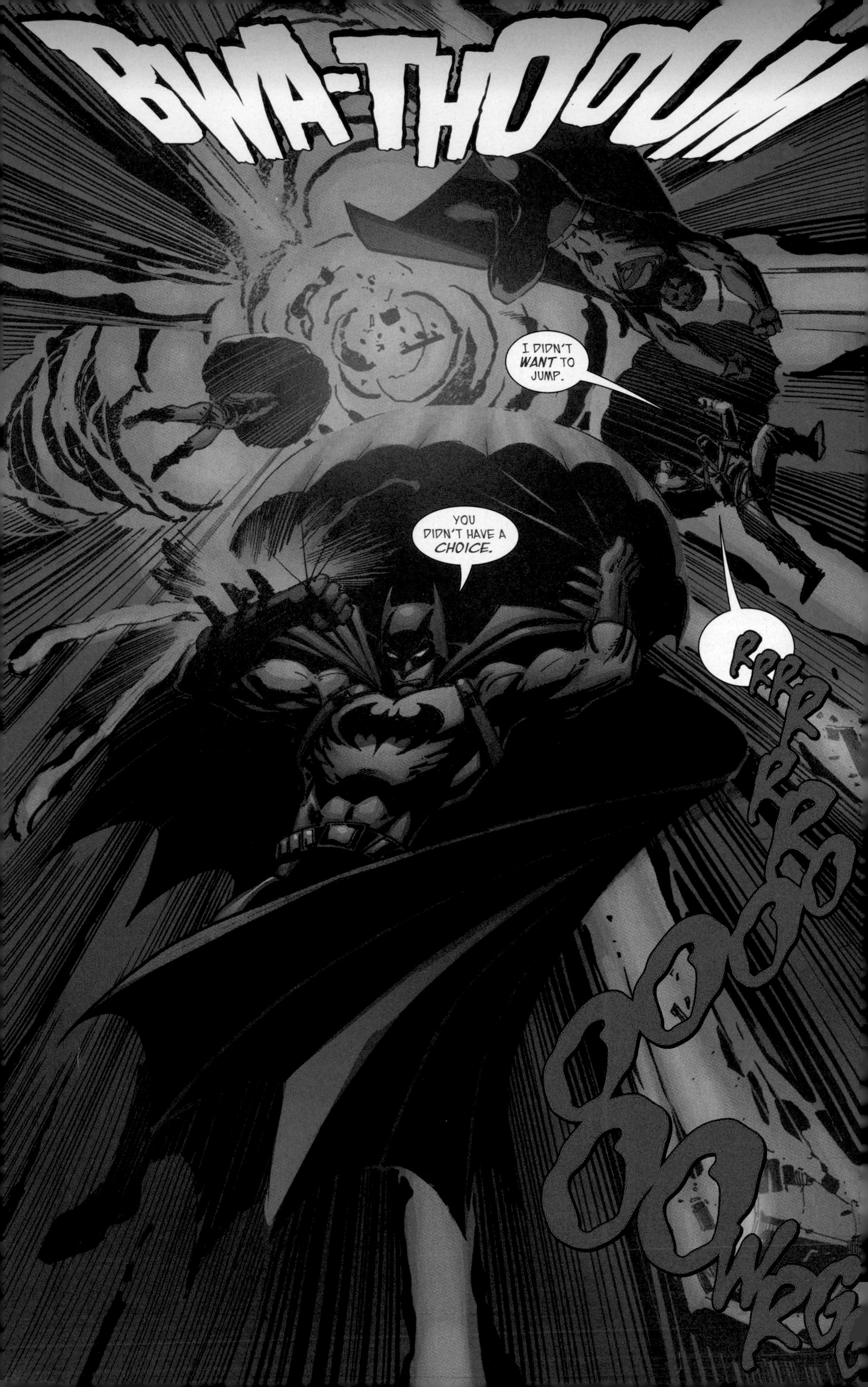
BWA-THOOOM
I DIDN'T *WANT* TO JUMP.
YOU DIDN'T HAVE A *CHOICE.*
RRRRRRRRGGGGGGGHHRG

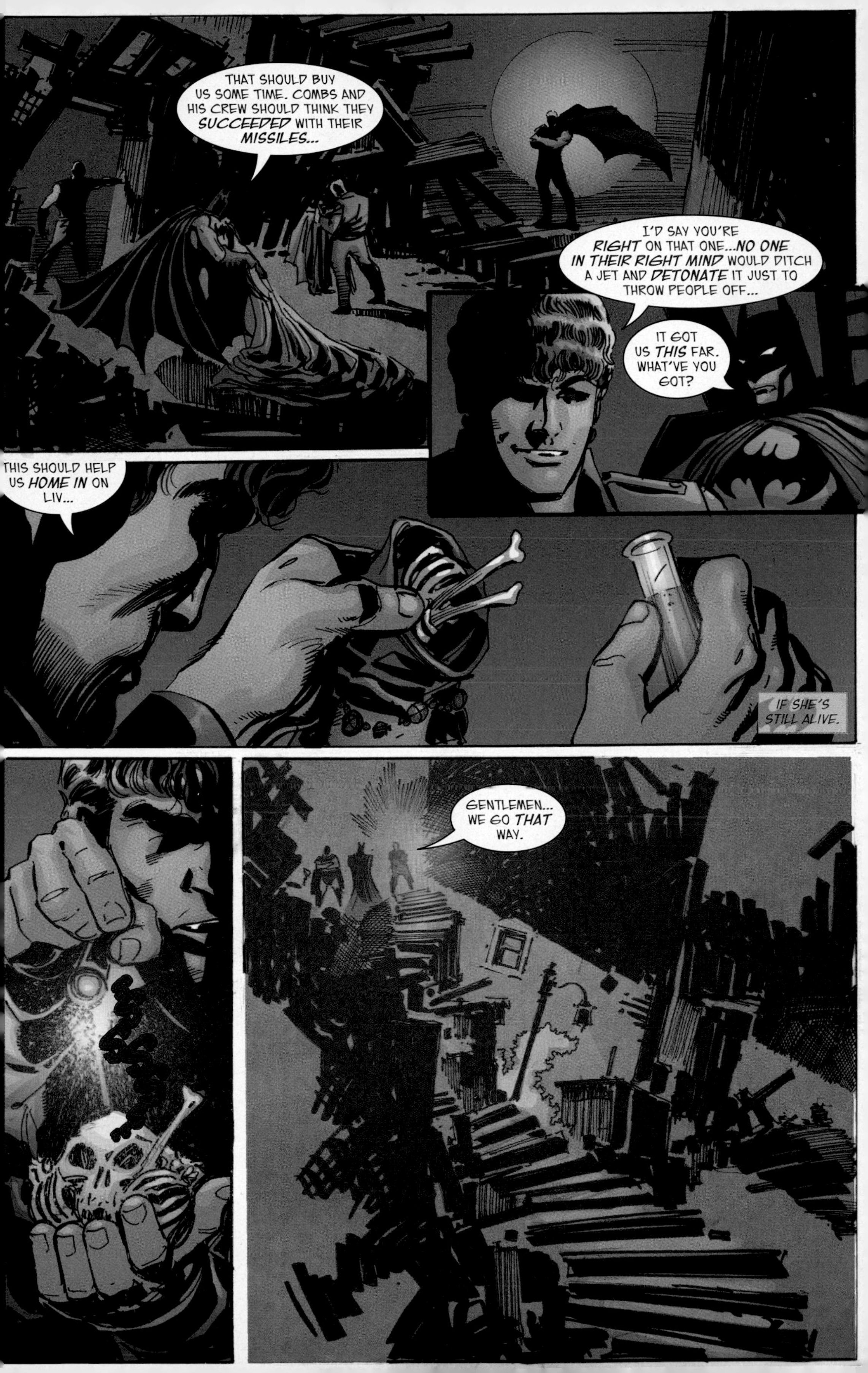
THAT SHOULD BUY US SOME TIME. COMBS AND HIS CREW SHOULD THINK THEY *SUCCEEDED* WITH THEIR *MISSILES...*
I'D SAY YOU'RE *RIGHT* ON THAT ONE...*NO ONE IN THEIR RIGHT MIND* WOULD DITCH A JET AND *DETONATE* IT JUST TO THROW PEOPLE OFF...
IT GOT US *THIS* FAR. WHAT'VE YOU GOT?
THIS SHOULD HELP US *HOME IN* ON LIV...
IF SHE'S STILL ALIVE.
GENTLEMEN... WE GO *THAT* WAY.

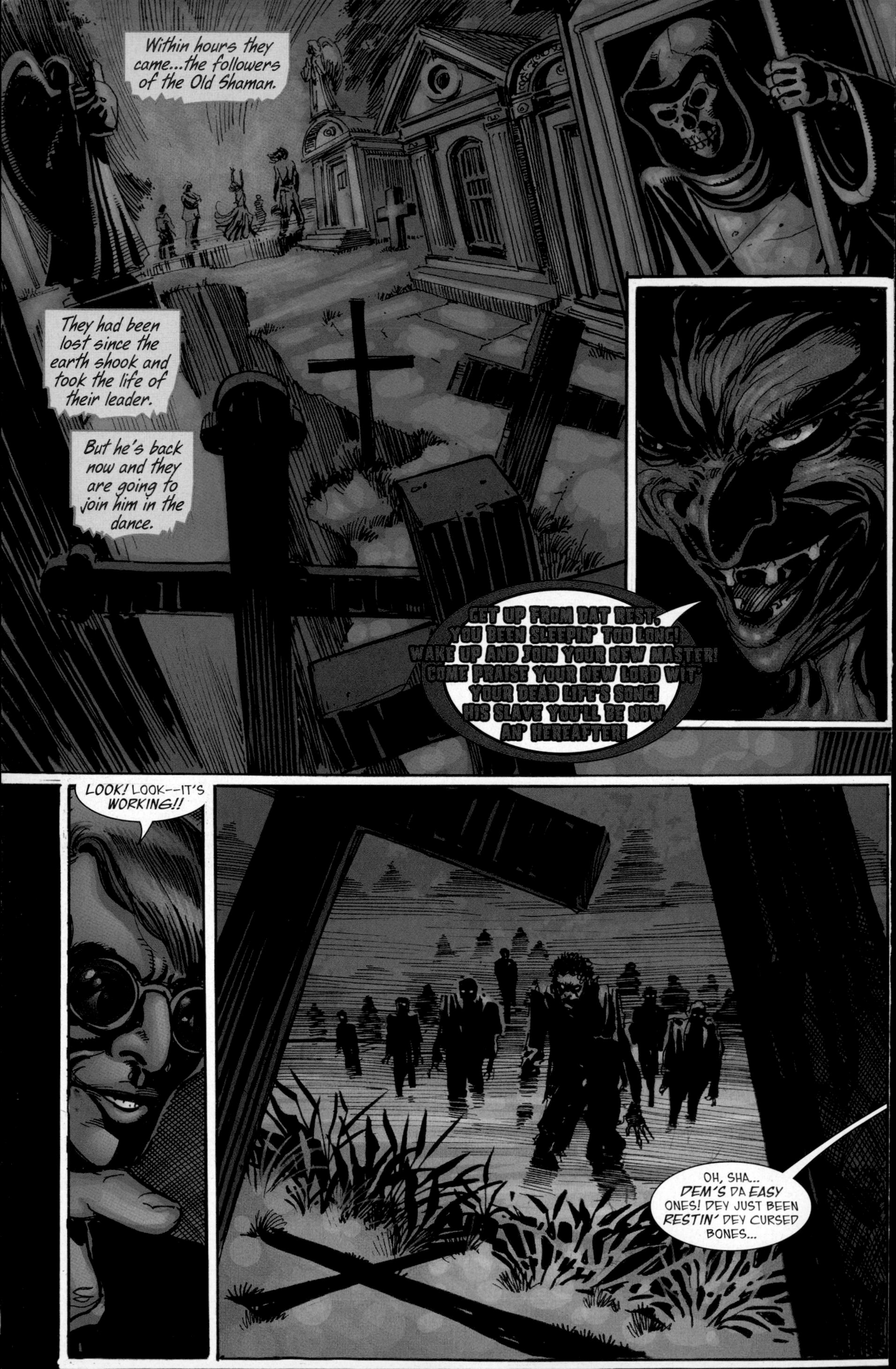
Within hours they came...the followers of the Old Shaman.
They had been lost since the earth shook and took the life of their leader.
But he's back now and they are going to join him in the dance.
GET UP FROM DAT REST, YOU BEEN SLEEPIN' TOO LONG! WAKE UP AND JOIN YOUR NEW MASTER! COME PRAISE YOUR NEW LORD WIT' YOUR DEAD LIFE'S SONG! HIS SLAVE YOU'LL BE NOW AN' HEREAFTER!
LOOK! LOOK--IT'S WORKING!!
OH, SHA... DEM'S DA EASY ONES! DEY JUST BEEN RESTIN' DEY CURSED BONES...

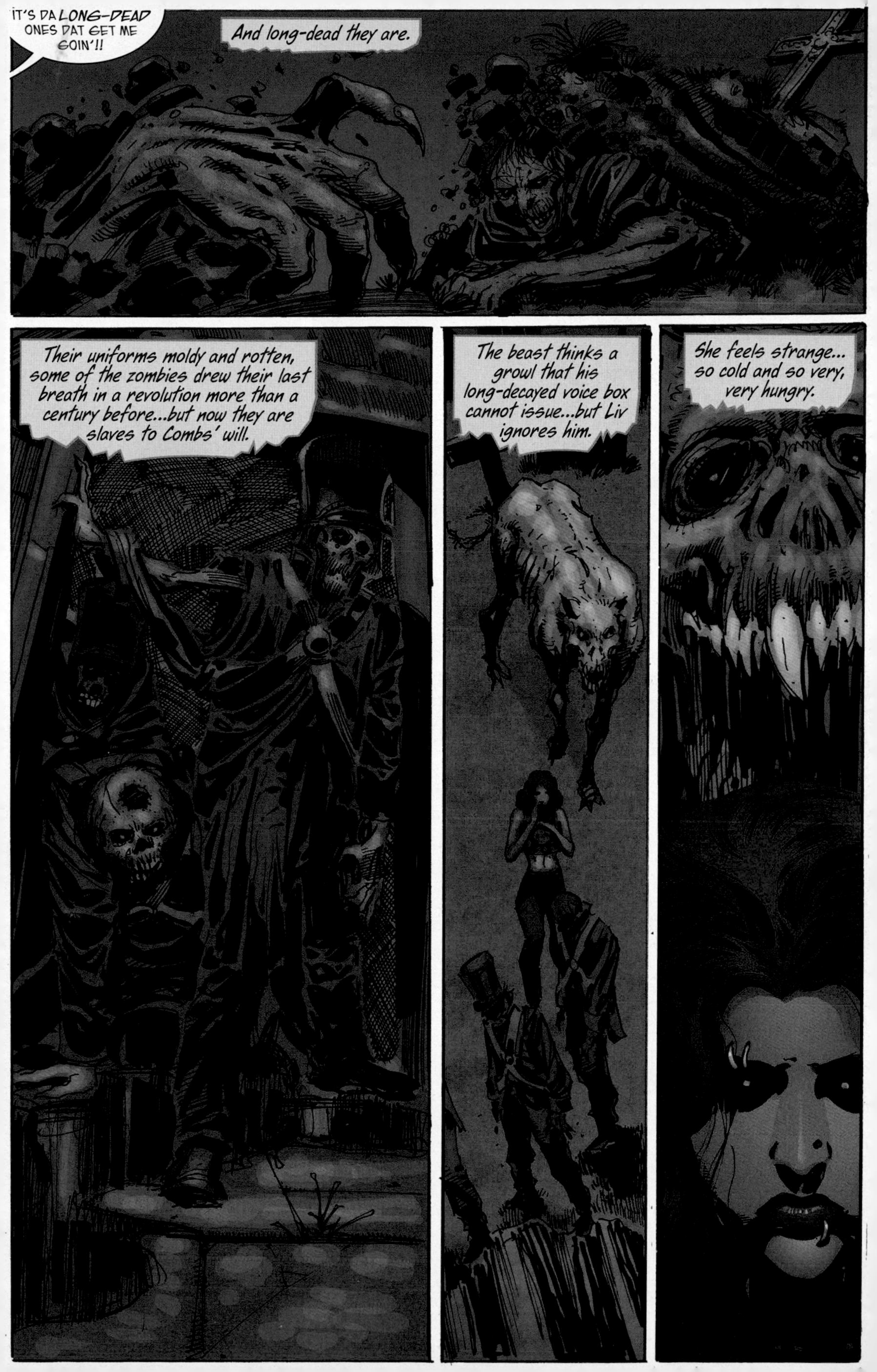
IT'S DA LONG-DEAD ONES DAT GET ME GOIN'!!
And long-dead they are.
Their uniforms moldy and rotten, some of the zombies drew their last breath in a revolution more than a century before...but now they are slaves to Combs' will.
The beast thinks a growl that his long-decayed voice box cannot issue...but Liv ignores him.
She feels strange... so cold and so very, very hungry.

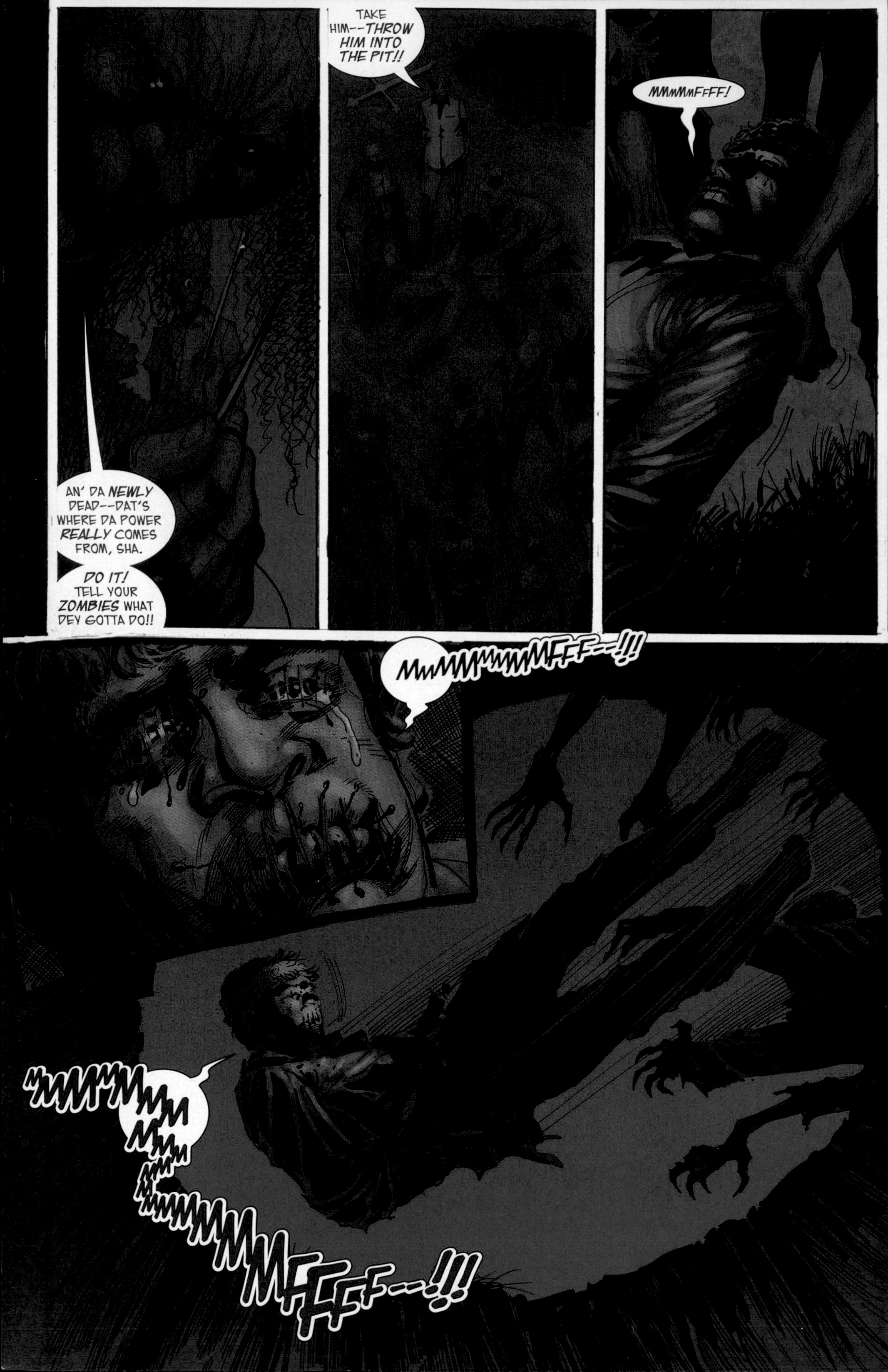
AN' DA NEWLY DEAD--DAT'S WHERE DA POWER REALLY COMES FROM, SHA.
DO IT! TELL YOUR ZOMBIES WHAT DEY GOTTA DO!!
TAKE HIM--THROW HIM INTO THE PIT!!
MMMMMFFFF!
MMMMMMMMMFFF--!!!
MMMMMMMMMMMMMMMMFFFF--!!!

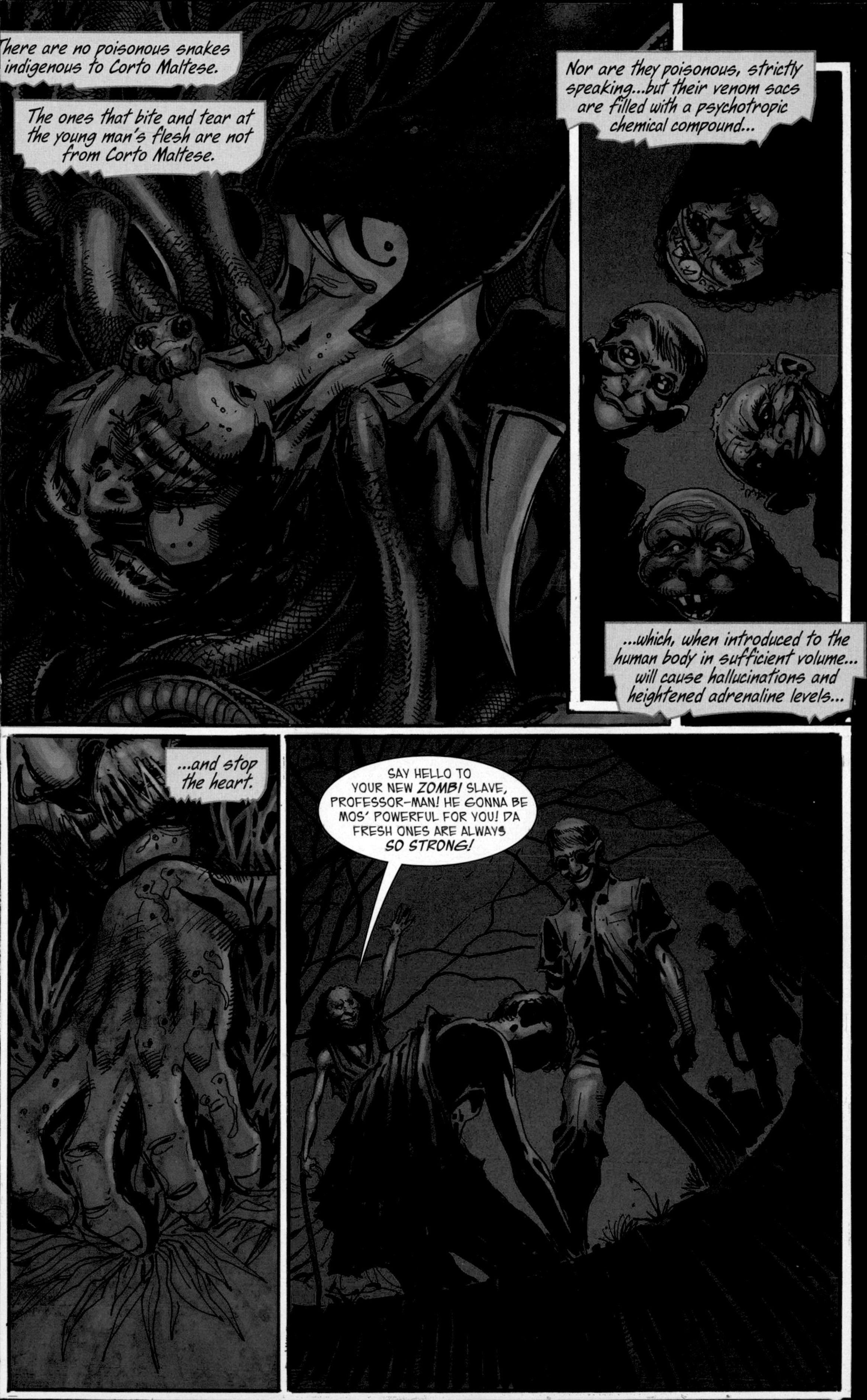
There are no poisonous snakes indigenous to Corto Maltese.
The ones that bite and tear at the young man's flesh are not from Corto Maltese.
Nor are they poisonous, strictly speaking...but their venom sacs are filled with a psychotropic chemical compound...
...which, when introduced to the human body in sufficient volume... will cause hallucinations and heightened adrenaline levels...
...and stop the heart.
SAY HELLO TO YOUR NEW ZOMBI SLAVE, PROFESSOR-MAN! HE GONNA BE MOS' POWERFUL FOR YOU! DA FRESH ONES ARE ALWAYS SO STRONG!

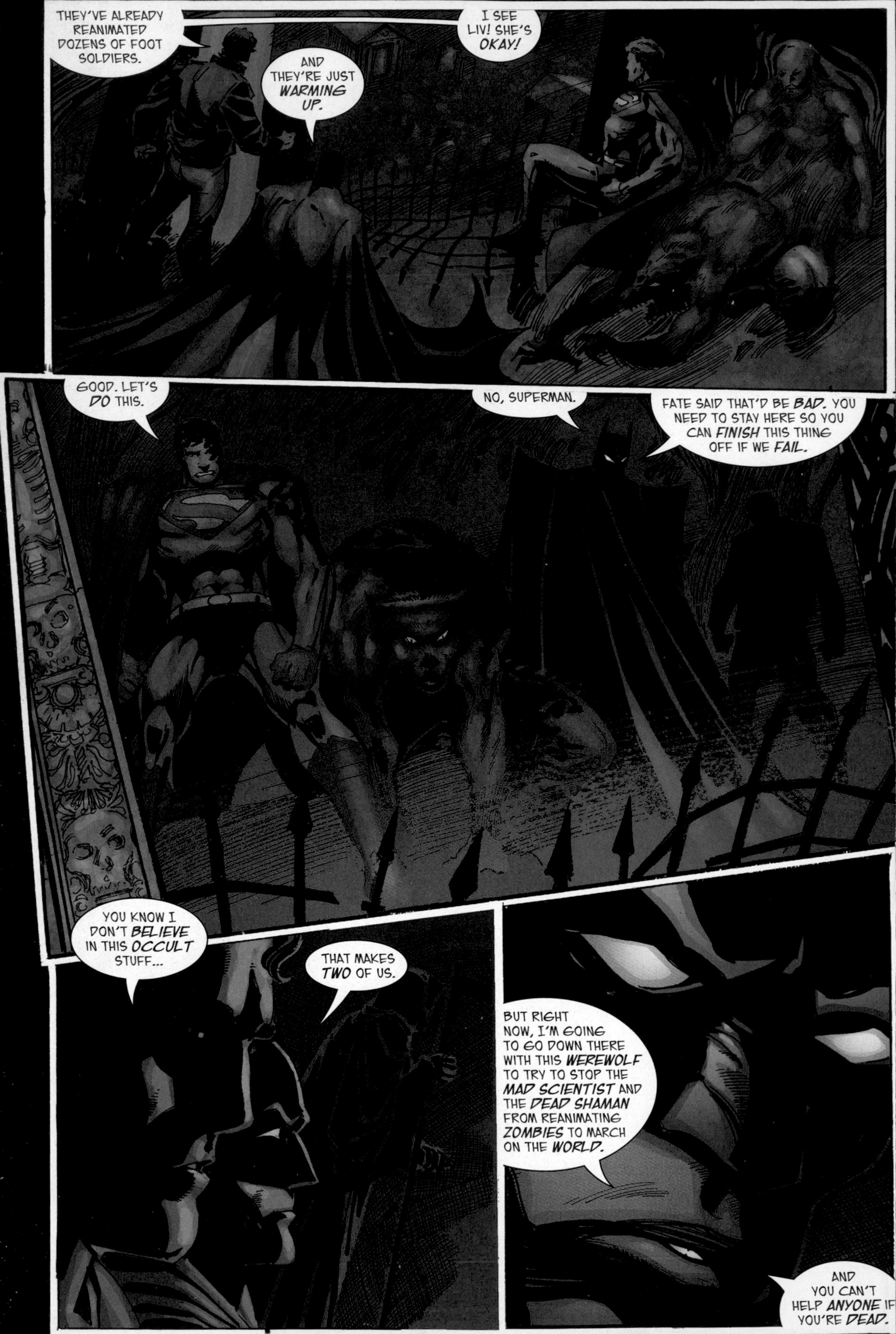
THEY'VE ALREADY REANIMATED DOZENS OF FOOT SOLDIERS.
AND THEY'RE JUST WARMING UP.
I SEE LIV! SHE'S OKAY!
GOOD. LET'S DO THIS.
NO, SUPERMAN.
FATE SAID THAT'D BE BAD. YOU NEED TO STAY HERE SO YOU CAN FINISH THIS THING OFF IF WE FAIL.
YOU KNOW I DON'T BELIEVE IN THIS OCCULT STUFF...
THAT MAKES TWO OF US.
BUT RIGHT NOW, I'M GOING TO GO DOWN THERE WITH THIS WEREWOLF TO TRY TO STOP THE MAD SCIENTIST AND THE DEAD SHAMAN FROM REANIMATING ZOMBIES TO MARCH ON THE WORLD.
AND YOU CAN'T HELP ANYONE IF YOU'RE DEAD.

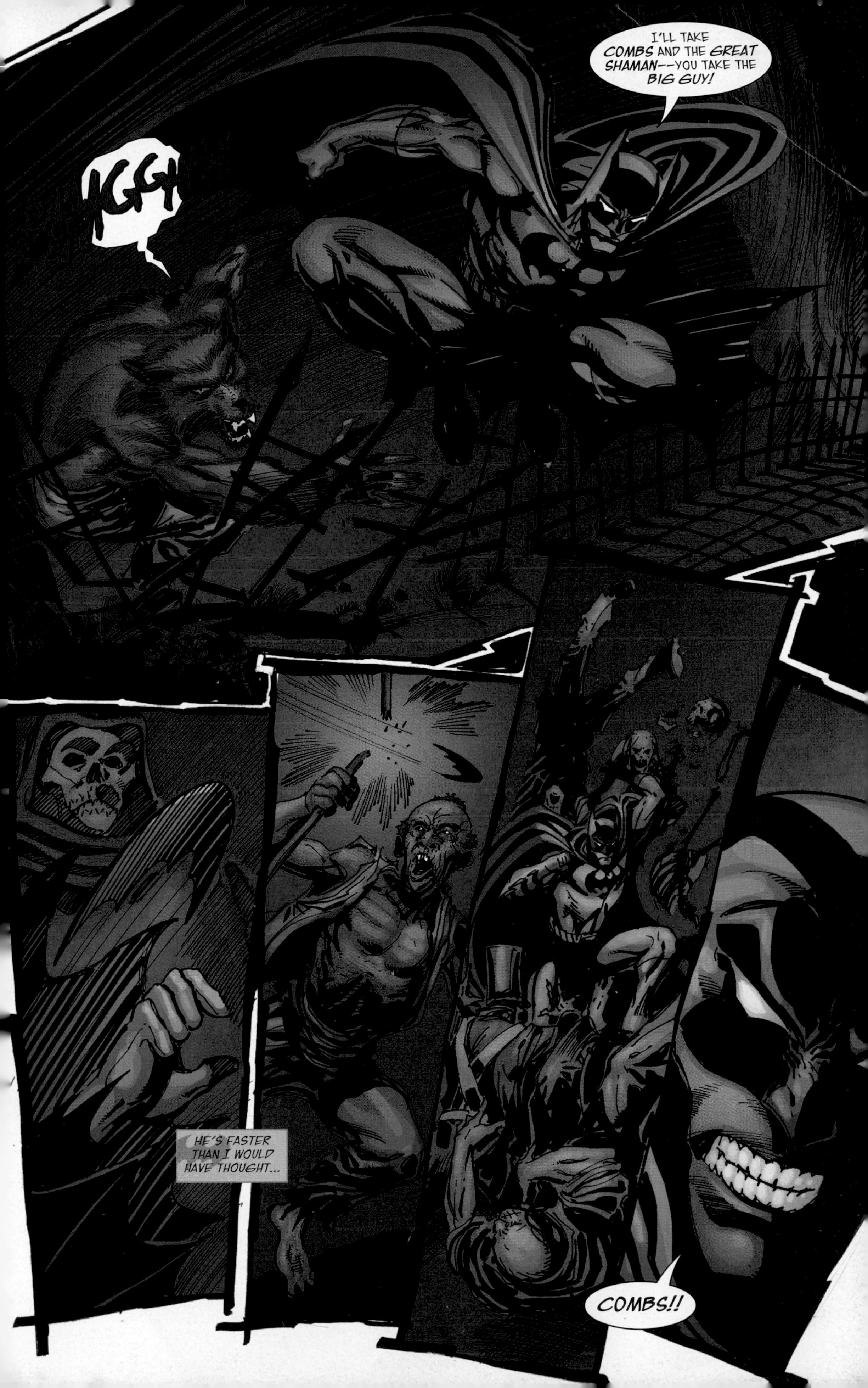
AGGH
I'LL TAKE COMBS AND THE GREAT SHAMAN--YOU TAKE THE BIG GUY!
HE'S FASTER THAN I WOULD HAVE THOUGHT...
COMBS!!

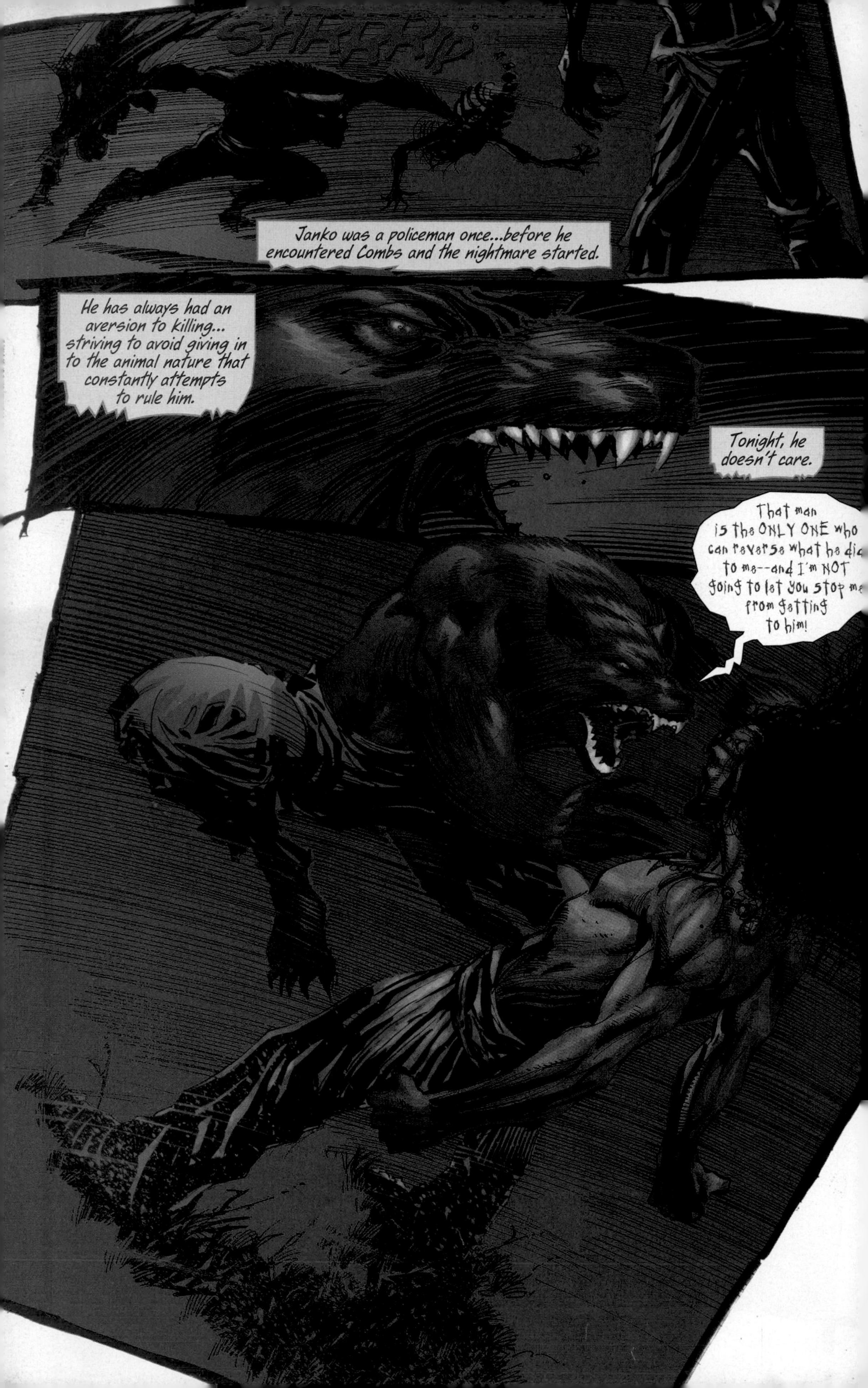

Janko was a policeman once...before he encountered Combs and the nightmare started.
He has always had an aversion to killing... striving to avoid giving in to the animal nature that constantly attempts to rule him.
Tonight, he doesn't care.
That man is the ONLY ONE who can reverse what he did to me--and I'm NOT going to let you stop me from getting to him!

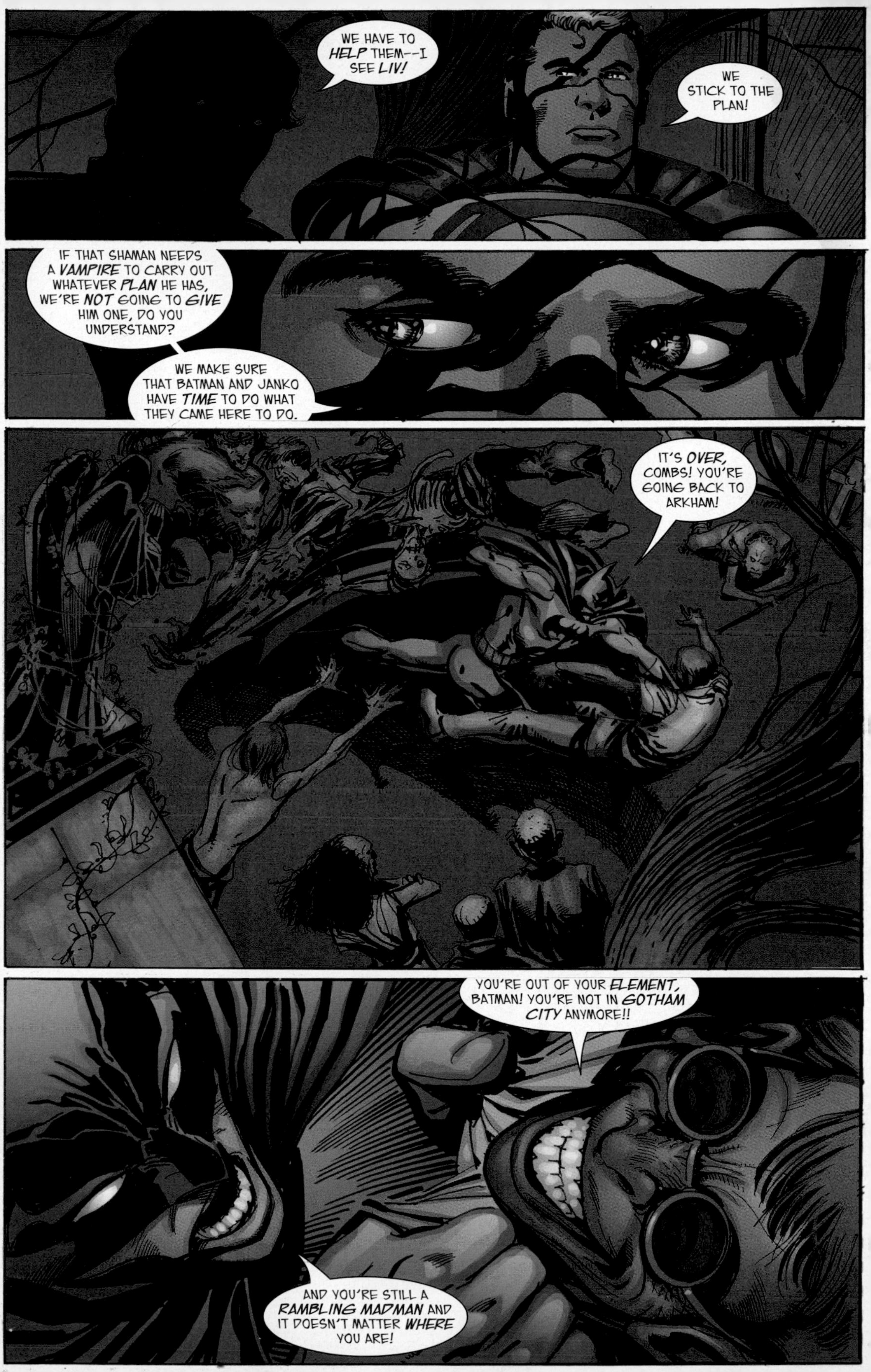
WE HAVE TO HELP THEM--I SEE LIV!
WE STICK TO THE PLAN!
IF THAT SHAMAN NEEDS A VAMPIRE TO CARRY OUT WHATEVER PLAN HE HAS, WE'RE NOT GOING TO GIVE HIM ONE, DO YOU UNDERSTAND?
WE MAKE SURE THAT BATMAN AND JANKO HAVE TIME TO DO WHAT THEY CAME HERE TO DO.
IT'S OVER, COMBS! YOU'RE GOING BACK TO ARKHAM!
YOU'RE OUT OF YOUR ELEMENT, BATMAN! YOU'RE NOT IN GOTHAM CITY ANYMORE!!
AND YOU'RE STILL A RAMBLING MADMAN AND IT DOESN'T MATTER WHERE YOU ARE!

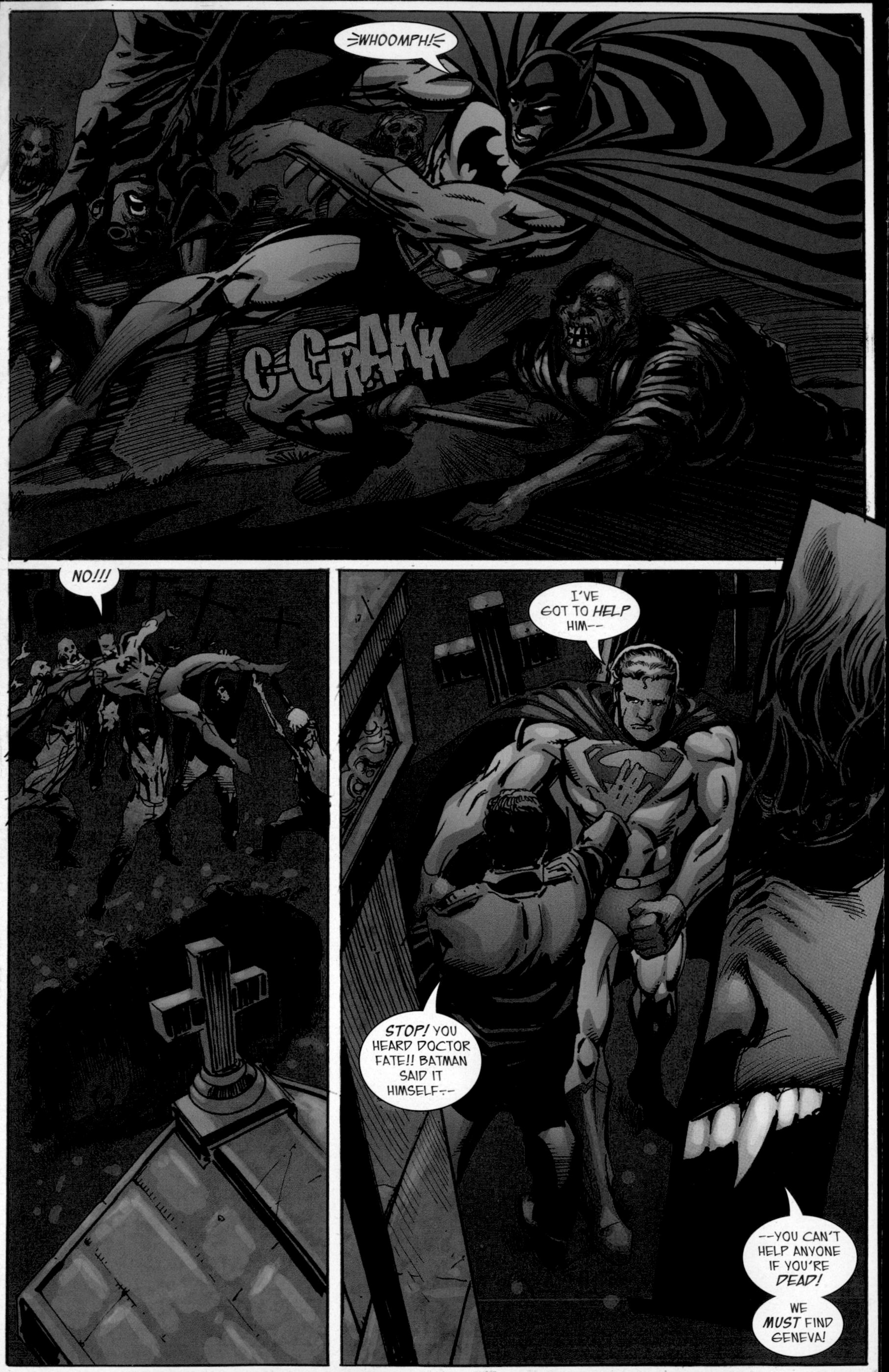
WHOOMPH!
C-CRAKK
NO!!!
I'VE GOT TO HELP HIM--
STOP! YOU HEARD DOCTOR FATE!! BATMAN SAID IT HIMSELF--
--YOU CAN'T HELP ANYONE IF YOU'RE DEAD!
WE MUST FIND GENEVA!

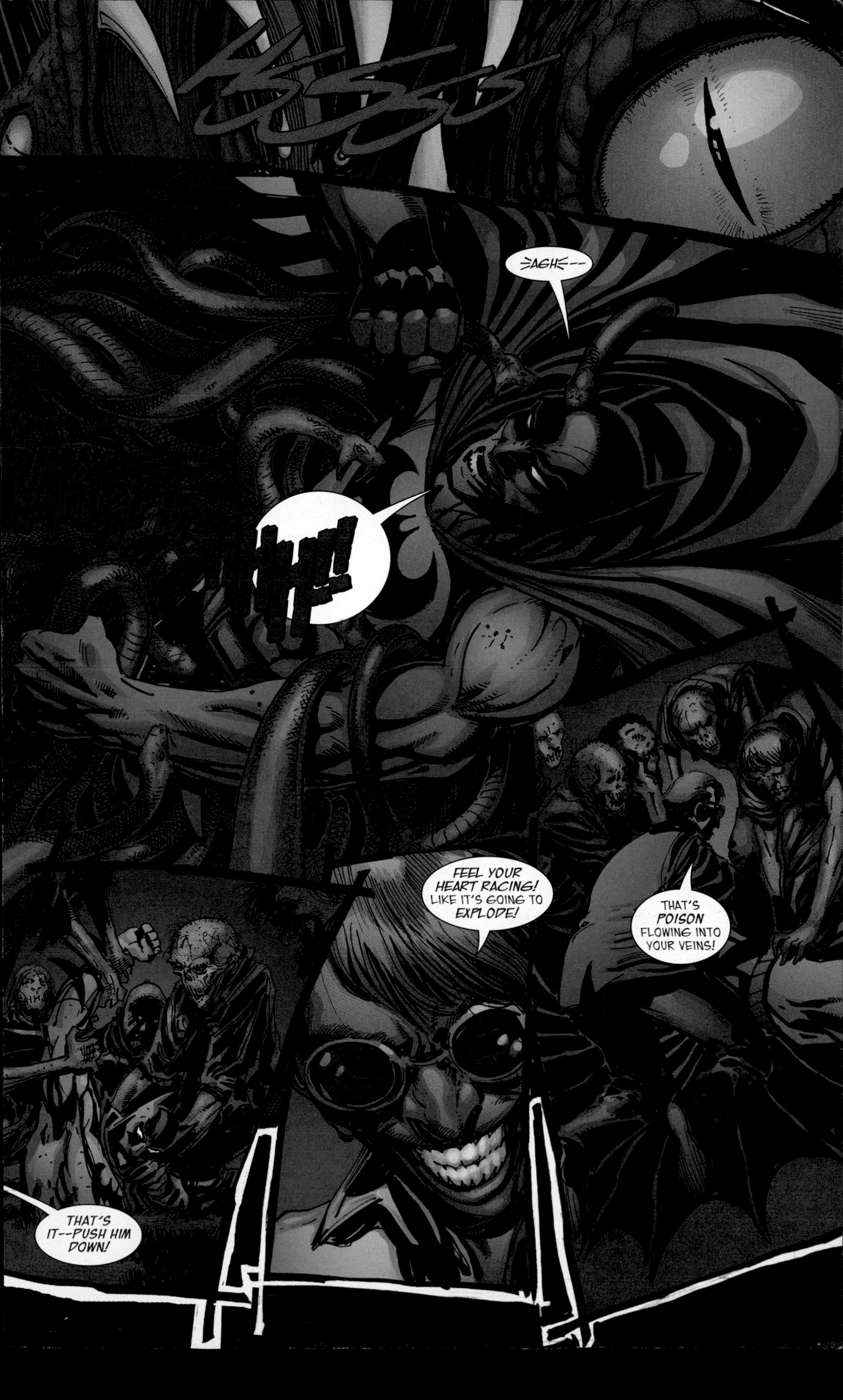

AGH---
FEEL YOUR HEART RACING! LIKE IT'S GOING TO EXPLODE!
THAT'S POISON FLOWING INTO YOUR VEINS!
THAT'S IT--PUSH HIM DOWN!

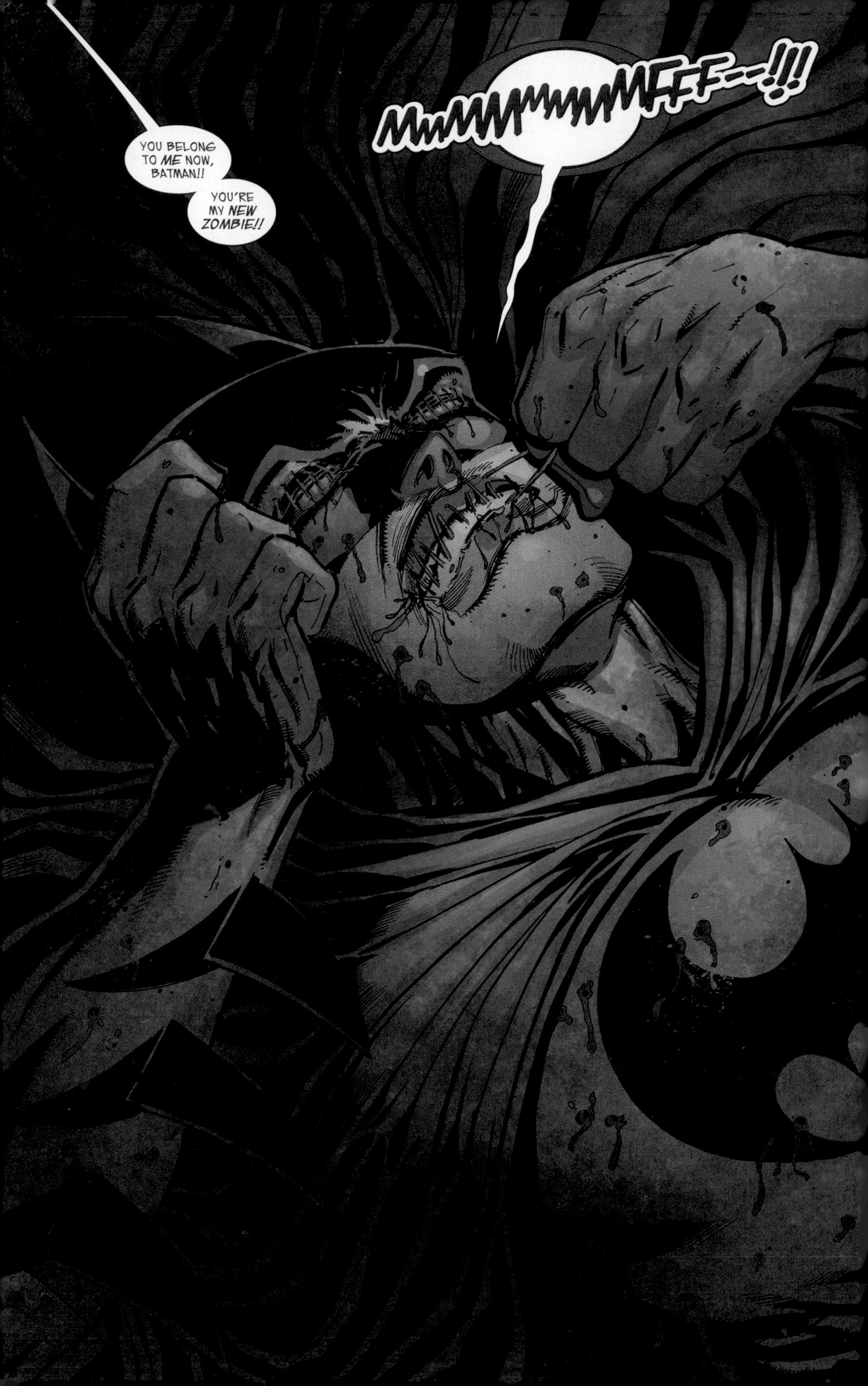
YOU BELONG TO ME NOW, BATMAN!!
YOU'RE MY NEW ZOMBIE!!
MMMMMMMMFFF--!!!

PART FIVE: **THE WAKING DEAD**

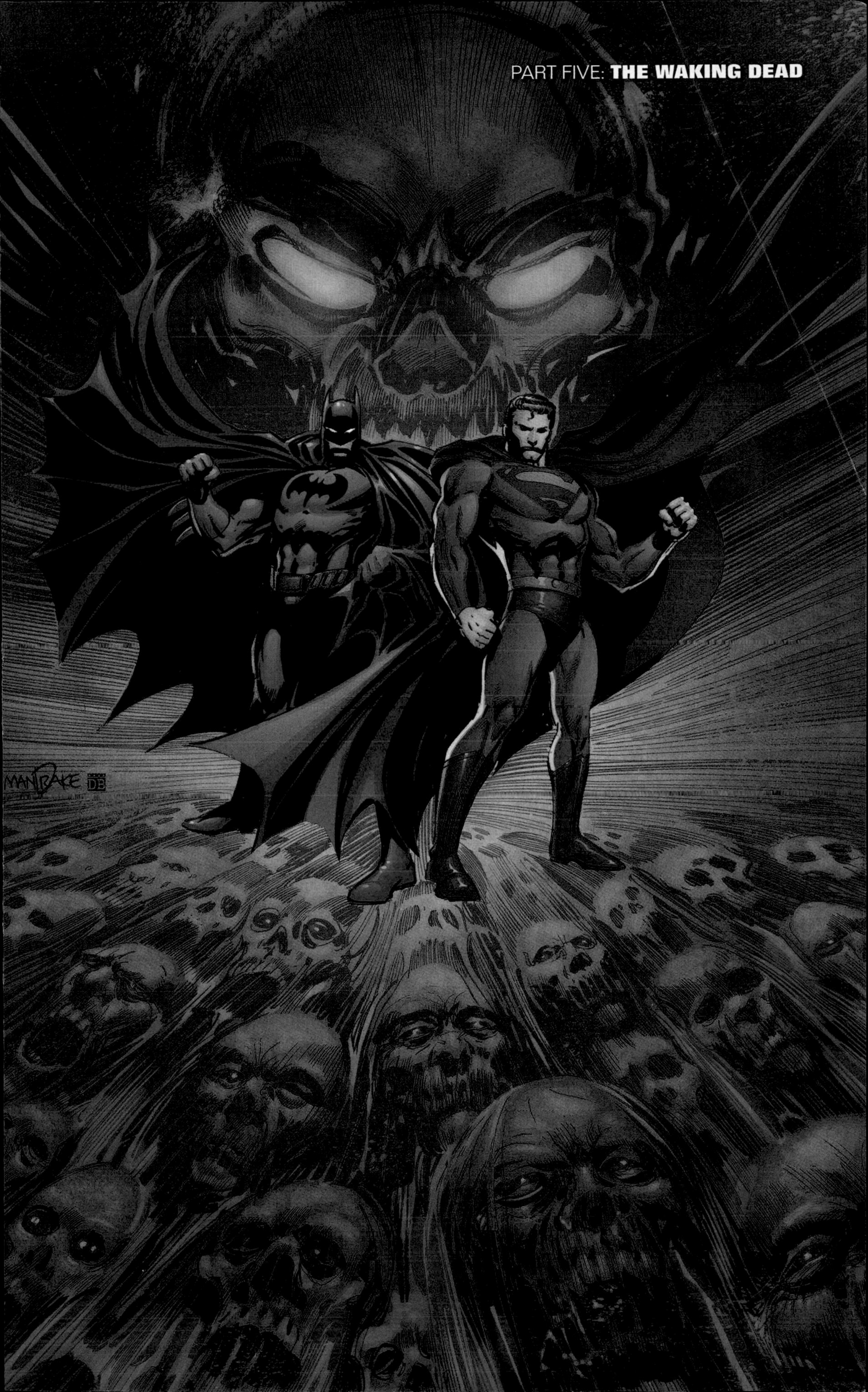

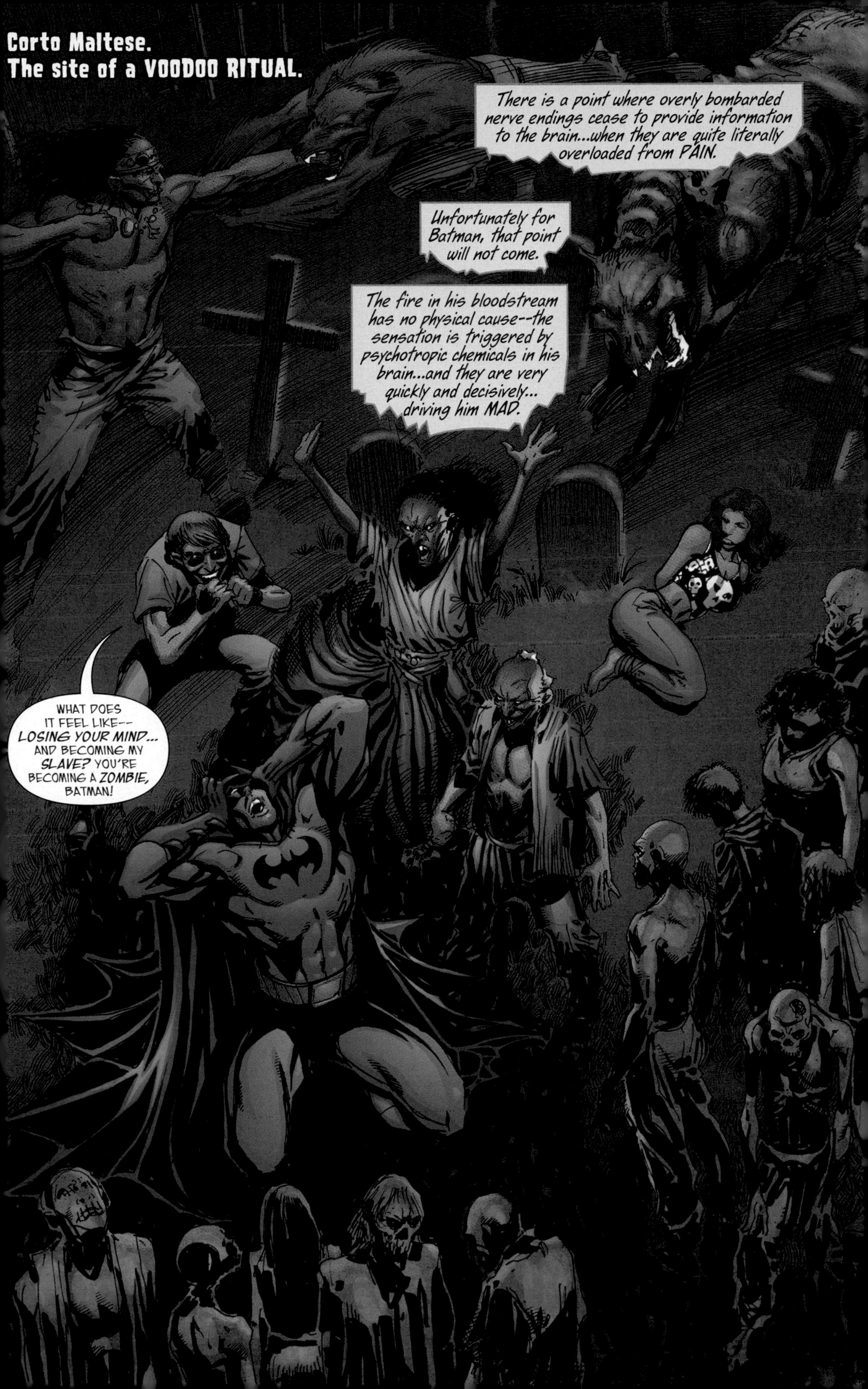
Corto Maltese.
The site of a VOODOO RITUAL.
There is a point where overly bombarded nerve endings cease to provide information to the brain...when they are quite literally overloaded from PAIN.
Unfortunately for Batman, that point will not come.
The fire in his bloodstream has no physical cause--the sensation is triggered by psychotropic chemicals in his brain...and they are very quickly and decisively... driving him MAD.
WHAT DOES IT FEEL LIKE-- LOSING YOUR MIND... AND BECOMING MY SLAVE? YOU'RE BECOMING A ZOMBIE, BATMAN!

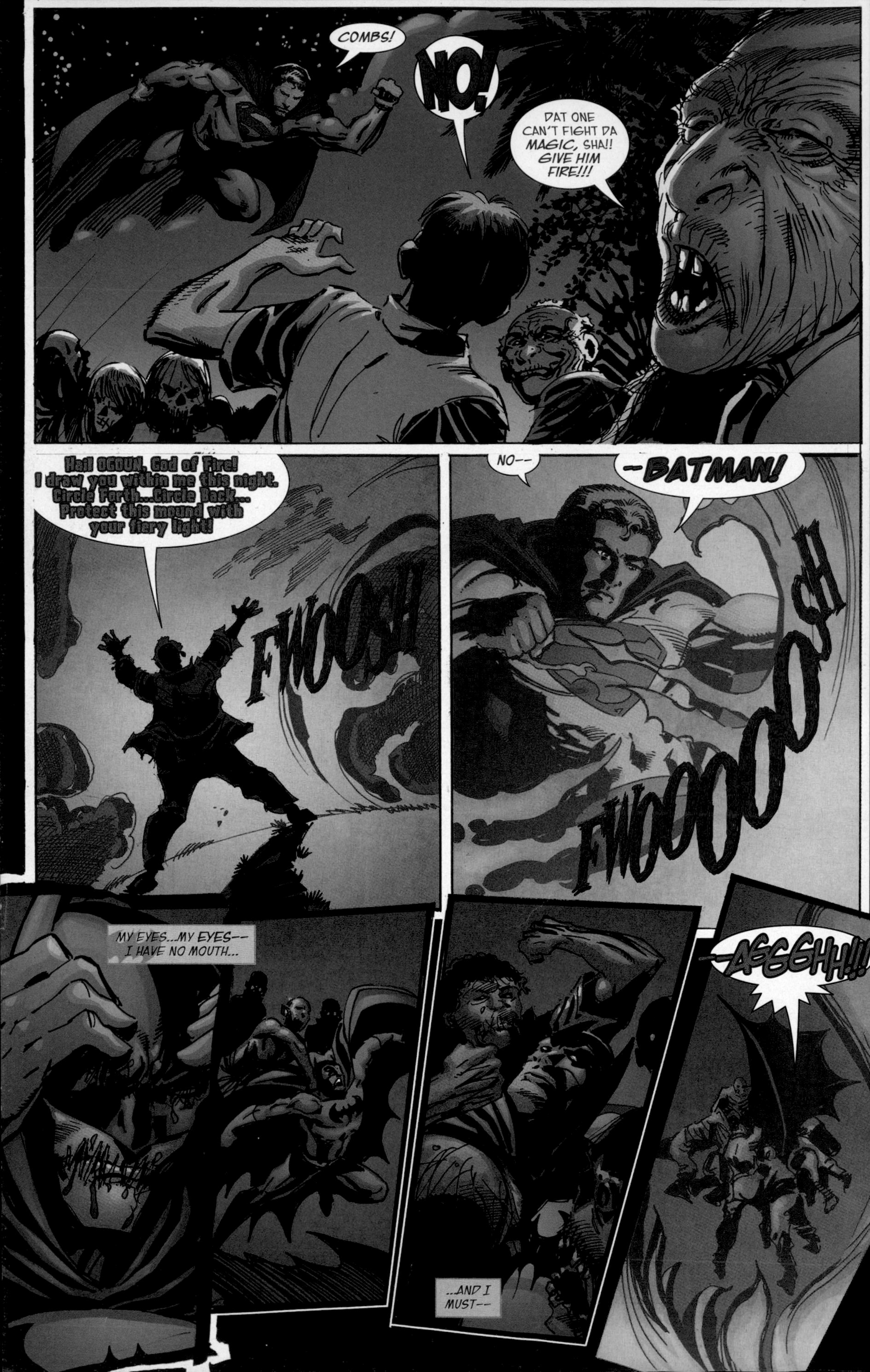
COMBS!
NO!
DAT ONE CAN'T FIGHT DA MAGIC, SHA!! GIVE HIM FIRE!!!
Hail OGOUN, God of Fire! I draw you within me this night. Circle Forth...Circle Back... Protect this mound with your fiery light!
FWOOSH
NO--
--BATMAN!
FWOOOOOOSH
MY EYES...MY EYES-- I HAVE NO MOUTH...
...AND I MUST--
--AGGGHH!!!

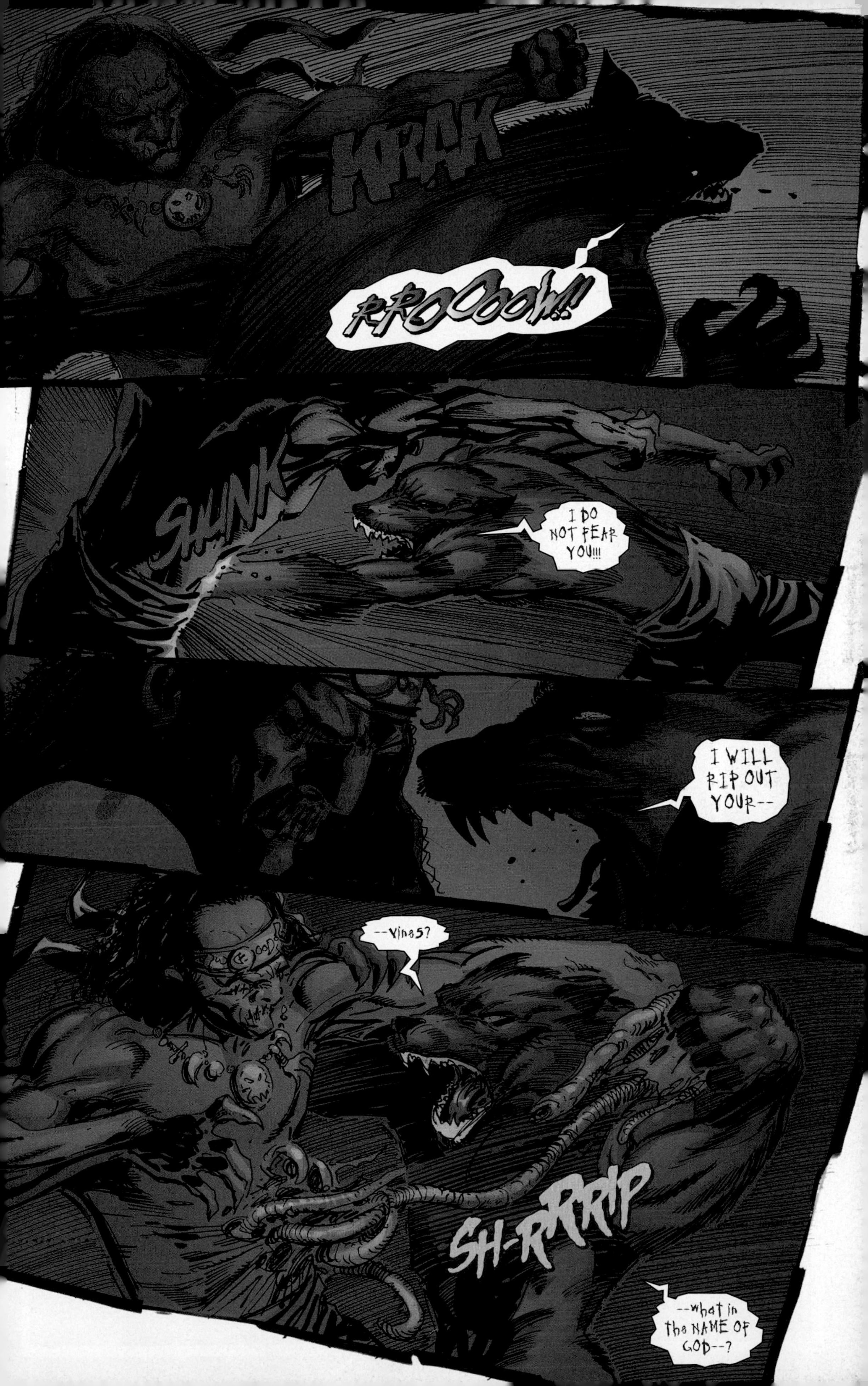

KRAK
RRROOOOOW!!
SHUNK
I DO NOT FEAR YOU!!!
I WILL RIP OUT YOUR--
--Vines?
SH-RRRIP
--what in the NAME OF GOD--?

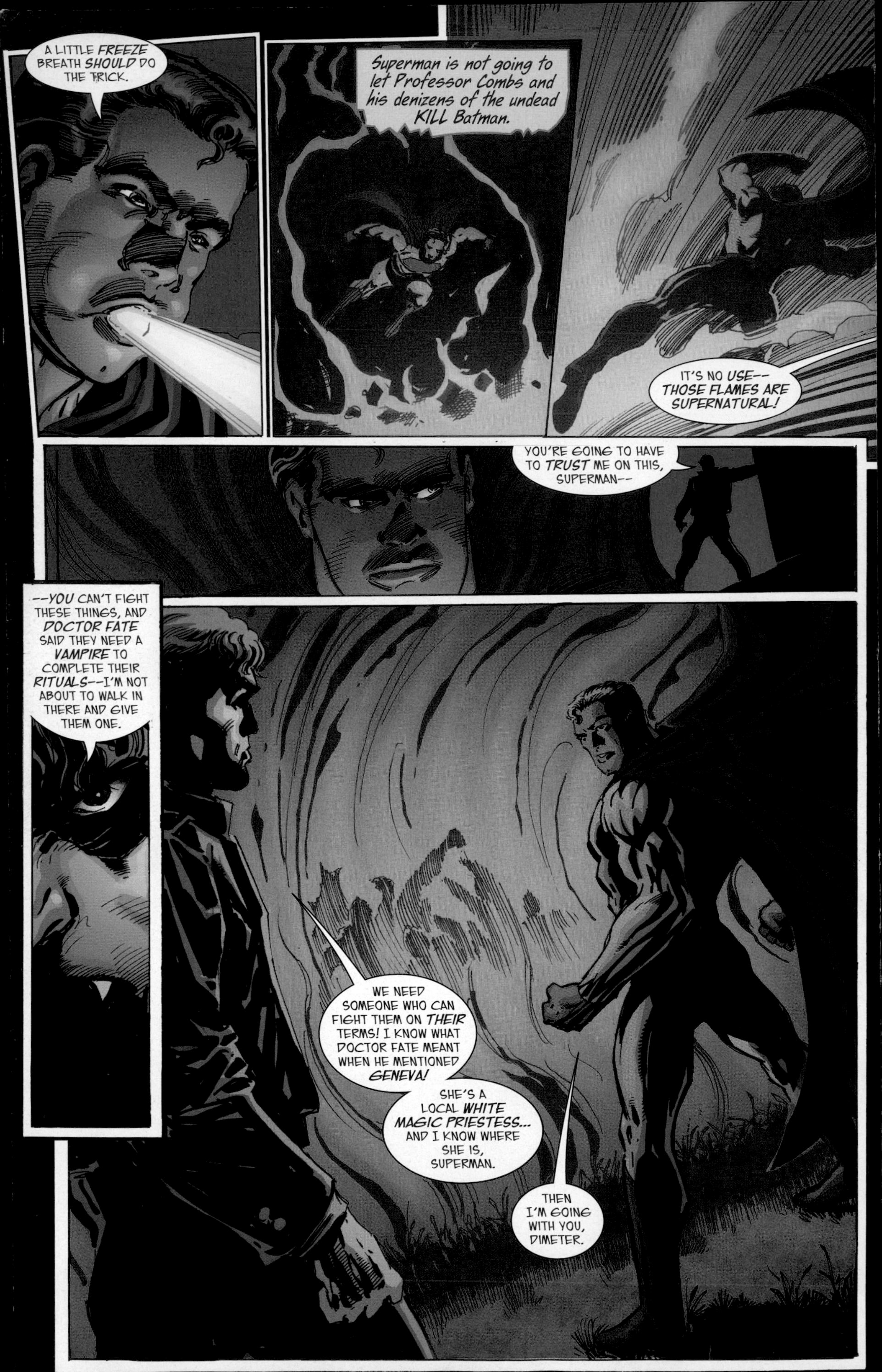
A LITTLE FREEZE BREATH SHOULD DO THE TRICK.
Superman is not going to let Professor Combs and his denizens of the undead KILL Batman.
IT'S NO USE-- THOSE FLAMES ARE SUPERNATURAL!
YOU'RE GOING TO HAVE TO TRUST ME ON THIS, SUPERMAN--
--YOU CAN'T FIGHT THESE THINGS, AND DOCTOR FATE SAID THEY NEED A VAMPIRE TO COMPLETE THEIR RITUALS--I'M NOT ABOUT TO WALK IN THERE AND GIVE THEM ONE.
WE NEED SOMEONE WHO CAN FIGHT THEM ON THEIR TERMS! I KNOW WHAT DOCTOR FATE MEANT WHEN HE MENTIONED GENEVA!
SHE'S A LOCAL WHITE MAGIC PRIESTESS... AND I KNOW WHERE SHE IS, SUPERMAN.
THEN I'M GOING WITH YOU, DIMETER.

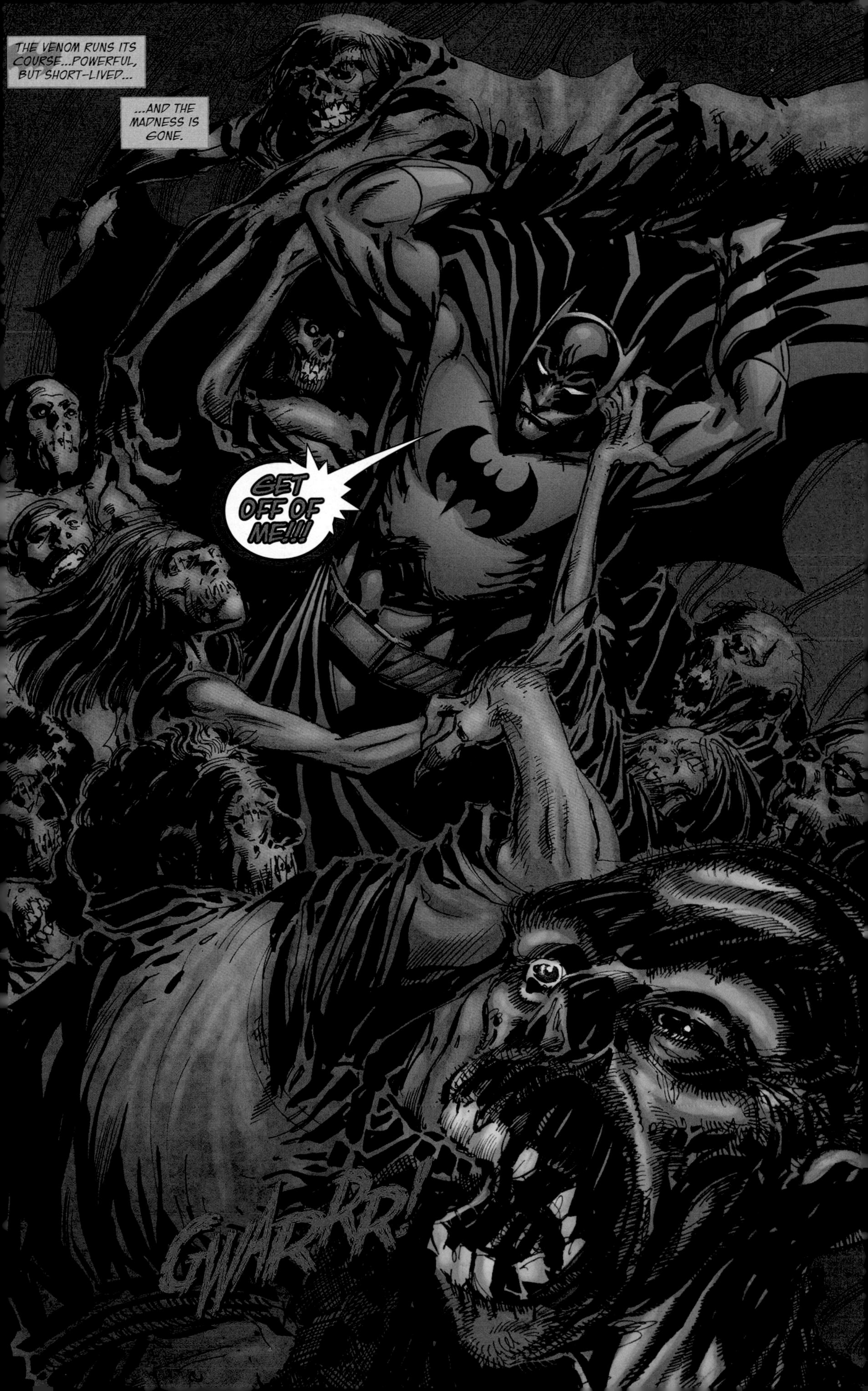
THE VENOM RUNS ITS COURSE...POWERFUL, BUT SHORT-LIVED...
...AND THE MADNESS IS GONE.
GET OFF OF ME!!!
GWARRR!

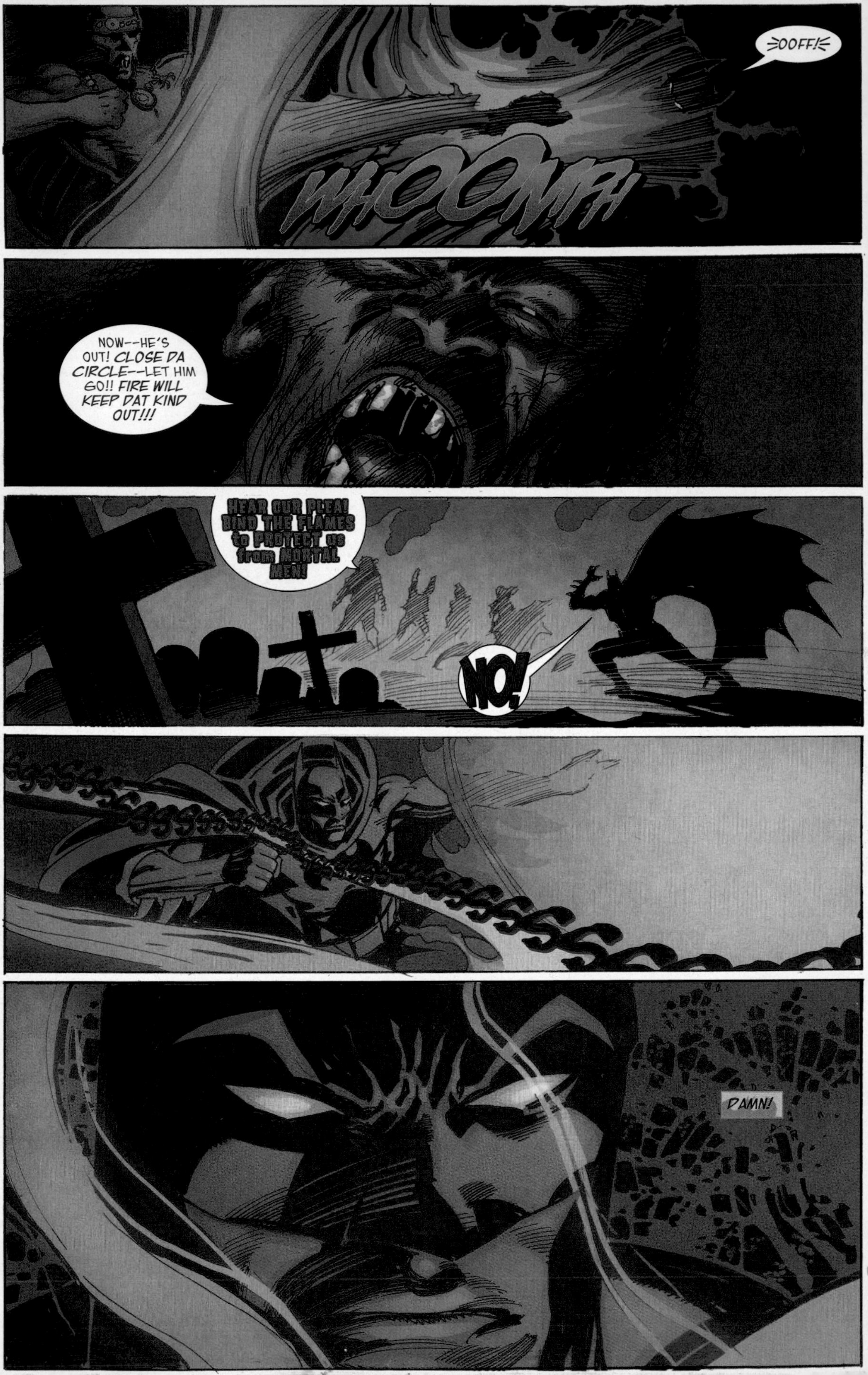

OOFF!
WHOOMPH
NOW--HE'S OUT! CLOSE DA CIRCLE--LET HIM GO!! FIRE WILL KEEP DAT KIND OUT!!!
HEAR OUR PLEA! BIND THE FLAMES to PROTECT us from MORTAL MEN!
NO!
DAMN!

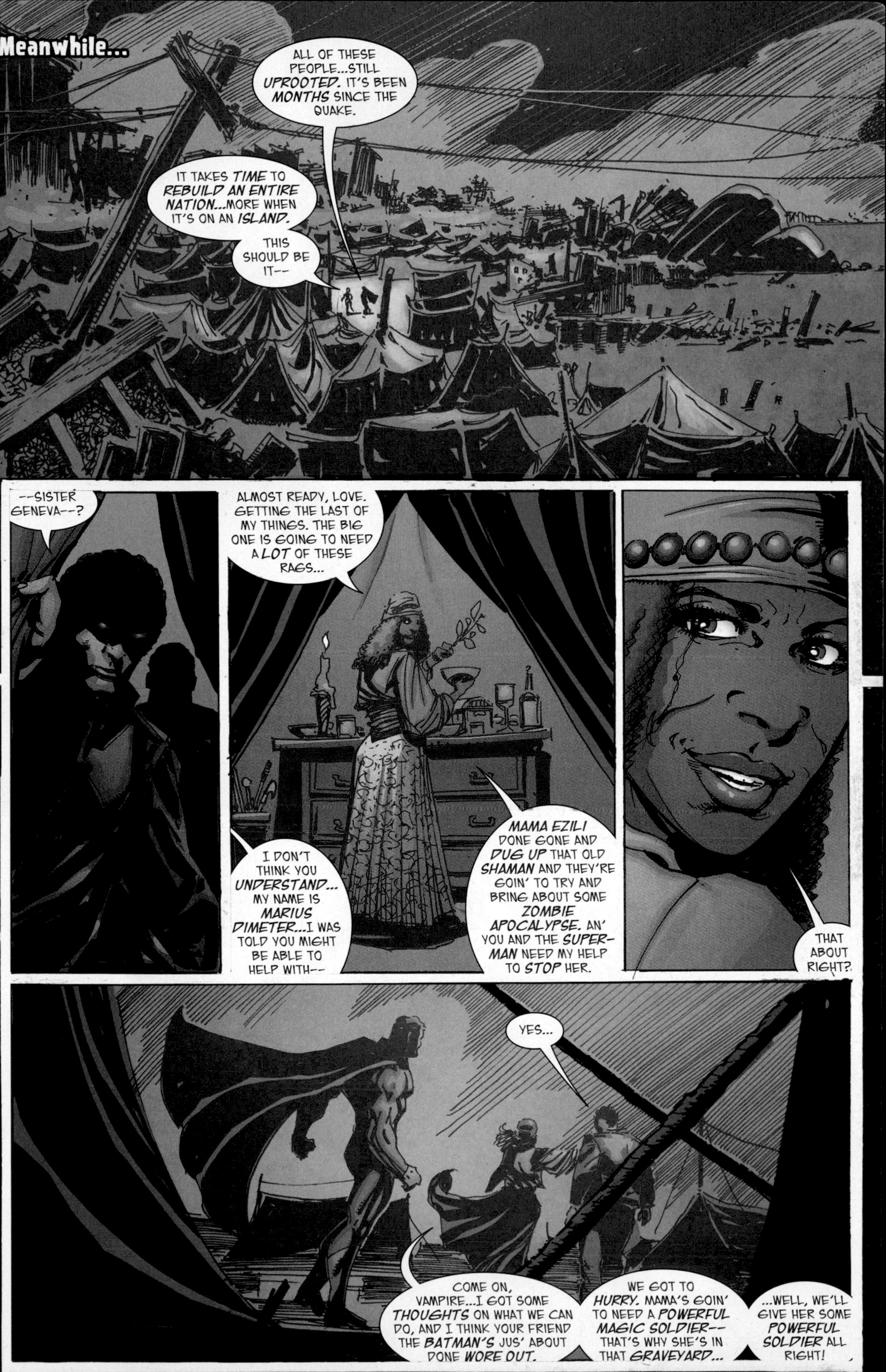
Meanwhile...
ALL OF THESE PEOPLE...STILL UPROOTED. IT'S BEEN MONTHS SINCE THE QUAKE.
IT TAKES TIME TO REBUILD AN ENTIRE NATION...MORE WHEN IT'S ON AN ISLAND.
THIS SHOULD BE IT--
--SISTER GENEVA--?
ALMOST READY, LOVE. GETTING THE LAST OF MY THINGS. THE BIG ONE IS GOING TO NEED A LOT OF THESE RAGS...
I DON'T THINK YOU UNDERSTAND... MY NAME IS MARIUS DIMETER...I WAS TOLD YOU MIGHT BE ABLE TO HELP WITH--
MAMA EZILI DONE GONE AND DUG UP THAT OLD SHAMAN AND THEY'RE GOIN' TO TRY AND BRING ABOUT SOME ZOMBIE APOCALYPSE. AN' YOU AND THE SUPER-MAN NEED MY HELP TO STOP HER.
THAT ABOUT RIGHT?
YES...
COME ON, VAMPIRE...I GOT SOME THOUGHTS ON WHAT WE CAN DO, AND I THINK YOUR FRIEND THE BATMAN'S JUS' ABOUT DONE WORE OUT.
WE GOT TO HURRY. MAMA'S GOIN' TO NEED A POWERFUL MAGIC SOLDIER--THAT'S WHY SHE'S IN THAT GRAVEYARD...
...WELL, WE'LL GIVE HER SOME POWERFUL SOLDIER ALL RIGHT!

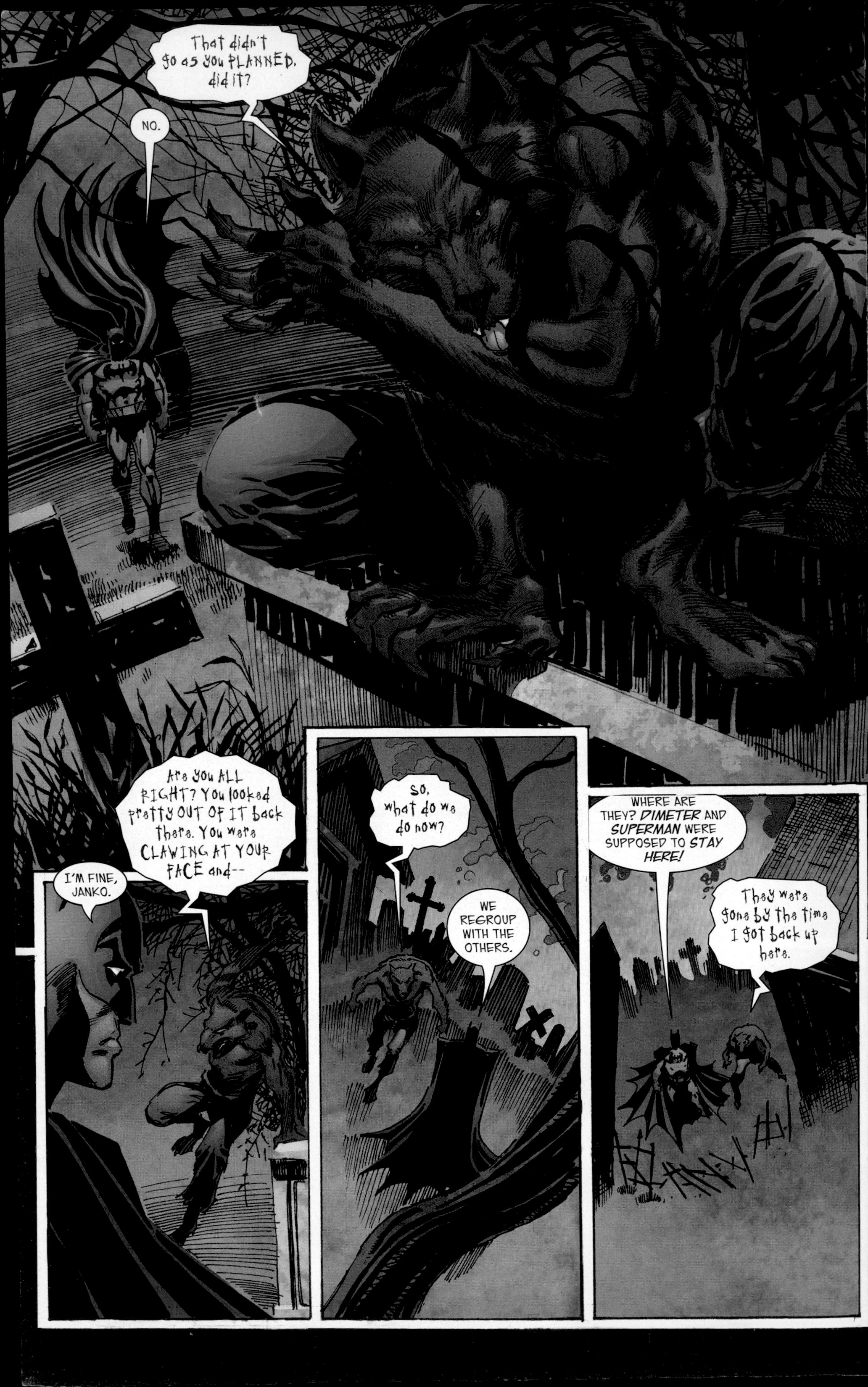
That didn't go as you PLANNED, did it?
NO.
Are you ALL RIGHT? You looked pretty OUT OF IT back there. You were CLAWING AT YOUR FACE and--
I'M FINE, JANKO.
So, what do we do now?
WE REGROUP WITH THE OTHERS.
WHERE ARE THEY? DIMETER AND SUPERMAN WERE SUPPOSED TO STAY HERE!
They were gone by the time I got back up here.

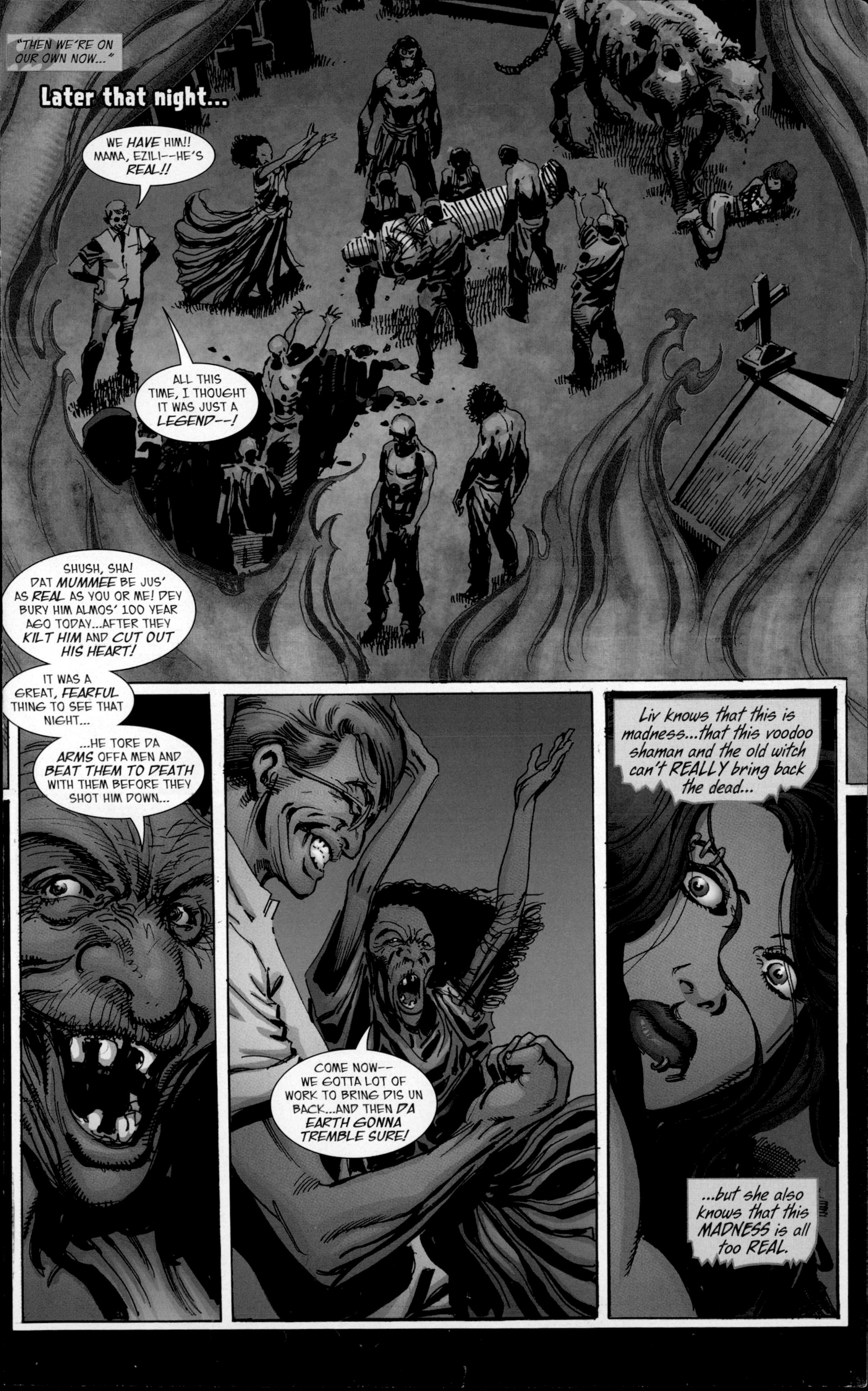
"THEN WE'RE ON OUR OWN NOW..."
Later that night...
WE HAVE HIM!! MAMA, EZILI--HE'S REAL!!
ALL THIS TIME, I THOUGHT IT WAS JUST A LEGEND--!
SHUSH, SHA! DAT MUMMEE BE JUS' AS REAL AS YOU OR ME! DEY BURY HIM ALMOS' 100 YEAR AGO TODAY...AFTER THEY KILT HIM AND CUT OUT HIS HEART!
IT WAS A GREAT, FEARFUL THING TO SEE THAT NIGHT...
...HE TORE DA ARMS OFFA MEN AND BEAT THEM TO DEATH WITH THEM BEFORE THEY SHOT HIM DOWN...
COME NOW--WE GOTTA LOT OF WORK TO BRING DIS UN BACK...AND THEN DA EARTH GONNA TREMBLE SURE!
Liv knows that this is madness...that this voodoo shaman and the old witch can't REALLY bring back the dead...
...but she also knows that this MADNESS is all too REAL.

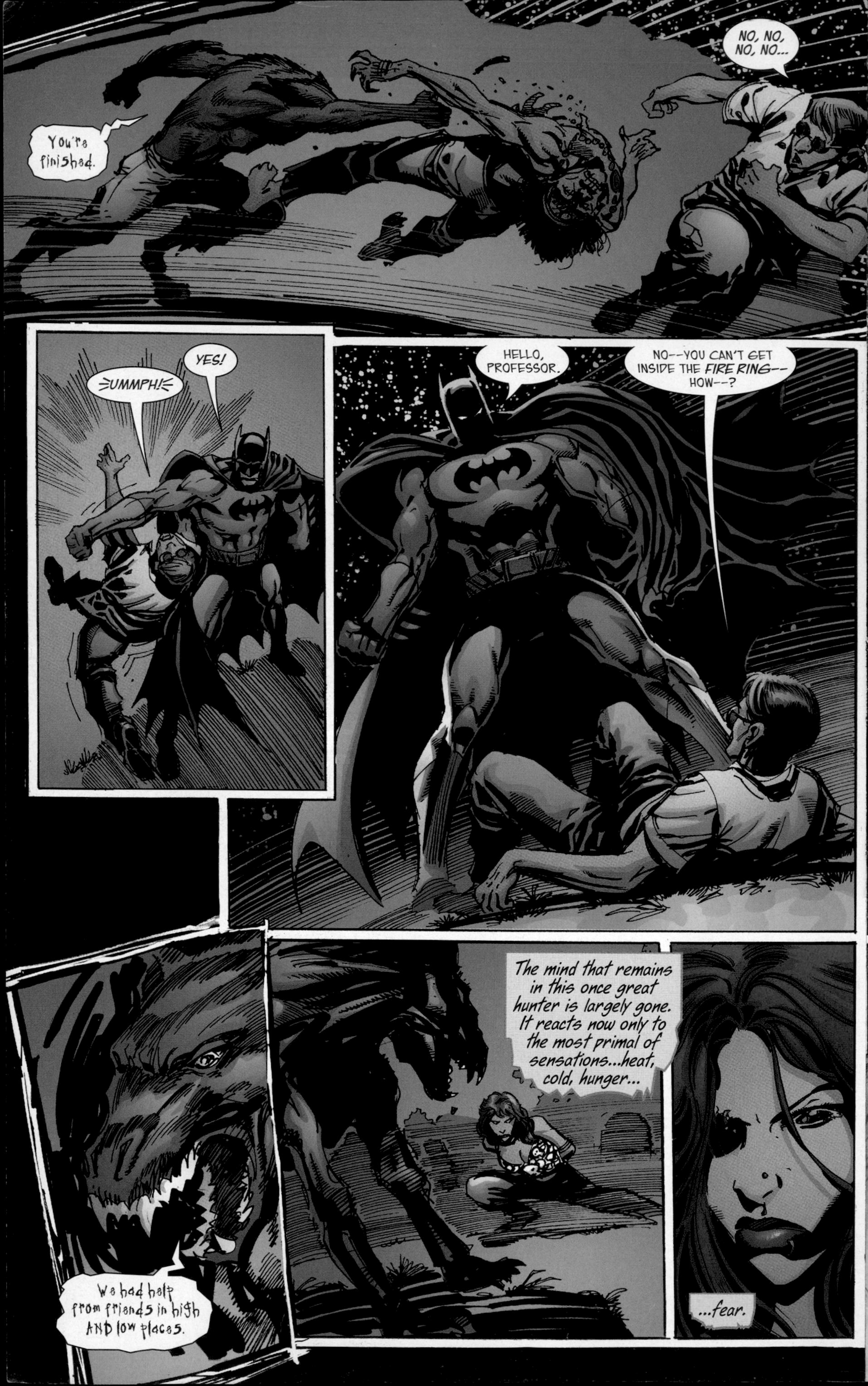
You're finished.
NO, NO, NO, NO...
YES!
UMMPH!
HELLO, PROFESSOR.
NO--YOU CAN'T GET INSIDE THE FIRE RING--HOW--?
We had help from friends in high AND low places.
The mind that remains in this once great hunter is largely gone. It reacts now only to the most primal of sensations...heat, cold, hunger...
...fear.

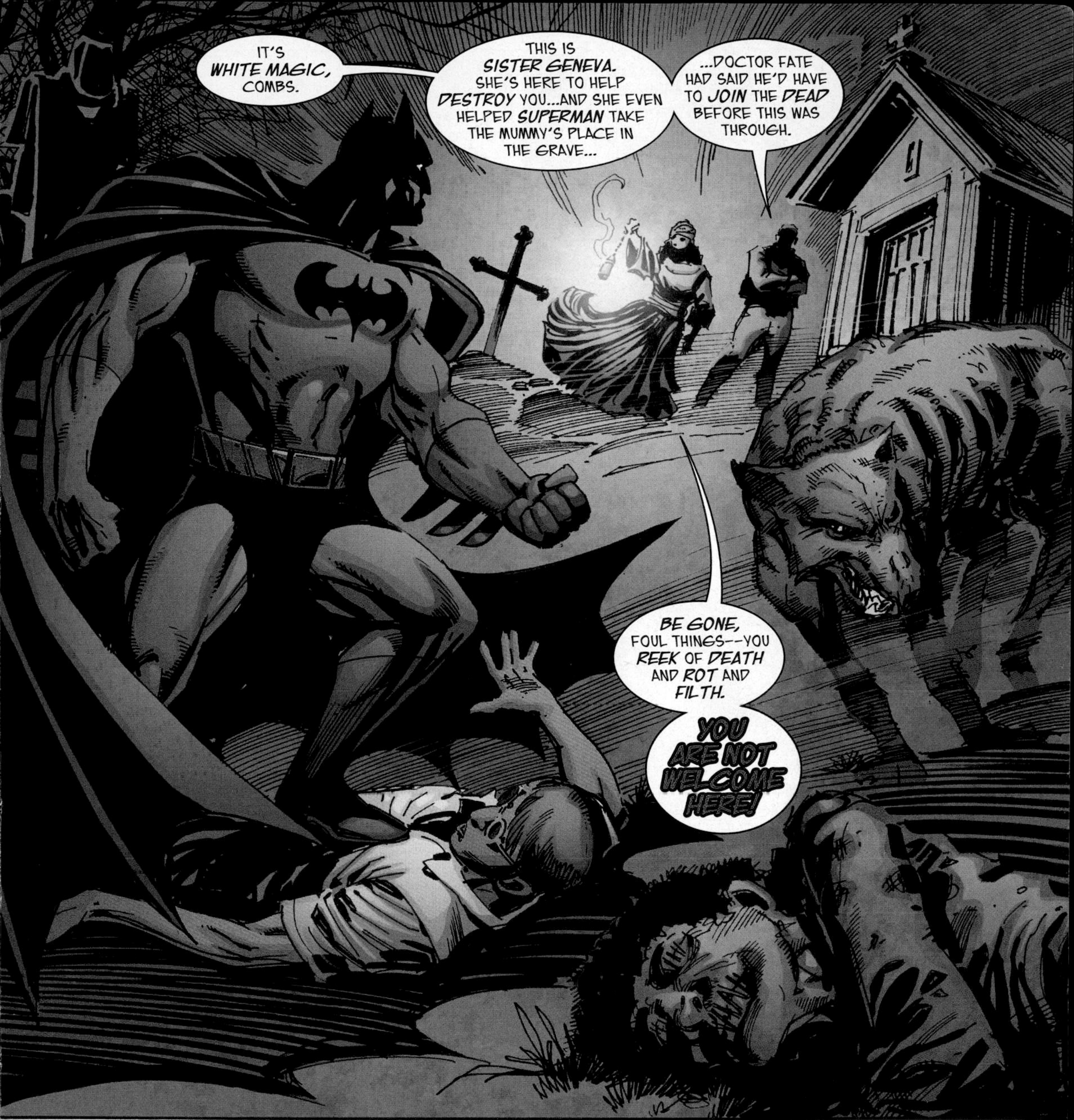
IT'S WHITE MAGIC, COMBS.
THIS IS SISTER GENEVA. SHE'S HERE TO HELP DESTROY YOU...AND SHE EVEN HELPED SUPERMAN TAKE THE MUMMY'S PLACE IN THE GRAVE...
...DOCTOR FATE HAD SAID HE'D HAVE TO JOIN THE DEAD BEFORE THIS WAS THROUGH.
BE GONE, FOUL THINGS--YOU REEK OF DEATH AND ROT AND FILTH.
YOU ARE NOT WELCOME HERE!

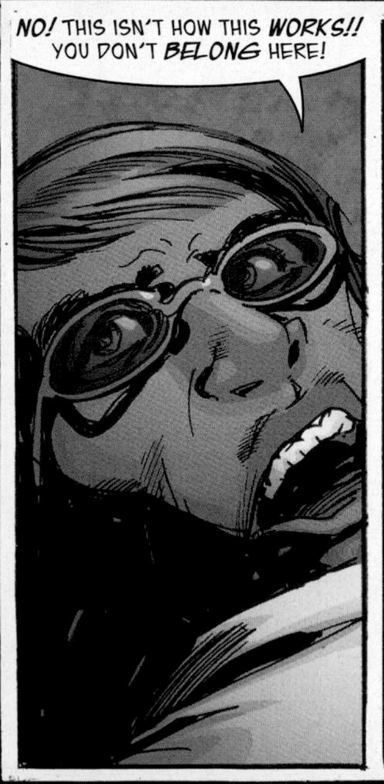
NO! THIS ISN'T HOW THIS WORKS!! YOU DON'T BELONG HERE!

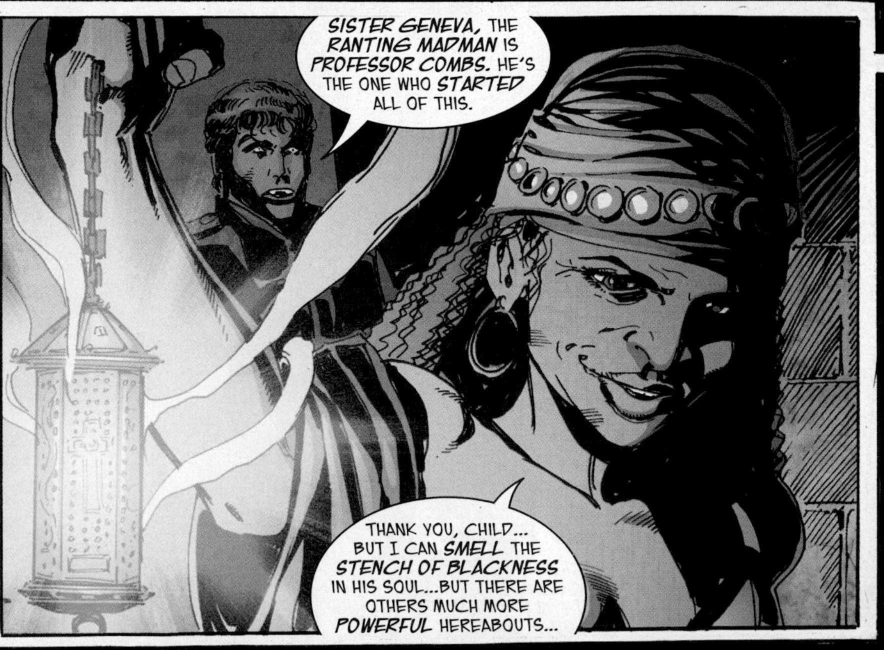
SISTER GENEVA, THE RANTING MADMAN IS PROFESSOR COMBS. HE'S THE ONE WHO STARTED ALL OF THIS.
THANK YOU, CHILD... BUT I CAN SMELL THE STENCH OF BLACKNESS IN HIS SOUL...BUT THERE ARE OTHERS MUCH MORE POWERFUL HEREABOUTS...

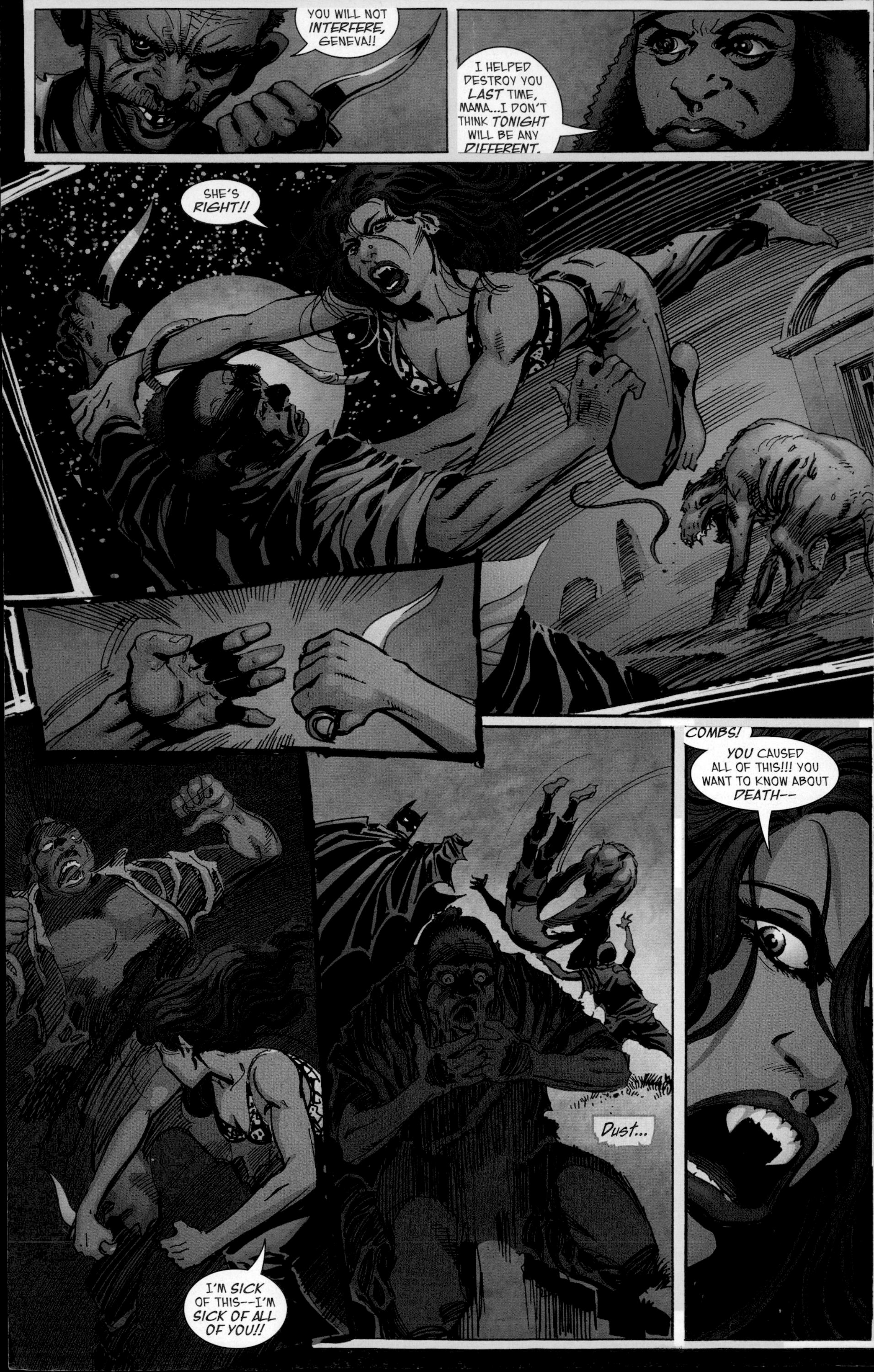
YOU WILL NOT INTERFERE, GENEVA!!
I HELPED DESTROY YOU LAST TIME, MAMA...I DON'T THINK TONIGHT WILL BE ANY DIFFERENT.
SHE'S RIGHT!!
I'M SICK OF THIS--I'M SICK OF ALL OF YOU!!
Dust...
COMBS!
YOU CAUSED ALL OF THIS!!! YOU WANT TO KNOW ABOUT DEATH--

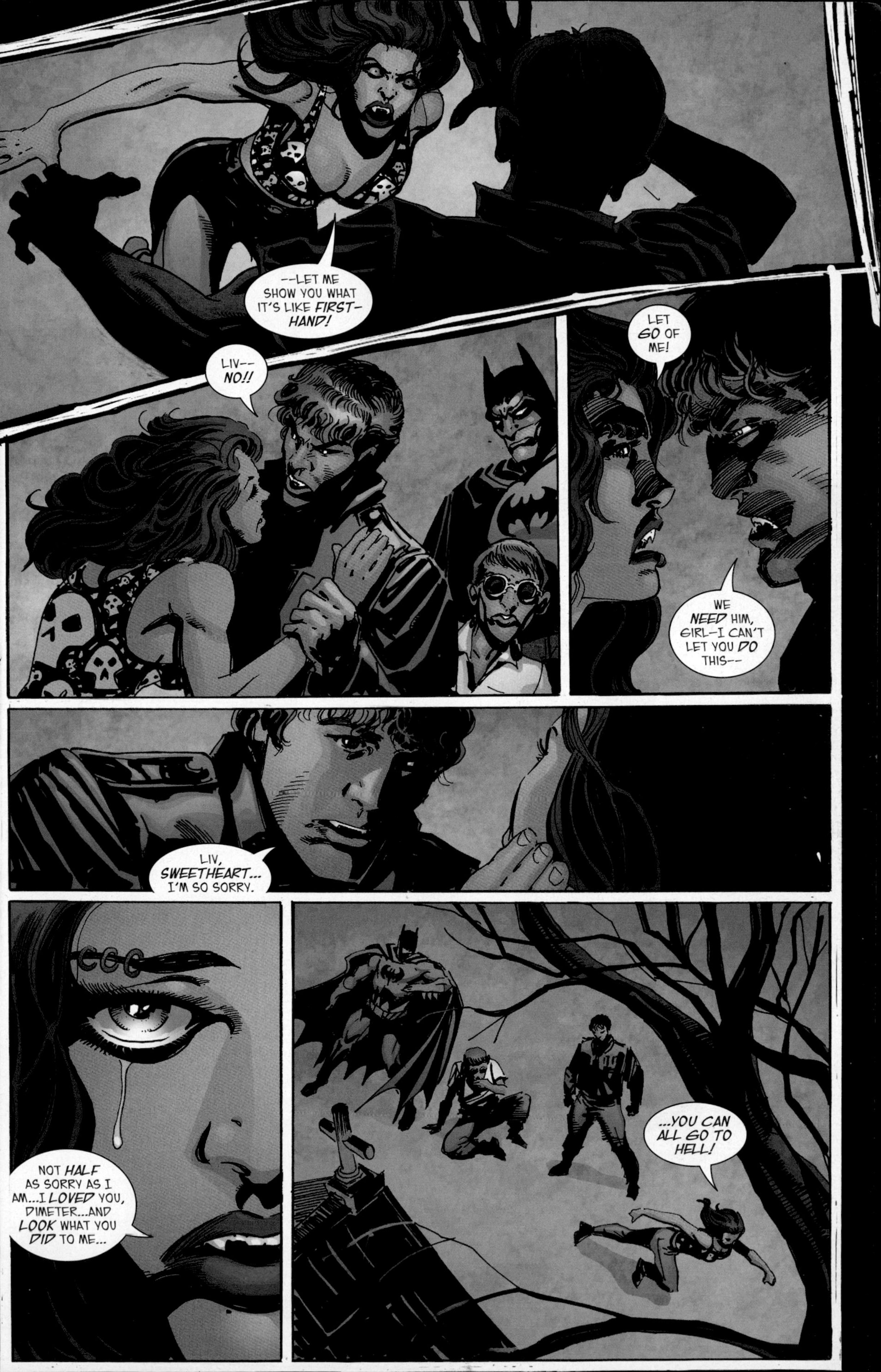
--LET ME SHOW YOU WHAT IT'S LIKE FIRST-HAND!
LIV-- NO!!
LET GO OF ME!
WE NEED HIM, GIRL--I CAN'T LET YOU DO THIS--
LIV, SWEETHEART... I'M SO SORRY.
NOT HALF AS SORRY AS I AM...I LOVED YOU, DIMETER...AND LOOK WHAT YOU DID TO ME...
...YOU CAN ALL GO TO HELL!

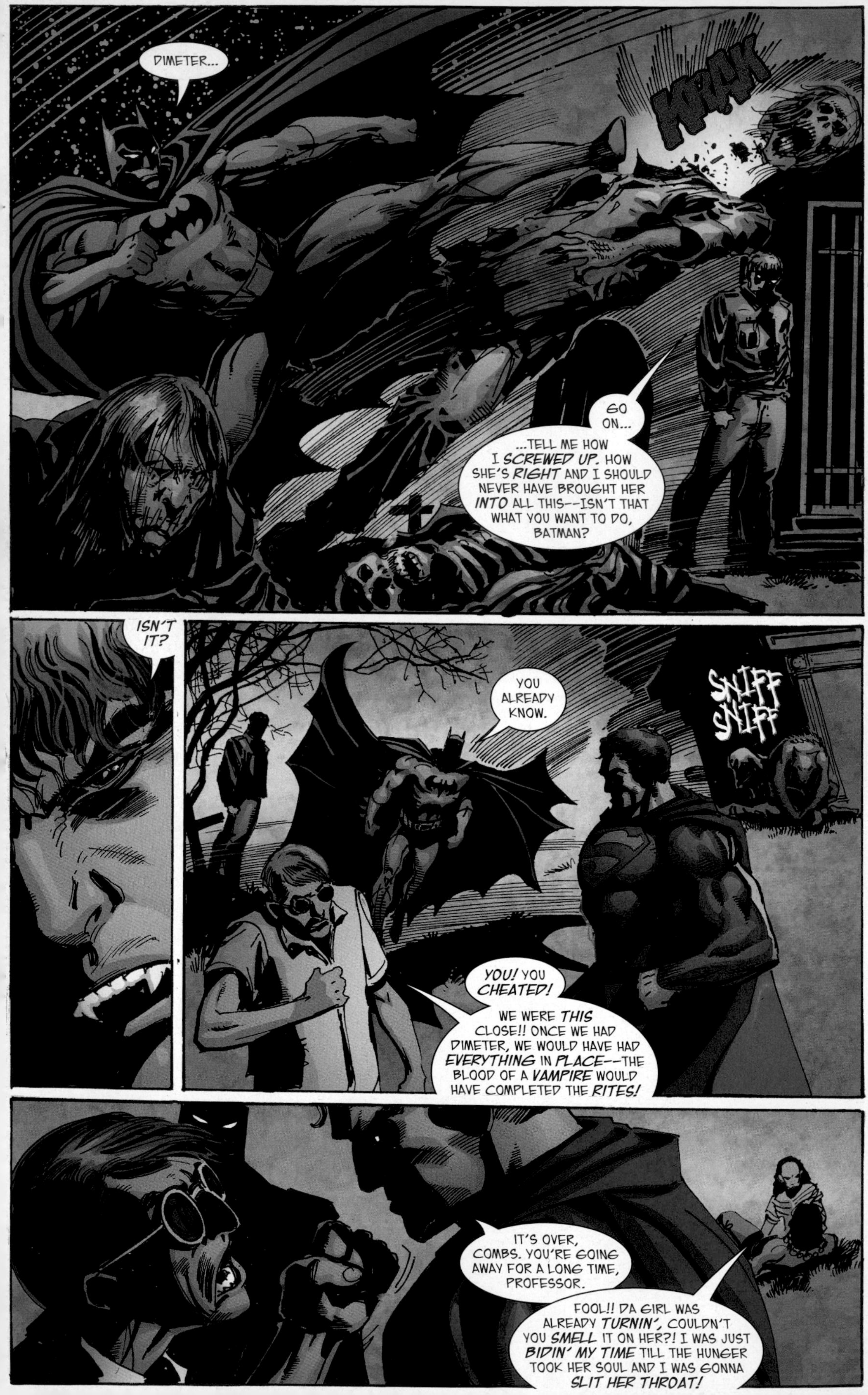
DIMETER...
KRAAK
GO ON...
...TELL ME HOW I SCREWED UP. HOW SHE'S RIGHT AND I SHOULD NEVER HAVE BROUGHT HER INTO ALL THIS--ISN'T THAT WHAT YOU WANT TO DO, BATMAN?
ISN'T IT?
YOU ALREADY KNOW.
SNIFF SNIFF
YOU! YOU CHEATED!
WE WERE THIS CLOSE!! ONCE WE HAD DIMETER, WE WOULD HAVE HAD EVERYTHING IN PLACE--THE BLOOD OF A VAMPIRE WOULD HAVE COMPLETED THE RITES!
IT'S OVER, COMBS. YOU'RE GOING AWAY FOR A LONG TIME, PROFESSOR.
FOOL!! DA GIRL WAS ALREADY TURNIN', COULDN'T YOU SMELL IT ON HER?! I WAS JUST BIDIN' MY TIME TILL THE HUNGER TOOK HER SOUL AND I WAS GONNA SLIT HER THROAT!

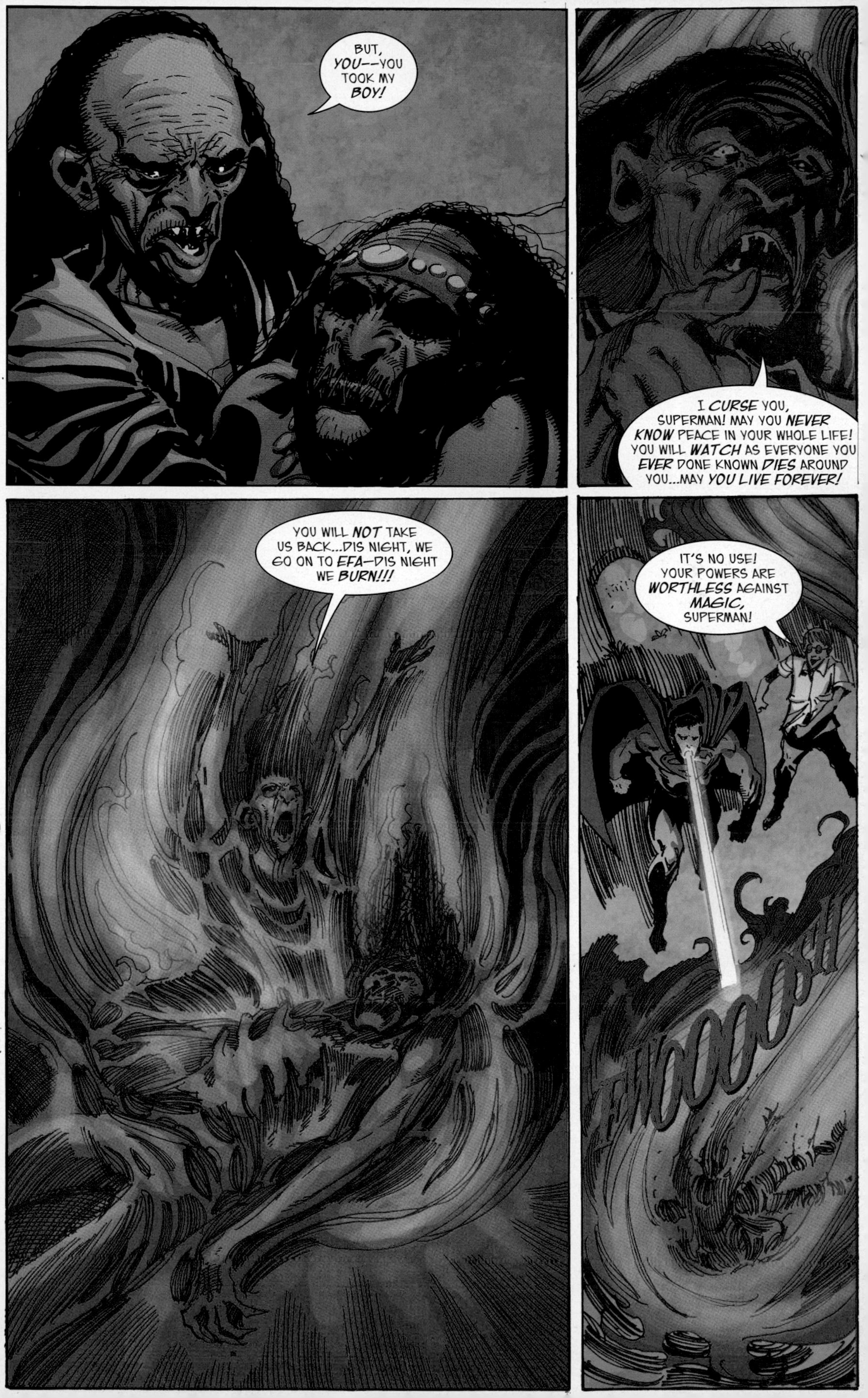

BUT, YOU--YOU TOOK MY BOY!
I CURSE YOU, SUPERMAN! MAY YOU NEVER KNOW PEACE IN YOUR WHOLE LIFE! YOU WILL WATCH AS EVERYONE YOU EVER DONE KNOWN DIES AROUND YOU...MAY YOU LIVE FOREVER!
YOU WILL NOT TAKE US BACK...DIS NIGHT, WE GO ON TO EFA--DIS NIGHT WE BURN!!!
IT'S NO USE! YOUR POWERS ARE WORTHLESS AGAINST MAGIC, SUPERMAN!
FWOOOOOSH

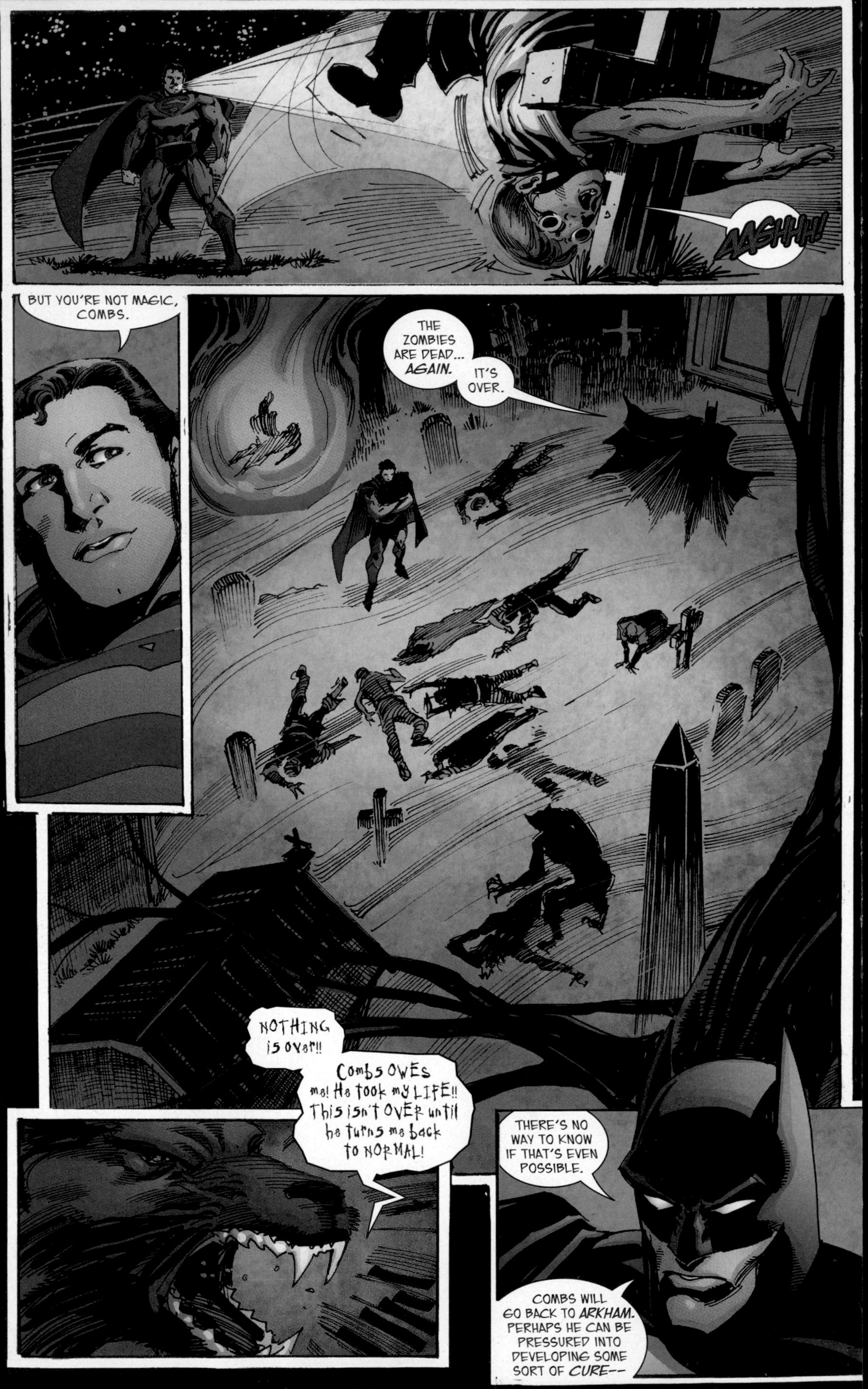
AASHHH!
BUT YOU'RE NOT MAGIC, COMBS.
THE ZOMBIES ARE DEAD... AGAIN.
IT'S OVER.
NOTHING is over!!
Combs OWES me! He took my LIFE!! This isn't OVER until he turns me back to NORMAL!
THERE'S NO WAY TO KNOW IF THAT'S EVEN POSSIBLE.
COMBS WILL GO BACK TO ARKHAM. PERHAPS HE CAN BE PRESSURED INTO DEVELOPING SOME SORT OF CURE--

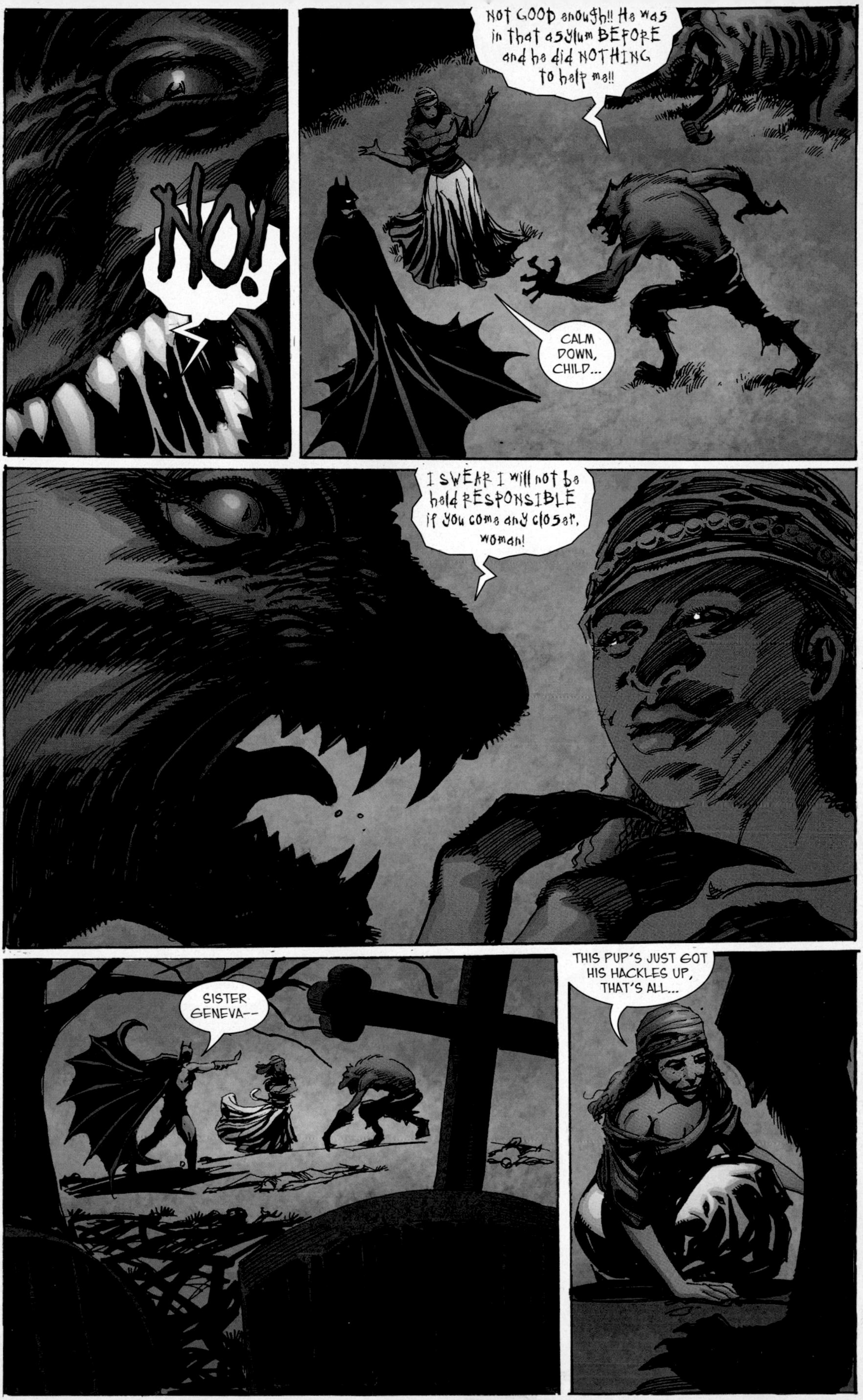
NO!
NOT GOOD enough!! He was in that asylum BEFORE and he did NOTHING to help me!!
CALM DOWN, CHILD...
I SWEAR I will not be held RESPONSIBLE if you come any closer, woman!
SISTER GENEVA--
THIS PUP'S JUST GOT HIS HACKLES UP, THAT'S ALL...

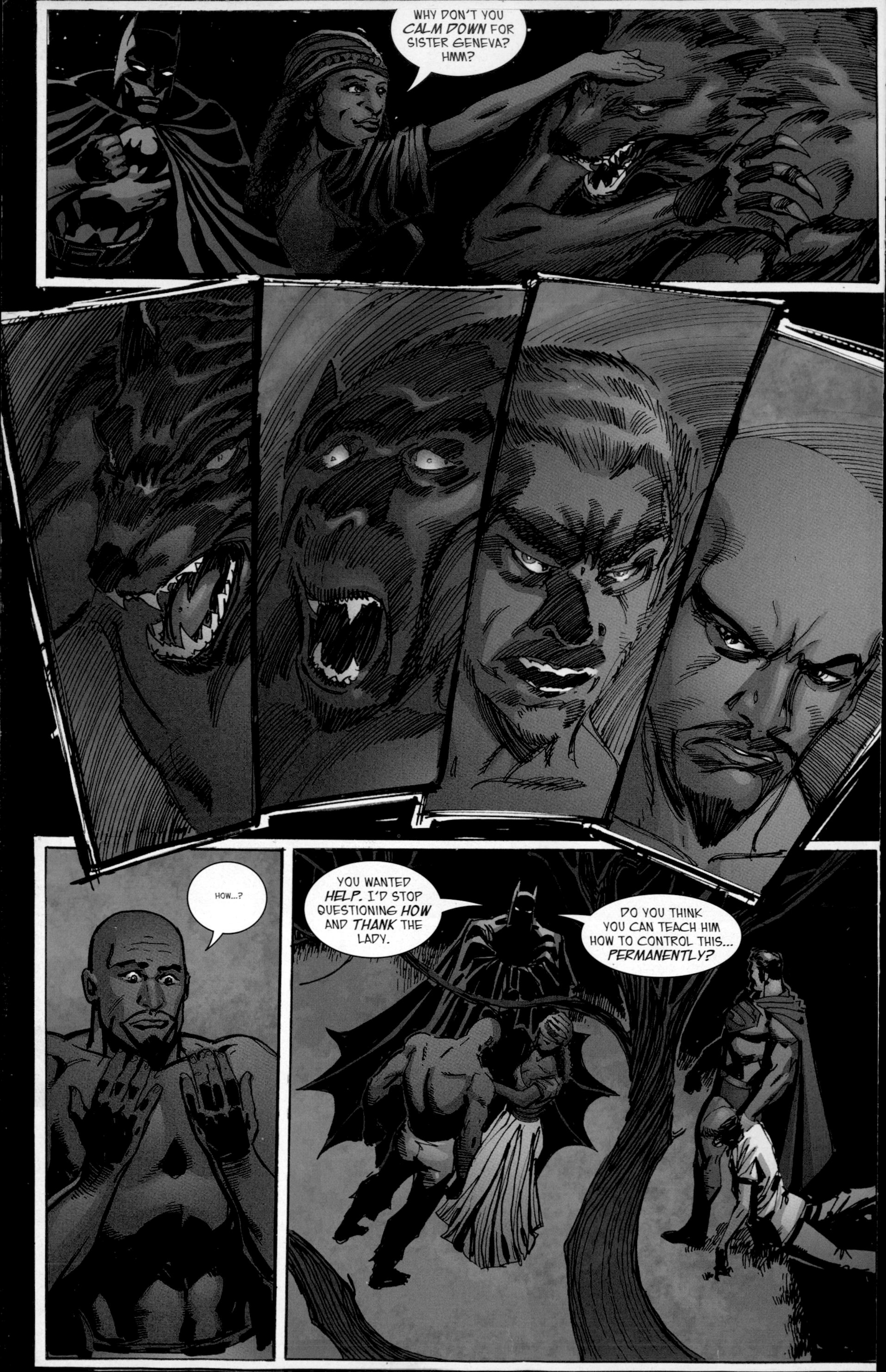
WHY DON'T YOU CALM DOWN FOR SISTER GENEVA? HMM?
HOW...?
YOU WANTED HELP. I'D STOP QUESTIONING HOW AND THANK THE LADY.
DO YOU THINK YOU CAN TEACH HIM HOW TO CONTROL THIS... PERMANENTLY?

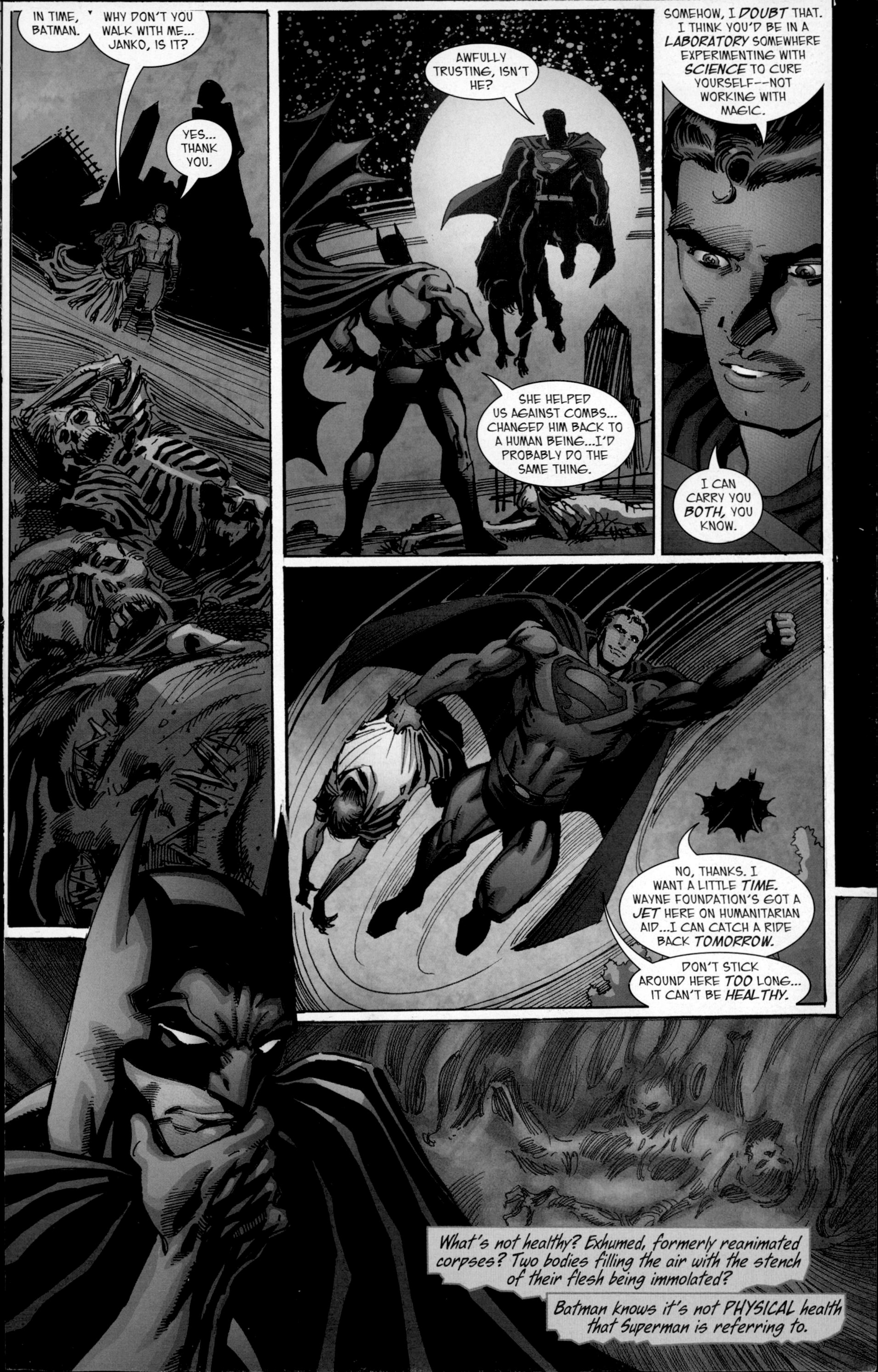
IN TIME, BATMAN.
WHY DON'T YOU WALK WITH ME... JANKO, IS IT?
YES... THANK YOU.
AWFULLY TRUSTING, ISN'T HE?
SHE HELPED US AGAINST COMBS... CHANGED HIM BACK TO A HUMAN BEING...I'D PROBABLY DO THE SAME THING.
SOMEHOW, I DOUBT THAT. I THINK YOU'D BE IN A LABORATORY SOMEWHERE EXPERIMENTING WITH SCIENCE TO CURE YOURSELF--NOT WORKING WITH MAGIC.
I CAN CARRY YOU BOTH, YOU KNOW.
NO, THANKS. I WANT A LITTLE TIME. WAYNE FOUNDATION'S GOT A JET HERE ON HUMANITARIAN AID...I CAN CATCH A RIDE BACK TOMORROW.
DON'T STICK AROUND HERE TOO LONG... IT CAN'T BE HEALTHY.
What's not healthy? Exhumed, formerly reanimated corpses? Two bodies filling the air with the stench of their flesh being immolated?
Batman knows it's not PHYSICAL health that Superman is referring to.

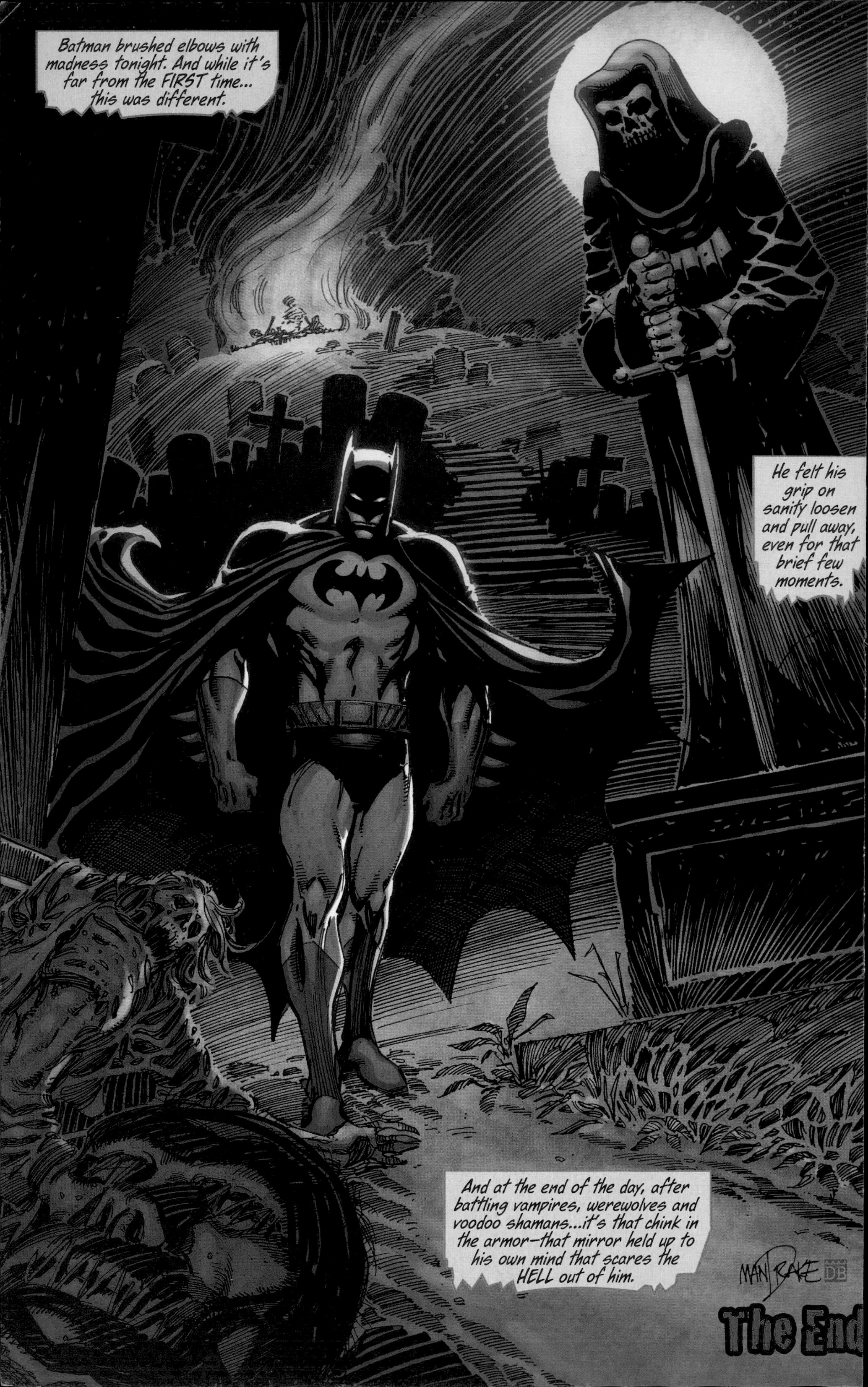
Batman brushed elbows with madness tonight. And while it's far from the FIRST time... this was different.
He felt his grip on sanity loosen and pull away, even for that brief few moments.
And at the end of the day, after battling vampires, werewolves and voodoo shamans...it's that chink in the armor—that mirror held up to his own mind that scares the HELL out of him.
MANDRAKE
DB
The End

MORE CLASSIC TALES OF THE DARK KNIGHT

BATMAN: HUSH

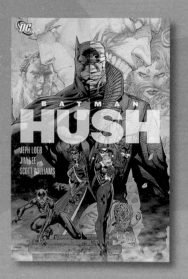

**JEPH LOEB
JIM LEE**

BATMAN: UNDER THE HOOD
VOLS. 1 & 2

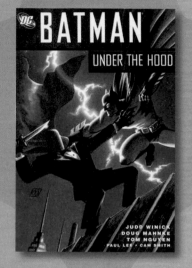

**JUDD WINICK
DOUG MAHNKE**

BATMAN:
THE LONG HALLOWEEN

**JEPH LOEB
TIM SALE**

BATMAN:
DARK VICTORY

BATMAN:
HAUNTED KNIGHT

BATMAN:
YEAR 100

**JEPH LOEB
TIM SALE**

**JEPH LOEB
TIM SALE**

PAUL POPE